ASIAN AMERICAN CHRONOLOGY

ASIAN AMERICAN CHRONOLOGY

CHRONOLOGIES OF
THE AMERICAN MOSAIC

Xiaojian Zhao

GREENWOOD PRESS
An Imprint of ABC-CLIO, LLC

A B C ⬤ C L I O

Santa Barbara, California • Denver, Colorado • Oxford, England

Library of Congress Cataloging-in-Publication Data

Zhao, Xiaojian, 1953–
    Asian American chronology : chronologies of the American mosaic / Xiaojian Zhao.
        p. cm.
    Includes bibliographical references and index.
    ISBN 978–0–313–34875–4 (hard copy : alk. paper) — ISBN 978–0–313–34876–1 (ebook)
1. Asian Americans—History—Chronology.   I. Title.
E184.A75Z47   2009
973'.0495—dc22   2009010170

13 12 11 10 9   1 2 3 4 5

This book is also available on the World Wide Web as an eBook.
Visit www.abc-clio.com for details.

ABC-CLIO, LLC
130 Cremona Drive, P.O. Box 1911
Santa Barbara, California 93116-1911

This book is printed on acid-free paper ∞

Manufactured in the United States of America

In memory of my parents

CONTENTS

PREFACE

Four decades ago, as part of the Third World student movement, Asian American students at San Francisco State University and the University of California at Berkeley launched a pan-Asian movement, which gave birth to the field of Asian American studies. Since then ethnically diverse curricula gradually developed in colleges and universities throughout the country, generating much academic interest in the experiences of Asians in the United States. The Asian population in the United States reached 12.5 million, or 4.5 percent of the total U.S. population, at the turn of the twenty-first century, up from 7.3 million and 3 percent of the U.S. population a decade earlier, but academic endeavors in the field have yet to meet the demand outside colleges and universities. It is common for Asian Americans to be viewed as Asians instead of Americans, and Asian American history is often considered as part of Asian history instead of American history. The growth of Asian American population and visibility necessitate a concise, reliable, and updated history of Asian Americans.

Asian American Chronology is designed to reach a broad audience. It provides both academic and nonacademic readers with a succinct history of a diverse American ethnic group. Significant events, activities, and individuals, from the prehistorical era to the present time, are categorized into specific themes and arranged chronologically by year or time period. Readers who are interested in a particular topic can trace changes over time by following the correlating subject entries throughout the book; those who are interested in certain historical events such as World War II or the Vietnam War, for example, can go directly to the relevant periods to find out what happened to Asian Americans in those times of rapid social change. The 31 subject categories are: agriculture and farming; architecture; art and performing arts; Asia and U.S. relations with Asia; civil rights and protests; community activities; crime; economics and employment; education and schools; family and gender; food and drink; health and disease; languages; laws and court cases; media and films; migration and immigration; military services; music and dance; obituary; politics and political activism; population; publications; race relations; religion and spirituality; science and scientists; settlement patterns; social organization; sports and recreation; trade; treaties; and wars, conquests, and exploration. These subject category entries will help readers learn about historical events and progress in the Asian American communities.

The transliteration of personal names in this book is sometimes inconsistent for a number of reasons. In most Asian societies, the family name precedes an individual's given name. Asians living in the United States often invert their family and given names following American and European practice, but some have chosen not to do so. For example,

Rhee is the family name of Syngman Rhee, a prominent Korean American community leader and the first president of the Republic of Korea, and Yao is the family name for Yao Ming, a Houston Rockets NBA star from China. Different transliteration systems and regional dialects also prevent consistency in translation and conversion. Chinese from Taiwan or pre-1949 China transliterate names according to the Wade-Giles system, while those from the People's Republic of China use the pinyin transliteration system, one that has been adopted by most academic institutions and educational programs in the United States and throughout the world.

ACKNOWLEDGMENTS

Several students at the University of California, Santa Barbara assisted me in various stages of this project. I thank Cathy Nguyen for conducting the initial research before her graduation. Katie Do was a freshman when she took over Cathy's position. The project would not have been completed in a timely fashion without her assistance in many tasks.

Katie Do, Pauline Vo, and Sue Lin read parts of the manuscript. Their comments helped me avoid many errors.

Most of the photographs are reprinted with the permission of the Library of Congress and the Associated Press. Phillip Ho, Maggie Gee, and Luella Louie kindly loaned me photos from their private collections and granted permission for reproduction. I also want to thank Pete Lew and Janice Louie for their assistance. Diane Fujino shared with me a 1930 advertisement from the Aokis' family business.

A major part of the book is built upon scholarly work produced by other researchers. I am indebted to all the scholars who laid the foundational work in the field of Asian American studies. The book benefited also from my many years of teaching experience at the University of California, Santa Barbara. Professor Emerita Sucheng Chan, who created most history courses before I joined the Department of Asian American Studies, not only introduced me to the field, but she also offered guidelines for teaching and generously shared with me many of her own notes and materials. I want to thank all the students who took my Asian American history survey course in the past 15 years. Their enthusiasm for Asian American history and their inquiries into many intricate issues have challenged me to a better understanding of the subject matter.

Several members of the Department of Asian American Studies at UCSB deserve special acknowledgment. Diane Fujino reminded me often that writing for a general audience is equally important as writing for an academic one. Arlene Phillips and Elizabeth Guerrero showed their patience when I was dealing with pressing deadlines, and I thank them for their many acts of kindness.

Mariah Gumpert of Greenwood Press persuaded me to undertake this project and guided me through the writing process. I want to thank her for her valuable feedback on the draft. I am also grateful to Elizabeth Claeys, whose superb copyediting skill greatly strengthened this book.

Xiaojian Zhao

INTRODUCTION

Beginning in the years of the California Gold Rush, tens of thousands of Chinese sailed across the Pacific in search of economic opportunities in North America. Chinese settlement in Hawaii took place decades earlier, long before the islands became a territory of the United States. Shortly after Japan was forced to open its doors to American and European powers, migration of Japanese to Hawaii and the U.S. mainland commenced. The expansion of American interest in Asia as well as the U.S. relationship with the British empire also led to the influx of migrants from Korea, the Philippines, and India. The pioneering migrants from Asia planted their roots in America before the arrival of many European groups; they and their descendents, and millions more who came later from East Asia, South Asia, Southeast Asia, and islands in the Pacific, are an important component of America's multiethnic mosaic.

Contributions of Asian Americans to the larger American society can hardly be overestimated. Chinese migrants were the first to cultivate sugarcane and develop sugar-making technology in Hawaii, and migrants from China, Japan, Korea, and the Philippines provided indispensable labor for the islands' plantation economy. In California and Pacific Northwest regions, Asian immigrants built the transcontinental railroads and many regional railways, turned deserts and swamps into arable land, and toiled in factories in the early stages of industrial development. For several decades, however, Asians were legally denied entry to this land of freedom and opportunity, and Asian immigrants were deprived of their civil rights. Many state and local discriminatory laws not only subjected Asian immigrants to economic hardships, but they also imposed segregation in education, housing, and job markets. To survive, Asians in the United States formed their own organizations and mutual aid networks, and they used their collective strength in the search for racial equality and social justice. Even before the civil rights movement of the 1960s, Asian Americans had already played an important part in shaping U.S. laws and policies, especially in areas of immigration. At a time when Japanese Americans were confined in internment camps during World War II, tens of thousands of young Japanese Americans served in the U.S. military. The ability of Asian Americans to utilize limited resources to negotiate for power and their basic civil rights under extremely difficult circumstances is quite remarkable.

The experiences of Asians in the United States recorded in this book are multifaceted, heterogeneous, and complex. Early Asian immigrants were predominantly peasants from rural areas of China, Japan, Korea, the Philippines, and India, while their compatriots who arrived after 1965 came from all walks of life and from far more diverse Asian Pacific regions. So much has happened since the first groups of Chinese immigrants landed on American soil. In a period of more than 150 years, many wars, conflicts, and revolutions have taken place throughout Asia. Declarations of victory or independence have led to the creation of some new nation states, changing national boundaries from time to time. The expansion of U.S. interests overseas and the involvement of Americans in Asian regional conflicts have greatly affected Asian immigration patterns and Asian American history. Because of their diverse regional, national, geopolitical, linguistic, cultural, and socioeconomic backgrounds, various Asian American groups have confronted different challenges in the United States. They have created various economic, social, cultural, and political structures and networks, making Asian American history intricate and intriguing at the same time.

The history of Asian Americans provides a window to America's past as a multiethnic nation. There are lessons to be learned, milestones to be celebrated, and new challenges to be met ahead. The significant progress that the Asian Americans have made is a living testimony of what America has to offer.

ABBREVIATIONS USED TO REPRESENT SUBJECT CATEGORIES

AGRI	Agriculture and Farming	MILI	Military Services
ARCH	Architecture	MUSI	Music and Dance
ARTS	Art and Performing Arts	OBIT	Obituary
ASIA	Asia and U.S. Relations with Asia	POLI	Politics and Political Activism
CIVI	Civil Rights and Protests	POPU	Population
COMM	Community Activities	PUBL	Publications
CRIM	Crime	RACE	Race Relations
ECON	Economics and Employment	RELI	Religion and Spirituality
EDUC	Education and Schools	SCIE	Science and Scientists
FAMI	Family and Gender	SETT	Settlement Patterns
FOOD	Food and Drink	SOCI	Social Organization
HEAL	Health and Disease	SPOR	Sports and Recreation
LANG	Languages	TRAD	Trade
LAWS	Laws and Court Cases	TREA	Treaties
MED	Media and Films	WARS	Wars, Conquests, and Exploration
MIGR	Migration and Immigration		

PRE-NINETEENTH CENTURY

13,000 B.C. to 10,000 B.C.

MIGR. The first human groups arrive in North America. At a time when rivers on earth are covered with glacial ice and sea levels are about 300 feet lower than they are now, some descendants of Siberian people cross the Beringia, a large landmass that connects Asia to Alaska. When the Ice Age ends, warmer global temperatures melt away the glacial ice in rivers and rising sea levels bury the Beringia, separating American continents from Asia. The first settlers of North America are cut off from their fellow human beings who remain in the Old World. Physical anthropologists have found that Native Americans share many distinctive traits with inhabitants of Siberia in northeastern Asia.

300–750

MIGR. Seafaring Polynesians, probably from Southeast Asia, settle the South Pacific Islands, including the remote northern Hawaii islands. Taro, coconuts, and bananas are introduced to the islands by the migrants.

618–907

ASIA. Tang dynasty begins in China. Canton centers China's maritime commerce, where thousands of foreign merchants trade. Canton remains the center of Chinese trade until the end of the Song (Sung) dynasty (960–1127).

900–1000

TRAD. Filipinos extend trade from Malaysia to China.

1127

ASIA. The Southern Song dynasty (1127–1279) begins in China.

TRAD. Chinese shipowners and merchants in the lower Yangzi (Yangtze) Valley and along the southern coast become active in international trade. Quanzhou (Ch'uanchou) in Fujian Province replaces Canton as the center for foreign commerce.

1492

WARS. Christopher Columbus lands in the New World while looking for a passage to India. This historic voyage brings European attention to the Americas. Colonies will soon be established in the New World.

1511

WARS. A Portuguese fleet conquers Malacca in Malaysia, marking the beginning of European expansion in Southeast Asia. In the fifteenth century Malacca will become a major regional commercial center where Chinese, Arab, Malay, and Indian merchants congregate. The Dutch will oust the Portuguese from Malacca in 1641. British presence in the city will begin in the late eighteenth century.

1521

ASIA. The Philippine Islands are discovered by Ferdinand Magellan, drawing European attention to the islands.

1526–1707

ASIA. The Mughal empire is founded in India, dominating nearly the entire Indian subcontinent at its height and controlling a population of nearly 150 million.

RELI. Religion is of great importance in Indian society. Two distinct social systems are developed under the Mughal empire, each based on its own religion. Above a traditional Islamic social structure sit the Mughal rulers. Muslim officials are prominent members of the society, and Muslim merchants enjoy special social prestige. The majority of the Mughal population, however, are Hindus. The Hindus are governed by a traditional caste system that defines social structure according to four varna castes of Brahman (priests), Kshatriya (nobility), Vaishya (merchants and artisans), and Shudra (laborers). An occupational caste system, *jati,* divides the Hindus into various social groups. There are, for example, scribal jati (lower officials), merchant jati, artisan jati, and peasant jati, each with its own regional or local identities. Those within the jati system interact economically and politically but seldom socially; members of a particular jati are born into their jati and will marry only within. A third religion, Sikhism, emerges as a resistance to Mughal oppression. This monotheistic religion is developed in north India as a syncretism of Islam and Hinduism. Sikhism is most appealing to commoners in northern India. A major Sikh uprising will bring the decline of the Mughals in the eighteenth century.

1543

ASIA. Japanese encounter Europeans for the first time, when some Portuguese land on a small island off the southern tip of Kyushu Island in southwestern Japan.

1549

RELI. Jesuit Francis Xavier starts Christian proselytizing in Japan. Catholic missionaries will convert about 300,000 Japanese by the end of the sixteenth century.

1560

ASIA. Oda Nobunaga (1534–1582) begins to unify Japan, ending Ahikaga rule in 1573.

1565–1815

MIGR. Some Filipino and Chinese sailors and stewards are hired by Spaniards for the Manila Galleon Trade between 1565 and 1815. Chinese luxury goods are shipped to Spain via Manila in the Philippines and Acapulco, Mexico, by large Spanish cargo ships called galleons. Some Filipinos settle in Acapulco in the late sixteenth century. In the seventeenth century, some Chinese merchants are found in Mexico City.

1565–1898

ASIA. The Philippine Islands are occupied by Spain from 1565 to 1898, interrupted by a brief partial occupation by Great Britain from 1762 to 1764. Spaniards name the islands after King Philip II of Spain. Catholic influence is widely spread on the islands.

LANG. About 87 native languages and dialects are spoken in the Philippines; all belong to the Malay-Polynesian linguistic family. The three principal indigenous languages are Cebuano, spoken in the Visayas; Tagalog, spoken mainly in the area around Manila; and Ilocano, spoken in northern Luzon. The national language, Pilipino, which will be promoted by the government in 1939, is based on Tagalog.

1587

MIGR. The Spanish galleon *Nuestra Señora de Esperanza* (Our Lady of Hope) lands in present-day California on October 18, with a few Filipino crew members on board.

1592–1598

WARS. Japan invades Korea with the ultimate goal of conquering China. This military aggression ends in 1598 with the death of the powerful Japanese warrior Toyotomi Hideyoshi, leaving Korea in ruins. China's Ming dynasty (1366–1644) is weakened due to its involvement in the war.

1600

ASIA. The Portuguese establish a colony in Macao.

1600–1602

TRAD. The British East India Company is established in 1600, two years before the founding of the United East India Company by Dutch merchants. Both companies enjoy great financial success. Five English ships sail from London to Asia, their cargoes worth 30,000 pounds sterling. Returning two years later, they carry spices and other goods worth more than one million pounds sterling. These two powerful joint-stock companies are major players in early global trade.

1603

ASIA. Tokugawa Ieyasu emerges as the leader of a unified Japan, indicating the beginning of the Tokugawa Shogunate. Shogun—military rulers—are now in control. During this time period Japan allows limited trade with Chinese merchants. Small numbers of Koreans and Dutch are permitted to reside on some of the islands.

1606

RELI. Anti-Christian decrees are first issued in Japan.

1636

WARS. The Manchu army invades Korea.

1638

ASIA. Japan begins a period of seclusion. This move was triggered by a rebellion involving about 20,000 Japanese Christians in 1637 and 1638. Many rebels are persecuted.

1640

ASIA. Japan closes its doors to most westerners.

1664

ASIA. The Qing dynasty (1644–1911) succeeds the Ming dynasty in China. Thousands of Ming loyalists flee abroad after the Manchu conquest. The Qing government forbids individuals to leave the country, although this new policy does not prevent Chinese from Fujian and Guangdong provinces from emigrating. Many migrants settle in Southeast Asia, while others will later move to Hawaii and the Americas.

1723–1731

TRAD. The British East India Company ships 200 chests of opium to China and Chinese emperor Yongzheng issues anti-opium edicts, providing severe punishment for the sale of opium and the opening of opium-smoking dens. The volume of opium trade, however, will continue to increase. It will total 5,000 chests in 1820, 16,000 chests in 1830, 20,000 chests in 1838, and 70,000 chests in 1858.

1760

TRAD. Canton replaces Quanzhou as the center for foreign commerce. Western merchants are permitted to trade with government-licensed Chinese merchants through the *cohong* system.

1762–1764

WARS. Great Britain occupies some parts of the Philippines, but its influence on the islands is limited compared to that of Spain.

1763

MIGR. Some Filipinos working for the Spanish in the Manila Galleon Trade between the Philippines and Mexico jump ship and settle in present-day Louisiana. They build small communities along the Mississippi River Delta.

1776–1783

WARS. The American Revolution takes place in British North America in 1776. The original 13 colonies gain independence from Britain in 1783.

1778

ECON. A highly sophisticated agricultural system including irrigation is built by the indigenous people on the islands of Hawaii at the time of Captain Cook's expedition. The main staple food cultivated is kalo (taro). Farmers and fishermen are ruled by *moʻi* (kings) of various regions on the islands. They exchange locally produced gifts and use stones, shells, and other materials to make tools and weapons. Metal, pottery clay, and textile fibers are absent. Hawaii will become a convenient stopover for westerners in the fur trade between the Pacific Northwest and Canton, leading to rapid economic and social transformation of the islands and people. Westerners will introduce metal tools, firearms, and foreign customs to the islands, as well as devastating disease to which the native population has no immunity.

WARS. Captain James Cook (1728–1779), a British explorer and navy commander, arrives in the Hawaii Islands. John Ledyard, an American sailor and explorer, is among his crew members.

1784

TRAD. At the Canton harbor, *Empress of China,* a commercial vessel outfitted by New York and Philadelphia merchants, opens trade between the new United States and China. The voyage is immensely successful, earning the investors a large profit. The United States is excluded from the European mercantilist system at the time; opportunities in the China trade encourage merchants from New York, Philadelphia, Boston, Baltimore, Providence, Salem, and other ports to send their own vessels. The vessels will leave Atlantic ports, sail around the Cape of Good Hope, and go across the Indian Ocean by way of the Dutch East Indies before reaching China. Americans will ship silver dollars, North American ginseng, sea otter furs, and sandalwood from Hawaii to China and will bring back tea, china, enameled ware, nankeens, and silks.

1785

MIGR. Some individual Chinese are found in Baltimore, Maryland and in Pennsylvania.

1787

LAWS. The Constitution of the United States is signed at the Pennsylvania State House in Philadelphia on September 17. The new government will become effective in March 1789, after the Constitution is ratified by each of the 13 colonies.

1789

MIGR. A small group of Chinese arrives on Hawaii. Most of those who migrate to Hawaii in the early years are from two Chinese southern provinces, Guangdong and Fujian, some with sugarcane cultivation experience and sugar-making skills.

TRAD. American merchants began to ship sandalwood from Hawaii to China. The Chinese will call Hawaii "the Sandalwood Mountains."

1790

LAWS. The first U.S. Naturalization Act is enacted, stipulating that only "free white persons" can gain American citizenship.

MIGR. A British trading vessel with an Asian Indian on board arrives in Salem, Massachusetts.

1791

LAWS. The Bill of Rights, consisting of 10 constitutional amendments, becomes part of the U.S. Constitution. These amendments provide civil rights to individuals, including freedom of religion, freedom of speech, freedom of assembly, freedom to bear arms, and freedom from unreasonable searches. The right to a fair trial by an impartial jury is also provided.

Nineteenth Century

1802

ECON. A Chinese "sugar master," Wong Tze-Chun, arrives in Hawaii, bringing with him sugar-making equipment and boiling pans.

1806

MIGR. Eight Japanese sailors on an American ship arrive in Hawaii. They are the first recorded Japanese to land on the Hawaii Islands.

1810

ECON. The discovery of sandalwood—a fragrant wood—in the mountains of Hawaii and its marketability in China lead to exploitation of the forest. The traditional subsistence way of life will soon be replaced by a monetary economy.

WARS. A *mo'i* (king) of the island of Hawaii, Kamehameha, unifies the Hawaiian islands with the assistance of western weapons and military advisers, ending wars among different regions and islands. The power of other chiefs is suppressed. Kamehameha declares himself king of Hawaii and will control trade until his death in 1819.

1814–1816

WARS. Nepal loses a war against the British.

1815

WARS. Filipino settlers in Louisiana join French pirate Jean Laffitte in the Battle of New Orleans against the British. This battle will lead to the American acquisition of Louisiana as a state.

1819

ASIA. Sir Thomas Stamford Raffles arrives in Singapore as an agent of the British East India Company, making the island known to westerners.

1820

ECON. Whaling ships begin to arrive in Hawaii's harbors, accelerating the process of commercialization in the islands in place of a rural, largely subsistence lifestyle and communalism. Commercial whaling will dominate Hawaii's economy until the 1860s.

RELI. Protestant missionaries from New England arrive in Hawaii. Calvinist Christianity will replace traditional indigenous religion and traditional culture on the islands, facilitating the introduction of western ideas, laws, institutions, and practices to the islands. Missionaries will establish schools and develop a Hawaiian alphabet.

1824

ASIA. Singapore is purchased by Great Britain. Within a year the city of Singapore becomes a major commercial port, with trade exceeding that of Malaya's Malacca and Penang combined.

TREA. Through the Anglo-Dutch Treaty, Britain gains possession of Malacca, a major regional commercial center in Malaysia, in exchange for territory on the island of Sumatra in what is today Indonesia.

WARS. The British invade Burma (Myanmar) and gain their first foothold. Two more wars of conquest will follow in the next few decades, until Burma is completely taken over by the British and annexed into India in 1885.

1826

ASIA. Great Britain forms the Colony of the Straits Settlements based on its strongholds in Singapore as well as Malaya's Malacca and Penang. The British will develop large-scale rubber and tin production in the colony. The Straits Settlements will become a British Crown Colony between 1867 and 1946.

TREA. Siam (Thailand) enters the Treaty of Amity and Commerce with Great Britain.

1830

POPU. The U.S. Census records three Chinese. This is the first time Asians appear in government documents. Because race and ethnicity are not included in the census questionnaire at the time, this record does not reflect the actual number of Chinese living in the United States. In 1840, eight Chinese will be recorded, and a decade later the number will reach 758. Chinese will be officially added to the census form in 1870.

1830–1840

ECON. Chinese sugar-making mills are established on the islands of Maui and Hawaii in the 1830s. By the 1840s, at least half a dozen such mills will be found there. The sugar masters use simple tools they brought from China to extract juice from sugarcane, and then they boil the juice and let the water evaporate. This primitive sugar-making method lays the foundation for the development of steam-powered machinery in the future. The Chinese are also the first to use contract laborers for large-scale sugarcane cultivation on the islands, which will be adopted by western plantation owners.

1831

EDUC. The first group of Hawaiian students starts their classes at Lāhaināluna, a mission school established to train native teachers. Some of the native students are in their thirties when they enter the institution to learn to read and write. Graduates of the school will play important roles in expanding western literacy and knowledge in the islands and in transforming Hawaii from a nonliterate society to a literate one. A few members of the first class of graduates will later serve as representatives in the legislature.

1833

ASIA. The United States begins diplomatic exchange with Siam.

MIGR. A small number of Filipinos settle in St. Malo at the mouth of the Mississippi River and establish a fishing village. This village will be destroyed by a hurricane 60 years later.

1839

EDUC. The Chiefs' Children's School, also known as the Royal School, is established in Hawaii. The school provides education to children of native rulers and descendents of noble families.

POLI. A constitutional monarchy is created by Kamehameha III in Hawaii. It will create its first written constitution a year later and establish a legislature and court system. The legislature will consist of a council of chiefs and an elected house of representatives.

WARS. The first Opium War (1839–1842) between China and Britain begins. Early British trade with China has been carried through the British East India Company. The British found limited markets for woolen goods and other merchandise in China but shipped large quantities of Chinese tea back to England. To reverse the trade deficit, the British have sold an increasing amount of opium to the Chinese. Many Chinese are addicted to the drug, and large amounts of silver flow out of China every year. To crack down on the opium traffic, Chinese imperial commissioner Lin Zexu (Lin Tse-hsu) confiscates and destroys thousands of chests of opium stored in the English merchants' storeships in Canton, triggering the war. Britain sends a naval squadron to China, seizes port after port, and occupies Canton. China is forced to enter the Treaty of Nanjing (Nanking) after its defeat in 1842.

1840

ECON. A significant change takes place in the land tenure system in Hawaii. Traditionally, all the land on the islands belonged to the king, while his commoners could cultivate the land freely. The westerners bring with them ideas of property ownership: they gradually gain access to land, first through informal grants from the king and then through formal leases, pressuring Kamehameha III for changes. Private ownership of land, which will be made possible after a land reform measure in 1848, will allow westerners to purchase land.

LAWS. The Kingdom of Hawaii produces its first constitution, providing a basis for representational government. Traditional chiefs and nobles are still powerful under the new government.

1842

ASIA. The United States recognizes the Kingdom of Hawaii and appoints Gerrit P. Judd (a missionary to Hawaii) as one of the four ministers of the islands. Judd will remain at this post until 1854. The growth of the sugar industry in Hawaii will attract great interest from American businessmen and consolidate commercial ties between the United States and Hawaii.

TREA. The Treaty of Nanjing, signed on August 29, concludes the first Opium War. Great Britain forces China to open Guangzhou (Canton), Xiamen (Amoy), Fuzhou (Foochow), Ningbo (Ningpo), and Shanghai as treaty ports to foreign commerce; abolish the cohong monopoly system in trade; limit the amount of tariff and customs dues the Chinese can charge; pay an indemnity of $21 million; cede the island of Hong Kong to Great Britain; allow Christian missionaries to preach in various localities; and grant Britain extraterritoriality, which makes British subjects and their employees immune to Chinese law. This treaty, which opens the door of China to western powers, is seen as China's first treaty of humiliation. It will affect Chinese history profoundly for many decades until World War II.

1843

MIGR. Manjiro Nakahama, also known as John Mung, is rescued at sea by an American vessel.

He is the first recorded Japanese to arrive in the United States. He will live in Fairhaven, Massachusetts and receive an education there. When Japan sends its first delegation to the United States in 1860, Mung will serve as an interpreter. He will die in Japan in 1898.

1844

TREA. The Treaty of Wang Hiya (Wangxia), the very first treaty between the United States and China, is signed on July 3. Although the United States has traded with China since shortly after the American Revolution, to most Americans China is still a mystery. After the Opium War, China agreed to grant the United States the same commercial privileges accorded Great Britain in the Treaty of Nanjing, but the U.S. government wanted to have its own diplomatic relationship with China. In 1843, President John Tyler appointed Caleb Cushing, one of the most knowledgeable scholars of the nineteenth century and an authoritarian on international matters, as the commissioner to China for the treaty negotiation. Cushing prepared his mission carefully—by the time he arrived in China, he had already mastered the Manchu language well enough to communicate with Chinese envoys without interpreters. In China, Cushing deals with Chinese diplomats with tact and discretion. He recognizes customary courtesies of the Qing empire and of his own position as a representative of the United States. In the Treaty of Wang Hiya China agrees to open five ports to American merchants and makes many concessions on issues regarding tariff and trade regulations. The extraterritoriality principle in the treaty makes citizens of the United States residing in China immune to Chinese laws. Cushing's mission to China is one of the most celebrated events in American diplomatic history.

1845–1847

LAWS. Organic Acts are enacted in Hawaii, penned by Attorney General John Ricord, a New York lawyer who arrived in the islands in 1844. These laws set terms for the government, providing separate ministries under the king. Three of the four first ministers are white Americans, including two previous missionaries.

1848

ECON. Gold is discovered along the American River, in north central California. About 100,000 people will flood in from different parts of the world in the next two years, including hundreds of Chinese.

ECON. The Great Mahele—land redistribution—takes place in Hawaii. Hawaiians are now allowed to buy or claim parcels of land and sell them to others. Prior to this reform, economic penetration by foreign interests was largely limited to trade. The privatization of land opens the doors for westerners to purchase large tracts of land, making it possible for the development of sugar plantations on the islands. Many Americans begin to invest in productive ventures in sugar plantations and mills. After the decline of the whaling trade, sugarcane growing and sugar production and exporting will dominate Hawaii's economy. Commercial agriculture will replace subsistence agriculture and rural communalism. Hawaii is now well on its way to integration into the global economy.

TREA. The Treaty of Guadalupe Hidalgo is signed between the United States and Mexico on May 20, transferring the northern third of Mexico to the United States. California also becomes part of the United States. It will be admitted to the Union on September 9, 1850.

1849

LANG. Cantonese is the official language spoken in the Chinese immigrant community because the majority of the early arrivals are Cantonese. These Chinese originate from three regions of Guangdong Province. Sanyi (Sam Yup) people are from areas west and north of the city of Guangzhou in the Pearl River Delta; Siyi (Sze Yup) people are from districts to the southwest of Sanyi; Xiangshan (Heungsan) natives are from a district between Guangzhou and the Portuguese colony of Macao, west of Hong Kong. Each subgroup of these Cantonese immigrants speaks its own dialect, but they all use the same Chinese language in writing.

MIGR. Chinese begin to arrive in California in large numbers during the Gold Rush. Most of the early arrivals are from Guangdong Province. Unlike the contract laborers in Hawaii, the Chinese in California are mostly independent laborers or merchants. Between 1849 and 1882, a total of 375,000 Chinese entries will be recorded. The bulk of these Chinese immigrants later will become a source of cheap labor for railroads, mines, fisheries, farms, orchards, canneries, garment shops, and cigar factories.

1850

ECON. The Royal Hawaiian Agricultural Society is established to increase the labor supply in Hawaii by looking outside. This government agency will be replaced by the Planters' Society and a bureau of immigration in 1864. Major steps will be taken to recruit workers from other countries.

LAWS. The Hawaiian government takes legislative measures to prevent indigenous people from leaving the islands for better economic opportunities outside. One forbids the people to depart without permission. Another law bars locals from working as sailors on outbound ships. The third one, "An Act for the Governance of Masters and Servants," aims to improve labor relations by setting rules for the treatment of apprentices; masters who violate the law are subject to judicial and administrative punishments. These laws indicate the importance of labor in Hawaii during this period of economic transformation.

LAWS. The Foreign Miners' Tax law is enacted to make California "for Americans." Although the law is an attempt to drive out the French, Mexicans, Hawaiians, Chileans, and the Chinese from the gold fields, the Chinese become a major target.

MIGR. Japanese Hikozo Hamada, also known as Joseph Heco, is rescued at sea by an American sailing ship. In Baltimore, Maryland, he will receive an American education and later become a naturalized American citizen.

POPU. The indigenous population in Hawaii declines rapidly after the islands' contact with westerners. Western diseases, to which the indigenous people have no immunity, are the main killers. Hawaiian natives pay a price in the process of commercialization as well.

Casualties are caused by cold weather on the mountains, where the locals are sent to cut sandalwood for Americans to trade with China. A new land system that deprives them of their traditional means of livelihood. The population in 1850 is only a fifth of what it was in 1778, when Captain Cook first landed on Hawaiian soil. Opportunities outside have also pulled some Hawaiians to leave the islands. The decline of the local population poses a big challenge to the development of a plantation economy, making importation of foreign laborers necessary for the new economy on the islands.

RACE. Groups of Chinese are invited to participate in President Zachary Taylor's "grand funeral pageant" in New York.

WARS. The Taiping Rebellion (1850–1864), one of the largest peasant uprisings in Chinese history, begins. Hong Xiuchuan (Hung Hsiu-chu'uan), a native of Guangxi Province, claims himself the younger brother of Jesus Christ and leads an uprising that sweeps through much of south and central China. About 10 million people are killed and much farmland destroyed. The turmoil is seen as one of the domestic causes that push many Chinese out of their homeland.

1851

SOCI. The first two Chinese district associations are formed in San Francisco. The Sam Yup Benevolent Association (Sanyi Huiguan) is known as the Canton Company; the other is the Sze Yup Benevolent Association (Siyi Huiguan). More district associations will be formed in later years. Each district association traces its origin to the immigrants' native place in China. Members of a district association usually share a common dialect. Members of a particular dialect group tend to settle in the same neighborhoods and enter similar occupations. The Heungsan natives who speak Hakka migrate to Hawaii in large numbers as plantation workers; those in California are mostly tenant farmers or nurserymen. The Sam Yup people are present in both Hawaii and the United States; many are merchants and entrepreneurs. The Sze Yup natives start in California as laborers. The district association is very important to the community, both

economically and socially, and it offers its members many benefits that are crucial to their survival. The association provides newcomers with temporary lodging and introduces them to jobs. It arbitrates disputes among its members, ensures the payment of debts, raises funds for projects of common concern, provides medicine, maintains cemeteries, covers burial expenses for the poor, and ships exhumed bones of the deceased to their home villages in China for final burial. Membership dues are also used to provide special funds for the elderly. Immigrants who share the same last name also form family/clan associations. Both the district associations and the family/clan associations provide social education for their members. They offer immigrants information unavailable elsewhere and teach them how to deal with the larger society and how to respond to the immigration authorities. Chinese family/clan associations will not be organized in Hawaii until 1889 and district associations will not appear until 1890.

1852

ECON. Thirty-seven Chinese entrepreneurs are found in Honolulu. They operate general merchandise stores, bakeries, and wholesale dry goods and wine businesses. Some companies own boats and vessels.

FAMI. The Hip Yee Tong, one of the fraternity organizations that controls the Chinese American underground, starts to traffic women from China to work as prostitutes. The rise of Chinese prostitution is largely due to the scarcity of women in the American West. Almost all Chinese prostitutes are brought to the United States against their will. Most are kidnapped, lured, or purchased from poor parents by procurers in China for $50 or less. Once in America, they are resold for as much as $1,000 per person. These women are forced by their owners to sign contracts with thumbprints, although few can read and therefore understand the terms of service. A typical contract states that the woman agrees to work without wages for a period of three to four years, and she will become free after the term. Should she get sick for more than 10 days, the woman will have to make up an extra month. Chinese prostitutes are usually between the ages of

16 and 25. Between 1852 and 1873, the Hip Yee Tong will traffic 6,000 women to America and net a profit of $200,000. Because the business is so lucrative, competing tongs often fight over the possession of certain prostitutes. Chinese tong wars become notorious in late nineteenth- and early twentieth-century America.

LAWS. California's Foreign Miners' Tax law is reenacted, aiming at mainly Chinese. The new tax requires a monthly payment of three dollars from every foreign miner, if the person does not desire to become a citizen. Because the 1790 naturalization law allows only "free and white" persons to become citizens, whether Chinese immigrants desire to become U.S. citizens is irrelevant. To enforce the law, tax collectors target Chinese miners in the gold fields, which works to encourage violent acts against Chinese miners. The Chinese miners are frequently robbed, harassed, and beaten, and some of them are killed.

MIGR. Reflecting Hawaii's first successful efforts in recruiting foreign laborers, 195 Chinese contract laborers arrive to work on the islands' sugar plantations. Each of the laborers from this group is under a five-year contract. Room, board, and transportation expenses are provided by the planters. The workers receive a monthly wage of three dollars. Contract laborers arriving after 1865 will be paid eight dollars per month and provided with working clothes and other necessities. Between 1852 and 1900, about 50,000 Chinese contract laborers and other individuals will arrive in Hawaii.

MIGR. More than 20,000 Chinese flock to San Francisco en route to the gold fields of the Sierra Nevada Mountains. In the following year, partly due to the enforcement of the Foreign Miners' Tax, fewer than 5,000 Chinese will arrive. More than 16,000 will come in 1854. The Chinese call San Francisco Jinshan (Gum San)—the gold mountain. These early arrivals are almost all male. Although many of them are married, few bring their wives with them.

RELI. Confucianism, Taoism, and Buddhism are all important elements of the popular Chinese religion. There are many religious festivals, but no regularly scheduled services are required.

An altar with a deity and a metal post for holding sticks of incense is often used for worship, and altars can be found in temples and other public gathering places as well as in private homes. Community organizations usually set aside a room with altars for their members to pray.

RELI. Missionary William Speer, after many years of service in China, opens a Presbyterian mission in San Francisco. He travels in California to convert Chinese immigrants. The mission will have more success later, after Augustus Loomis's arrival in 1859. Loomis's followers include both Chinese and Japanese immigrants. Many Asian immigrants are converted, becoming Baptists, Methodists, and Congregationalists.

1853

ASIA. American naval officer Matthew Perry sails into Edo (Tokyo) Bay with the mission of "opening" Japan for American navigation, trade, and diplomacy. Japan is forced to negotiate and enter a treaty with the United States.

TREA. The United States signs a treaty with Japan in Kanagawa, ending 200 years of Japan's policy of national isolation. In the treaty, which is produced under the pressure of Matthew Perry's military presence, Japan provides privileges to the United States similar to those China gives to the British in the Treaty of Nanjing. In the next few years Japan will sign additional treaties with other western powers. These "unequal treaties" will be removed in the 1890s as Japan emerges as a world power.

1854

SOCI. Chinese immigrants in Hawaii organize a funeral society, the very first community organization of their own on the islands. The society provides funeral services for Chinese who die in Hawaii. Ceremonial burial procedures include a parade following traditional Chinese rituals.

1855

EDUC. Yung Wing becomes the first Chinese person to graduate from an American college when he graduates from Yale College (now Yale University). Born in 1828 to a peasant family in a little village in south China, Yung Wing began his education at age seven in classes taught by Protestant missionaries. He was a student at Morison Educational Society's school for boys in 1841. When the school principal, Samuel Robbins Brown, returned to the United States in 1847, Yung and two classmates came with him. Yung started at the Manson Academy in Monson, Massachusetts, before attending Yale College. While still in college, in 1852, he became a citizen of the United States. A prominent figure in both the United States and China, he will return to China to establish an educational mission in 1872. Following in Yung's footsteps, 120 young Chinese boys will receive education in Connecticut and Massachusetts between 1872 and 1882.

LAWS. The Married Women Law, the first legislation regarding women's citizenship status, grants an alien woman American citizenship upon her marriage to an American citizen. The law does not specify whether a female American citizen can keep her legal status upon marriage to a foreigner. This law, its two amendments, and a related U.S. Supreme Court decision will be highly contested in the first three decades of the twentieth century.

LAWS. In *People v. George W. Hall,* the California supreme court reverses the conviction of George Hall for the murder of a Chinese person on the grounds that the conviction is based on evidence provided by Chinese witnesses. The Criminal Proceedings Act of 1850 prohibited blacks, mulattos, and Native Americans from testifying in court. The judge rules that since Native Americans came from Asia to Alaska crossing the Bering Strait, the Chinese should be treated the same. The prohibition will be incorporated into the state's Civil Procedure Code in 1863. Chinese testimony against white individuals will not be allowed until the state law is amended in 1872.

1856

WARS. The second Opium War (1856–1860), between China and a joint force of Great Britain and France, begins. Taking advantage of an incident in which Chinese soldiers search a ship formerly of Hong Kong registry, the British will attack Canton and seize the port city in 1857, pressuring the Qing ruler to sign a new treaty. To assure the new treaty will be absolutely on British terms, the British and French will attack again, with the assistance of

American naval Commodore Josiah Tattnall, despite the neutral stance of the United States. On October 18, 1860, the British will burn to the ground Yuan Ming Yuan, the summer palace of the Chinese emperor, in the Beijing suburbs, forcing China to agree to all terms in the Treaty of Tianjin (Tientsin).

1858

TREA. Great Britain and France force China to sign the Treaty of Tianjin in the midst of the second Opium War (1856–1860). To force China to agree to all terms in the treaty, the British will burn to the ground Yuan Ming Yuan, the exquisite summer palace of the Chinese emperor in the Beijing suburbs, on October 18, 1860. China will reaffirm the treaty and give additional concessions. The finalized treaty will impose extraordinarily strict terms on China. China will agree to open trade in four new Yangzi treaty ports (Hankou, Jiujiang, Nanjing, and Zhenjiang) in addition to the six existing treaty ports; legalize opium; pay an additional indemnity and lower further its customs duty of foreign goods; cede Jiulong (Kowloon)—territory on the Chinese mainland opposite Hong Kong—to Britain; and permit missionaries to proselytize in the interior of China. China also will agree to let a British ambassador reside in Beijing (Peking). By the terms of the most-favored-nation clause, all British gains will also be shared by the other major foreign powers.

WARS. France begins its conquest of Vietnam, starting in the south.

1859

EDUC. A segregated school for Chinese children is established in San Francisco. Because there are few Chinese children in the city, classes will be held only in the evenings a year later. This facility will be closed in 1871. For more than a decade thereafter, Chinese students in the city will be denied the right to public education. A new segregated school for Chinese students will be built in 1886.

WARS. France begins an effort to conquer Cambodia and Laos.

1860

FOOD. Food is of great importance to Chinese people. Most Chinese immigrants originate from the rice-growing provinces of Guangdong and Fujian, where rice, instead of wheat products, is served in most meals. The immigrants consume fresh and dry vegetables and meat from pigs, ducks, and chickens. The rich sea resources along the Pacific coast create opportunities for Chinese fishermen, and the immigrants enjoy a great variety of fish and seafood, including rare delicacies such as abalone and sea cucumbers. Meat, fish, and vegetables are often stir-fried, steamed, or boiled with other Chinese ingredients. Among the food products that the Chinese merchants import from China are rice, noodles, beans, tea, vinegar, soy sauce, wine, cooking oil, bean paste, dried mushrooms, bamboo shoots, cured eggs and pork, sausages, salted fish, and dried shrimp. The most well-known Chinese dish in America is chop suey, a stir-fry of sliced meat and vegetables. As a tradition, Chinese restaurants in the United States usually serve free tea to meal purchasers.

POPU. The U.S. Census records 34,933 Chinese. Only 1,784 of them are female.

SPOR. Gambling, prostitution, and opium smoking are the three most popular forms of recreation among the Chinese bachelors in the United States.

1861

RACE. The Joint Select Committee Relative to the Chinese Population of the State of California praises the Chinese for their contribution of $14,000,000 to the state's economy. The report points out that while the Chinese help build the economy, they are not in any way acting as competitors.

WARS. The battle at Fort Sumter in Charleston, South Carolina marks the beginning of the U.S. Civil War.

1862

RACE. According to an 1862 committee report of the California state legislature, 88 Chinese miners are murdered, including 11 killed by collectors of the Foreign Miners' Tax.

SOCI. Six Chinese district associations join force and organize a federation called Gongsuo, known by mainstream American society as the Chinese Six Companies. This organization will be renamed as the Chinese Consolidated Benevolent Association in 1882 and become the voice of the entire Chinese American community.

1863

WARS. British ships bombard the city of Kanoshima in Japan in retaliation for the death of an Englishman.

WARS. France claims Cambodia as its protectorate. It will turn Cambodia into a colony in 1884.

1864

WARS. Japanese cannons installed at the straits of Shimonoseki are destroyed by joint western naval forces.

1865

ECON. About 3,000 Chinese workers are hired by the Central Pacific Railroad Company to construct the west half of the transcontinental railroad. The workers provide the hard labor and perform difficult and dangerous tasks. To remove a huge rock outcrop called Cape Horn, Chinese workers are lowered by rope from the tops of cliffs to chisel holes in the rock and stuff them with black powder. They are then pulled up by fellow workers after the powder is ignited. Some Chinese perish in the explosions. Many more will be buried by avalanches during the winter of 1867 in the high Sierras. The Chinese laborers will work through harsh winters in the high Sierras as well as on the hot and dry plateaus of Nevada and Utah until the transcontinental railroad is completed in 1869.

SOCI. To protect their economic interests, Chinese in San Francisco organize several craft and labor guilds. Laundrymen, shoemakers, and cigarmakers all form their own guilds.

1866

WARS. Seven French ships appear in Korean waters. Five American ships will follow in 1871, as well a Japanese ship in 1875. These early attempts to open Korea for trade and diplomacy meet with military resistance from the Koreans.

1867

CIVI. Chinese railroad workers strike in June against the Central Pacific Railroad Company. About 10,000 Chinese are recruited to construct

Track work takes place in Nevada as Central Pacific forces build the western link of the first transcontinental railroad, now a part of the Southern Pacific system, in 1868. Rail layers shown in the foreground were followed by gangs of Chinese laborers who spaced and spiked the rail to the ties. [AP Photo/Southern Pacific News Bureau]

the transcontinental railroad heading eastward. The Chinese workers are paid $30 a month, while white workers are paid the same monthly wage plus board. About 2,000 Chinese working in the high Sierras organize a strike, demanding a monthly wage of $40. They also demand 10 hours a day for outdoor work and 8 hours a day for working inside the tunnels, and they want the freedom to quit their jobs. The railroad company cuts off the food supply, forcing the strikers to give up after a week.

1867–1870

MIGR. About 40,000 Chinese arrive in the United States, partly as a result of active recruitment efforts by the Central Pacific Railroad Company.

1868

ASIA. The Meiji Restoration takes place in Japan. Leaders in favor of learning the ways of

the west come into power. The feudal system is abolished. The teenage Emperor Meiji is restored to paramount status. The reform leads to fundamental changes in Japanese society, signifying the beginning of westernization and modernization. The new government imposes a new system of land taxation, requiring farmers to pay taxes based on the value of their land instead of the value of their crops. This fixed land tax secures revenue for the government, but many farmers will lose their land. The samurai, who have ruled Japan since the twelfth century, are no longer in power, but the ex-samurai still living receive compensations from the new government. The Meiji reform also creates western-style legal and educational systems, providing universal education for both males and females. To build a military force, the government will also pass a conscription law. The law will allow citizens overseas to be exempted from military service, giving young Japanese men more incentive to migrate.

RELI. Shintoism and Buddhism are the two dominant religions in Japan. Unlike Buddhism, Shintoism is not concerned with afterlife issues, but the two religions are often seen by Japanese adherents as closely linked. Shintoism will gain prominence during and after the Meiji Restoration up until after World War II, as the government uses religion to spur patriotic and nationalistic feelings. Buddhism is a popular religion among Japanese immigrants.

TREA. The United States and China reach an agreement known as the Burlingame Treaty. Anson Burlingame, a former Massachusetts congressman, is appointed by President Lincoln as the U.S. minister to the Qing government. He wins the confidence of the Chinese rulers because of his personal charm and genial sympathy for China. In 1867, China had asked Burlingame to head a Chinese delegation to negotiate new treaties with western powers. Representing China, Burlingame signs a treaty with the U.S. government in July 1868. The pact secures greater privileges for American citizens in China. Two important provisions of the treaty also provide protections for Chinese immigrants in America. In one article both countries recognize the inalienable human right to change domiciles and allegiance, as well as the mutual advantage of free migration. Another article grants Chinese people visiting or residing in the United States the same privileges, immunities, and exemptions enjoyed by the citizens or subjects of the most-favored nations. The Burlingame Treaty later will become a major obstacle for the anti-Chinese forces in the United States. In 1880 the United States will renegotiate the Burlingame Treaty with China and gain the unilateral right to limit Chinese immigration, thereby clearing the way for federal exclusion laws.

1869

ECON. The first group of Japanese to arrive on the U.S. mainland settles in Gold Hill (Coloma) near Sacramento, California. The Japanese establish the Wakamatsu Tea and Silk Farm Colony on 600 acres, sowing tea seeds and planting mulberry shoots brought from Japan. This experiment is short-lived because the crops fail to survive in the dry California soil.

ECON. The transcontinental railroad is completed on May 10, leaving 10,000 Chinese laborers unemployed. Discharged railroad workers seek work in agriculture.

MIGR. Several hundred Japanese laborers arrive in Hawaii, Guam, and California. They are recruited and sent by American Eugene Van Reed, a German company, and the Dutchman Edward Schnell. There are 141 men, 6 women, and 1 child brought to Hawaii to work on sugar plantations. These pioneers to Hawaii are treated poorly, and the Japanese government dispatches two officials to bring 40 of them home. Japan will ban all emigration after the incident.

RACE. The Knights of Labor, an American labor organization, is formed by Philadelphia tailors to counteract the growing power of big industries. This organization and the Workingmen's Party are major opponents of immigration, and they make immigrant workers scapegoats for labor problems.

1870

ECON. California is one of the world's leading wheat producers, and Chinese provide the labor for cultivating, harvesting, and packing wheat as well as other crops for the growers. Chinese farm laborers form small groups and find work through their own labor contractors. In California's Central Valley as well as in smaller coastal villages, in Washington's Yakima Valley, Oregon's Hood River Valley, and in other farm communities in states west of the Rocky Mountains, some lease land and become tenant farmers. The farmers concentrate on labor-intensive vegetables, strawberries, and tree fruits. In the Sacramento-San Joaquin Delta, they grow potatoes, onions, and asparagus. In Santa Barbara, California, Chinese workers provide long-term labor to local farmers in the early stages of agricultural development. They build houses and pave roads for their employers, and they tend a large variety of crops. Residing in farm houses on the premises of their employers, they work closely with the growers and perform domestic chores for them as well when needed.

ECON. Chinese in San Francisco enter a variety of occupations. About 40 percent of the gainfully employed find work in light manufacturing industries, making shoes, boots, slippers, women's apparel, cigars, and other items in small factories. They are also hired by small manufacturers along the Pacific coast. A good number of Chinese also find work as cooks in private homes and hotels.

ECON. Self-employment is common among the Chinese immigrants. In San Francisco and elsewhere, Chinese create a niche in laundering, largely because there have been few women in California during and after the Gold Rush. By 1870, there are 3,000 Chinese laundrymen in California, catering to mainly non-Chinese customers. Their number will increase to 5,000 a decade later. Chinese laundry businesses will expand to other states as well. Some Chinese also operate restaurants and grocery stores in cities and towns. Laundry, restaurant, and grocery are the three major enterprises in the ethnic economy before World War II.

LAWS. A new naturalization law extends citizenship eligibility to aliens of African nativity and to persons of African descent. The law does not mention the status of alien Asians.

LAWS. In San Francisco, the board of supervisors passes an ordinance to impose additional fees on laundry businesses. An entrepreneur with one horse for a delivery wagon is subject to a $2 fee every three months. The fee is $4 for those who use two horses. If a laundryman uses no horse at all, his fee is $15. Although the ordinance makes no mention of race or nationality, the Chinese are singled out because they do not have horses for delivery wagons.

POPU. The 1870 census records 63,199 Chinese in the United States. Among them, 4,566 are female.

RACE. Chinese become scapegoats as a nationwide recession leads to the rise of unemployment on the west coast.

1871

RACE. In Los Angeles's Chinatown, violence erupts against the Chinese on October 24. Two Chinatown factions fight over possession of a Chinese woman, attracting a crowd of observers. Some people in the crowd start firing at the Chinese. The Chinese run to a house to hide, but a mob cuts through the walls to shoot at them. Police arrive to find 15 Chinese lynched, 4 shot, and 2 wounded. The mob loots the residence for gold and other valuables. To take the rings from a Chinese herbalist, the mob cuts off his fingers. Eight men are convicted for the crime, but all are released a year later.

1871–1899

MIGR. A total of 491 immigrants from India are recorded.

1872

EDUC. Thirty young boys form the first contingent of the Chinese Educational Mission under the leadership of Yung Wing. They arrive in Hartford, Connecticut and are assigned to live with various local families. This group of students plans to start a 15-year term of study in the United States.

1873

EDUC. Zun Zow Matzmulla graduates from the U.S. Naval Academy. He is the first Japanese midshipman to attend the institution.

1873–1884

LAWS. San Francisco's board of supervisors passes 14 ordinances to restrict Chinese laundry operations. These ordinances find various ways to impose extra financial burdens on Chinese laundrymen. One such ordinance forbids them to dry laundry on rooftops.

1874

MUSI. The hula dance, which features a rhythmic, hip-swaying movement, is reinstalled in Hawaii while King Kalakaua is in power. This dance was banned by Christian missionaries in previous decades. Traditional Hawaiian music and the custom of wearing grass skirts also become popular during this time period.

1875

AGRI. California farmer Seth Lewelling develops a new cherry variety and names it the Bing cherry, after his farm hand Ah Bing. The latter probably plays a part in the experiment.

LAWS. The U.S. federal government enacts the Page Law, forbidding the entry of Chinese, Japanese, and Mongolian contract laborers, prostitutes, and felons. Although the law stipulates an end to the importation of contract laborers and prostitutes, its strict implementation, with the collaboration of American consuls in Hong Kong, will make it extremely difficult for the wives of Chinese immigrants to come to the United States. Female applicants are charged fees for their applications and have to undergo examinations by the American consuls at the port of departure. Many women are turned away. The combination of financial burden and the humiliation these women are forced to endure in the process discourages many Chinese women from applying for entry. The number of female Chinese immigrants will decline significantly after 1875. From 1869 to 1874, an average of 626 Chinese women were admitted annually; between 1875 and 1881, the number will fall to 265.

TREA. The United States ratifies a reciprocity treaty with the Kingdom of Hawaii, permitting the shipment of sugar to America duty-free. Sugar produced in the islands is now at an advantage in competition with other foreign sugar. The growth of the sugar industry will accelerate at a fast pace and become almost totally dependent on the American market. The importation of laborers to work on the plantations will be more urgent, since there is a shortage of labor on the islands. The Hawaiian population, which was between 300,000 and 500,000 at the time of Cook's arrival, will shrink to fewer than 60,000 by the end of the 1870s. Between 1876 and 1890, 55,000 Chinese and Japanese laborers will be imported to the islands to work on the plantations. This treaty will be renegotiated in 1887, when Hawaii will agree to let the United States build a naval base in Pearl Harbor.

1876

ASIA. Japan forces Korea to sign the Treaty of Kanghwa after its ship was driven away by Korean shore batteries in 1875. In the treaty Japan gains the right to trade in three ports, operate pawn shops, and lend money. Korea also gives the Japanese the right to extraterritoriality. Korea agrees to declare itself an independent state under the pressure, undermining its relation with China in terms of *sadae* ("serving the great").

HEAL. An epidemic of smallpox strikes San Francisco in the summer, taking 450 lives and infecting more than 1,600 individuals by October. John Mears, the city's health officer, blames the spread of the disease on the presence of Chinese residents in the city.

MIGR. Public resentment of Chinese in California leads to a congressional investigation, which brings on anti-Chinese sentiment at the national level. A total of 128 witnesses are called to hearings before the Joint Special Committee to Investigate Chinese Immigration; not a single Chinese is asked to testify. Most of the individuals who testify in front of the committee are anti-Chinese. They allege that cheap Asian laborers have lowered the standard of living. They also argue that the Chinese are unassimilable. Those who are in favor of Chinese immigration are usually employers of laborers. Charles Crocker, one of California's Big Four and an employer of a large number of Chinese on behalf of the Central Pacific Railroad Company, thinks that Chinese are reliable and steady people with aptitude and capacity for hard work. William W. Hollister, a California landowner of 75,000 acres, is the first to bring Chinese laborers to farm in his Santa Barbara ranch. He voices his support for Chinese immigration and says that without Chinese workers he would not be able to succeed in farming at all. Some religious groups also give testimonies favorable to the Chinese. Methodist Reverend Otis Gibson argues that, under God, all men are born free and equal. Merchants interested in trade with China offer their pro-Chinese stands as well. But the anti-Chinese labor groups, the politicians who need their votes, and the news media gain overwhelming support from the majority of Californians. They argue that the Chinese drive white men out of the labor market, causing their families to starve. The joint special committee supports the California position and recommends that the government restrict Chinese immigration.

RACE. Anti-Chinese violence breaks out in Chico, California. Arsonists burn a soap factory and a barn to the ground, because the owners have hired Chinese laborers or leased land to them. Several homes and businesses of the Chinese in Chico as well as the neighboring town of Nord are set on fire. Four Chinese are murdered and another two are injured.

1878

LAWS. The court decides in *In re Ah Yup* that Chinese immigrants are ineligible for citizenship because they are neither white nor black.

1879

EDUC. The University of Santa Tomas, a Spanish university in the Philippines, founds the School of Midwifery, providing higher education for Filipino women for the first time. Under Spanish rule only a small number of Filipino girls are able to receive primary education, provided by

charitable institutions. The development of nursing programs in the Philippines prepares some Filipino women to immigrate to the United States.

LAWS. President Rutherford B. Hayes vetoes the Fifteen Passenger Bill, which seeks to allow only 15 Chinese per ship to enter the United States.

1880

ECON. Fifty-nine percent of Chinese are still working in the gold fields. Stores operated by Chinese merchants provide the miners with foodstuffs, herb medicine, and clothing, as well as social and recreational services.

POPU. The 1880 census records a total of 105,465 Chinese in the United States, including 4,779 females.

TREA. The Burlingame Treaty is renegotiated by representatives of the United States and China. It gives the United States unilateral power to "regulate, limit or suspend" the "coming or residence" of Chinese laborers. The new treaty will

---

Testimony of William W. Hollister, a Farmer in Santa Barbara, California, on Chinese Immigration

"Of course, the question becomes one of labor. The Chinaman occupies a position in this matter simply incidentally. I look upon the whole question of labor as involved in this investigation. I can see it in no other light. In other words, it becomes a question simply whether we have enough labor or not in California. My own conviction is, from my experience in this State for twenty years, that we never have had a sufficient amount of reliable, patient, kindly labor. The field of labor is so enormous that I do not see when the time will come when it shall be fully filled. My opinion is that there is not a tithe of the laborers in California that ought to be here now, of any and all nationalities. With me and my labor it does not matter a straw. I am entirely regardless of the color or complexion of the man who does my work, white or black or particolored, or any complexion, simply requiring that the men shall work patiently and kindly. I ask nothing more from him. As to the character of the labor of the country, my experience in this State makes me put Chinamen entirely ahead of all others. The character of the man is better. His willingness to perform what the proprietor wants done is beyond question better than that of any other man."

Source: Report of the Joint Special Committee to Investigate Chinese Immigration, 44th Congress, 2d Session, Senate Report No. 680, February 27, 1877, 767.

be ratified quickly, removing a major obstacle for Chinese exclusion legislation.

WARS. Conflicts between Britain and the Burmese monarch intensify until Burma falls completely under British control in 1885.

1881

EDUC. In June, the Chinese government ends the Educational Mission and orders all the teachers and students in the program to return to China immediately. About 100 students are studying in the United States at the time; the majority of them are in the beginning of their training in colleges and technical schools. Most of these students will later establish distinguished careers in China.

MIGR. Hawaii's King Kalakaua visits Japan during his world tour. The king tries to persuade Japan to lift emigration restrictions, but the Japanese emperor is not moved. Hawaii will send two more representatives to Japan in the following two years, but both efforts are fruitless. Japan will not remove its emigration ban until 1885.

RELI. Sit Moon, a converted Christian, becomes the first Chinese pastor of a church in Hawaii. There are several Japanese pastors in Hawaii, including Miyama Kanichi, a Methodist-Episcopal evangelist in Honolulu; Sokabe Shiro, the pastor of the Honomu Church on the island of Hawaii; and the well-known pastor Takie Okumura.

1882

LAWS. On May 6, President Chester Arthur endorses the Chinese Exclusion Act, suspending the immigration of Chinese laborers for 10 years. For the first time, the federal government bars the entry of a group of people on racial grounds. The law signifies the beginning of a 61-year-long Chinese exclusion, ending the history of the United States as a country of free immigration. The law does not apply to Chinese laborers already in the United States or those who may come within 90 days after it is enacted. Under the 1880 treaty obligations, Chinese teachers, students, merchants, tourists, and their servants,

as well as diplomats, are exempted from the restriction. Valid certificates issued by the Chinese government will be required for these groups to gain entry to the United States. The law also stipulates that no state or federal court shall grant citizenship to Chinese, making Chinese aliens ineligible for citizenship.

The Chinese Exclusion Act will be amended several times. Each amendment will add more restrictions and close loopholes. An 1884 amendment will require certificates for Chinese who left the country to reenter. The 1888 amendment (the Scott Act) will void all certificates previously issued by the government and prevent Chinese immigrants who had left the United States from reentering. An 1892 amendment (the Geary Act) will extend the exclusion for another 10 years and require all alien Chinese to carry certificates of residence. The amendment of 1902 will extend exclusion for yet another 10 years. In 1904, a final amendment will make Chinese exclusion permanent. All Chinese exclusion legislation will be repealed in 1943. Chinese exclusion laws will effectively block entry of new immigrant laborers. They will also make it extremely difficult for male Chinese already residing in the United States to form families. Under the exclusion legislation Chinese population in the United States will have negative growth, from 107,488 in 1890 to 77,504 in 1940.

SOCI. The Chinese Consolidated Benevolent Association (CCBA) is established in San Francisco on November 19, in place of the existing federation of district associations known as the Chinese Six Companies. Hierarchically above the family/clan and district associations, the CCBA is often compared to the ancient Irish Order of Hibernians or the Scandinavian Association. It is formed in response to immigrants' increasing demand for help in dealing with anti-Chinese legislation. The CCBA provides leadership for the immigrants and is recognized by the larger American society as the voice of the ethnic community. It hires lawyers to fight against anti-Chinese legislation. It will also establish Chinese language schools and issue "exit permits" to those who want to return to China. There will be 37 branches of the CCBA by 1947.

TREA. Admiral Robert W. Shufeldt signs the Treaty of Kanghwa with Korea, securing for the United States the same privileges that Korea gives to Japan. Korea will sign similar treaties with Great Britain, Germany, Russia, Italy, and France shortly after.

1882–1886

RACE. Anti-Chinese agitation gains momentum in Hawaii, and some restrictive measures are issued. Opponents of Chinese labor argue that the increase of Chinese on the islands poses challenges to the survival of native Hawaiians, and they blame the Chinese for introducing diseases to the native population. The 18,000 Chinese compose about a quarter of the Hawaiian population. Although the planters are satisfied with Chinese laborers, they do not want the Chinese to become too dominant. They want to diversify the labor force by bringing in workers from other countries.

1884

ASIA. American medical missionary Horace N. Allen arrives in Korea. This cosmopolitan American plays an important role in the United States' contact with Korea. For many years Allen is the only foreigner who is allowed to visit King Kojong and the queen in their royal palace, and his personal connection helps American Protestant missionaries to spread the gospel in the kingdom and his friends to gain lucrative concessions and franchises, including the Unsan gold mines. Allen will become a diplomat, serving as secretary of the American legation in Seoul between 1890 and 1897 and the American minister to Korea between 1897 and 1905.

EDUC. The first Chinese language school in the United States is established in San Francisco for the children of immigrants. The school is sponsored by the Chinese Consolidated Benevolent Association.

LAWS. An amendment to the Chinese Exclusion Act requires each Chinese merchant to present a Section 6 certificate issued by the government of China at the port of entry.

LAWS. A federal circuit court for the district of California turns down two petitions of Chinese women, preventing Chinese laborers from sending for their wives. The 1882 Chinese Exclusion Act does not bar the entry of Chinese women. Because women in China do not usually work for wages, they are not considered laborers. But immigration authorities do not let wives of Chinese laborers join their husbands in the United States. Two Chinese women take their cases to court in 1884. In the case of Ah Quan, the court rejects her position, ruling that a wife of a Chinese laborer can be allowed to enter only if she can prove she was in the United States before June 6, 1882, and that the wife and minor children should be classified the same as the husband or father. In the case of Ah Moy, the justice hands down a similar ruling, concluding that a woman should be accorded laborer status upon her marriage to a laborer, even if she has never worked outside the home. Thus the court denies a laborer the right to bring in his Chinese wife and children.

1885

EDUC. Chinese in San Francisco battle for the right to public education. After the closing of the first segregated Oriental School for Chinese children in 1871, Chinese were deprived of the right to public education for 14 years. In 1884, the American-born Mamie Tape had tried to attend a local school in San Francisco, but the school principal rejected her because she was Chinese. Mamie's mother, Mary Tape, was a Chinese orphan brought to the United States by American missionaries at age 11. Her husband, Joseph Tape, also came to California at a young age and occasionally works as an interpreter for Chinese labor contractors. The Tape family resides outside Chinatown, and their American-born children speak English more fluently than Chinese. The Tapes take the case of their daughter to the San Francisco board of education. However, not only does the board uphold the decision of the school, but it also rules that any school principal or teacher who admits a "Mongolian child" will be dismissed. The Tapes take another step and file their grievances in court. The case becomes the focus of a heated public debate in San Francisco. Many people are shocked to learn that nearly 1,000 Chinese children are denied public education. Both the San Francisco superior court and the California supreme court rule in the Tapes' favor, arguing that denying a child born in California to Chinese parents entry to a California public school would violate state law and constitutional law. The school still refuses to accept Mamie. It pushes through state legislation establishing a separate facility for Chinese students. The new Oriental School is opened in a rented room above a grocery store in Chinatown.

FAMI. More Japanese than Chinese laborers migrate to Hawaii and the United States with their wives. Believing that family will bring stability to the immigrant communities, the Japanese government encourages men to bring their wives. Women make up about 22 percent of the Japanese population in Hawaii and 7 percent on the mainland. Later, Japan will agree to terminate the emigration of its male laborers but will allow parents, wives, and children of the laborers already in the United States to go to the United States until 1920.

LAWS. In *Yick Wo v. Hopkins,* the Chinese successfully establish a case in the U.S. Supreme Court against discrimination. A San Francisco city ordinance requires laundries housed in wooden buildings to be licensed (violators are subject to a $1,000 fine or six months in jail). All Chinese laundries are located in wooden structures, and all of their license applications are rejected by the board of supervisors. The board, however, grants licenses to all 80 non-Chinese applicants with only one exception. Yick Wo has been in the laundry business since 1863. Although his license application is denied, he keeps his business open because he has in his possession valid certificates from fire and health officials, indicating his laundry has passed the city's fire and sanitation inspections. The police arrest him. *Yick Wo v. Hopkins* is a class action suit sponsored by Tung Hing Tong, the guild of Chinese laundrymen. The lawyer for the plaintiff argues in front of the U.S. Supreme Court justices that the ordinance is arbitrary and discriminatory and that the Chinese are denied due process of law. The defense lawyer argues that the city's police have the power to regulate laundries and that the ordinance in question is nondiscriminatory because the Chinese are not mentioned. Invoking the Fourteenth Amendment, the high court rules in favor of the Chinese plaintiff. It decides that to divide laundries arbitrarily into two classes is a denial of equal protection under the law. The court rules that a discriminatory law against any party, even if the party is not named

---

Protest Letter by Mary Tape, Mother of Mamie Tape, April 8, 1885 (The Letter Is Read before the Board and Reprinted in Full in the Local Newspapers)

"Dear Sirs: I see that you are going to make all sorts of excuses to keep my child out off the public schools. Dear sirs, Will you please tell me! Is it a disgrace to be born a Chinese? Didn't God make us all!!! What right! Have you to bar my children out of the school because she is a Chinese descend. They is no other worldly reason that you could keep her out, except that I suppose, you all goes to churches on Sundays! Do you call that a Christian act to compel my little children to go so far to a school that is made in purpose for them . . . You have expended a lot of the Public money foolishly, all because of a one poor little child . . . . It seems no matter how a Chinese may live and dress so long as you know they Chinese. Then they are hated as one. There is not any right or justice for them . . . . May you Mr. Moulder [the San Francisco school superintendent], never be persecuted like the way you have persecuted little Mamie Tape. Mamie Tape will never attend any of the Chinese schools of your making! Never!!! I will let the world see sir What Justice there is When it is govern by the Race prejudice men!"

Source: Alta, April 16, 1885, 1.

in the law, is unconstitutional. The ruling implies that equal protection guaranteed by the Constitution applies to both U.S. citizens and aliens. This landmark supreme court case has a long-lasting impact on American legal history.

MIGR. Japanese contract laborers begin to arrive in Hawaii in large numbers to work on sugar plantations. This is made possible by American Robert Walker Irwin, who reaches an agreement with the Japanese government to allow its subjects to go abroad. A cosmopolitan American, Irwin is instrumental in Japanese migration to Hawaii. Serving as consul general and special agent of the board of immigration for the Kingdom of Hawaii, he is also a foreign advisor to Mitsui Bussan, a Japanese import-export company, as well as the Japanese government. Irwin is in charge of the initial recruitment and arranges to have the first shipload of Japanese contract laborers sail for Hawaii. The monthly wage for a male laborer is $9 and a female laborer $6. Wages will increase to $15 a month for men and $9 for women. Workers in the fields are required to work 10 hours a day, while 12 hours of work is expected for those in the sugar mills. The workers can take Sunday off. Passage to Hawaii, lodging, fuel, medical care, and interpreter services are provided. The Japanese are brought to fill the increasing demand for plantation labor, as well as to undermine the dominance of the large Chinese population. Irwin's involvement in Japanese migration to Hawaii, known as the Irwin Convention, will last for 10 years. By 1894 there will be 29,000 Japanese laborers brought to Hawaii. Japanese workers will become the largest single ethnic group on the islands.

RACE. Mob violence takes the lives of 28 Chinese and wounds 15 in Rock Springs in Wyoming Territory in September. About 600 Chinese are employed by a coal mining company. The violence erupts when the Chinese workers decide not to join a strike organized by white workers.

RACE. An anti-Chinese group meets in Seattle in Washington Territory, ordering the evacuation of all Chinese by November 1. Two days after the deadline, Tacoma residents evacuate 600 Chinese by force and take them to a railroad station in Lake View. The forced removal causes the death of two men. The Chinese are transported by railroad to Portland. Tacoma Chinatown is burned down two days later.

RACE. Arsonists set fire to several buildings in San Francisco's Chinatown, killing 13 people.

WARS. France annexes Vietnam. Although Vietnam's emperors retain their paramount status, they have little power to rule.

WARS. Great Britain gains complete control of Burma and annexes it to India. British control of Burma will continue until 1948.

1886

MIGR. Philip Jaisohn (1864–1951) arrives in the United States. Born as Suh Jae-pil in Korea, he will receive his medical degree in 1892. Returning to Korea four years later, he will found the first Korean newspaper and become an advocate for Korean independence. His work in medical research and pathology, as well as his nationalist ideas, will be highly regarded in both Korea and the United States.

RACE. Seattle residents force an evacuation of Chinese. A mob congregates in February and marches into Chinatown. About 350 Chinese are loaded into wagons and taken to the docks to be shipped away. Interference by the court and the territorial government, together with the assistance of a citizens group and small contingents of the Seattle Rifles and the University Cadets, is not enough to disperse the mob. Some Chinese decide to leave. The rest of them return to Chinatown to face continuous harassment. Violence is prevented only because martial law is declared and a curfew order is imposed, and only because of the presence of federal troops.

RACE. Anti-Chinese violence takes place all over the American West in the mid-1880s. Murder or expulsion of Chinese occurs at Snake River Canyon in Idaho; in Denver, Colorado; in Portland, Oregon; and in Squaw Valley, Coal Creek, Black Diamond, Tacoma, and Puyallup in Washington. In California, many Chinese dwellings are set on fire, and Chinese farm laborers in many agricultural areas are forcibly removed.

1887

ASIA. Hawaii's constitution becomes effective, assuring the planters and businessmen of control over the government of the kingdom. Investment and profit in the sugar industry will increase, and American businessmen will gain political power on the islands.

PUBL. *When I Was a Boy in China,* authored by Lee Yan Phou (1861–1938), is published. Brought to the United States by the Chinese Educational Mission in 1873, the author received education in Springfield, Massachusetts and New Haven, Connecticut. A Yale College graduate, he was invited to write the book by the Lothrop Company in Boston. The book is an encyclopedic account of Chinese civilization, covering such subjects as philosophy, education, literature, religion, ceremonies, family, food, and pastimes.

1888

LAWS. The Scott Act, another amendment of the Chinese exclusion legislation, is signed into law by President Grover Cleveland. The original Chinese Exclusion Act allowed reentry of Chinese who left the United States to visit their families in China. Thousands of Chinese are out of the country with government-issued reentry certificates, but this new law voids all certificates. Chinese laborers in the United States can no longer visit their families and return freely.

1889

LAWS. *Chae Chan Ping v. United States* challenges the Scott Act. The 1882 exclusion law allows Chinese laborers already residing in the United States to stay as well as giving them the freedom to visit China and return. In an 1888 amendment known as the Scott Act, however, the government changed its early decision and voided all previously issued return certificates. An estimated 20,000 laborers visiting China at the time were affected. Chae Chan Ping, who had in his possession a government-issued return certificate, was on his way back to the United States from China when the new law became effective. The U.S. Supreme Court reviews Chae's case and rejects his petition, arguing that the government can regulate immigration and revoke the right of Chinese laborers to return.

RELI. The vast majority of Japanese immigrants are Buddhists, and many of them belong to the Nishi Hongwanji—the West School of the Temple of the Original Vow. The first Nishi Hongwanji priest arrives in Hawaii in 1889. With funds donated from Japanese plantation workers, he builds a small temple in Hilo. Another priest, Imamura Yemyo, will organize the Young Men's Buddhist Association (YMBA) in 1898 and start a night school to teach English to the workers. A bigger temple will be built in Hilo in 1898, and another one in Honolulu in 1900. Two Nishi Hongwanji missionaries will arrive in San Francisco in 1899. YMBAs will be set up in San Francisco, Sacramento, and Fresno, as well as a Buddhist Women's Association under the North American Buddhist Mission, which will be renamed several times, first as the Buddhist Church of San Francisco in 1905, then as the Buddhist Mission in 1906, and as the Buddhist Churches of America in 1944. Some of the services will be conducted in English.

1890

AGRI. Chinese in Hawaii enjoy some success in agriculture. Poor working conditions and abusive luna (overseers) discourage Chinese sugar plantation workers from renewing their contracts. Some former contract laborers become independent farmers. They are most successful in rice farming and truck gardening. Rice is the second most important source of income in Hawaii's economy. Largely due to Chinese farmers, rice acreage has increased from 1,000 acres in 1875 to 7,500 acres. The growth will reach 9,000 acres in 1900.

ECON. The McKinley Tariff grants duty-free status to all foreign sugar, removing the special privilege enjoyed by Hawaiian sugar producers in the previous two decades. This will undermine the profits of investors in the sugar industry.

POPU. The census of 1890 records 107,488 Chinese in the United States, with an imbalanced sex ratio of 26.8 to 1. Partly because of the enforcement of the Page Law and Chinese exclusion legislation, it is extremely difficult for Chinese women to gain entry, making Chinese America a predominately bachelor society.

POPU. The 1890 census finds more than 2,039 Japanese on the U.S. mainland.

SPOR. Gambling is a popular form of recreation for both Chinese and Japanese immigrants, while prostitution provides female companionship for lonely male laborers.

1892

ASIA. Tonghak (eastern learning) believers in Korea begin to hold demonstrations against the government. First appearing in the 1860s, Tonghak leaders advocated eastern learning instead of western learning in order to cope with the might of foreign imperial powers. This syncretistic religious group gained many followers in the late 1880s, including members of the *yangban* (Korea's ruling class). The movement will turn into a large-scale revolt, called the Tonghak Rebellion, in 1894. The Korean government will call China to send troops to help crack down on the rebellion.

LAWS. The Geary Act extends Chinese exclusion for 10 years and requires alien Chinese to carry registration cards. This law allows the police and immigration authorities to arrest and deport Chinese without search warrants. Both Chinese laborers and merchants are affected, and hundreds of them will be arrested and some deported.

LAWS. In *Fong Yue Ting v. United States,* the Chinese challenge the Geary Act unsuccessfully. Three Chinese involved in deportation proceedings for violation of the Geary Act file their grievances with the U.S. Supreme Court, backed by the entire Chinese American community. The high court decides that the government has the right to regulate immigration, compel aliens to register, and deport those who do not comply with the law.

PUBL. The first Japanese-language newspaper in Hawaii appears in Honolulu.

1893

SOCI. About 20 Japanese shoemakers in San Francisco organize a Shoemakers' League, which becomes the first Japanese trade association in the United States. The league makes cooperative purchases and sets rules for marketing on behalf of all the members.

WARS. Hawaii's Queen Liliuokalani is overthrown in January in a virtually bloodless coup led by American, German, and British businessmen. At the instigation of the U.S. minister to Hawaii, John L. Stevens, U.S. Navy and Marine forces move ashore from the USS *Boston,* in Honolulu Harbor at the time. A provisional government is established under Sanford B. Dole, the son of a pioneer missionary to Hawaii, and Stevens declares Hawaii a U.S. protectorate. A mission is dispatched to Washington, D.C., to negotiate a treaty for annexation of the islands by the United States. President Grover Cleveland, however, is not interested in the annexation and launches an investigation of American involvement in the overthrow. Denied the support of the White House, the annexation treaty is pushed aside. Not until the election of Republican President William McKinley in 1896 and the outbreak of the Spanish-American War will enthusiasm for expansion be renewed.

1894

WARS. The Sino-Japanese War (1894–1895) starts in Korea. It is a response to the presence of Chinese military in Korea, which had been called in by the Korean government to suppress the Tonghak Rebellion. Japan sends an even larger contingent of troops to the peninsula and wins the war against China. Japan will establish its domination of Korea after the war and take control of Formosa (Taiwan).

WARS. France forms the French Indochina Union after its conquest of Vietnam, Cambodia, and Laos is completed. Southeast Asia integrates into the French empire.

1895

MIGR. After the Irwin Convention, the recruitment of Japanese workers to Hawaii is privatized. Emigration firms charge fees for their services, helping applicants to obtain passports, purchase tickets, and prepare for medical examinations. About 125,000 Japanese will leave for Hawaii between 1894 and 1908. Fifteen percent of the recruited laborers are female.

1896

EDUC. Japanese in Hawaii start the first Japanese language school in Hawaii, led by Reverend Takie Okumura at Makiki Christian Church in Honolulu.

HEAL. The San Francisco board of health decides to inspect all arriving passengers when deaths from bubonic plague are reported, but Chinese and Japanese are singled out for detention in quarantine. When two cases of the disease are found in Honolulu's Chinatown, the Hawaii board of health sends 4,500 Chinese to a quarantine camp and burns Chinatown to the ground.

SPOR. Japanese sugar plantation workers in Hawaii organize the first Hawaii Grand Sumo Tournament in Honolulu. Sumo is a Japanese form of wrestling and one of the most important sports to people in Japan and Japanese emigrants. The Hawaii Grand Sumo Tournament facilitates inter-plantation activities.

WARS. An uprising led by the radical Katipunan in the Spanish-occupied Philippines takes place. Leader Emilio Aguinaldo is arrested and forced into exile. He will be brought back to Manila by Americans during the Spanish-American War.

1898

LAWS. Chinese immigrants win a landmark case, *United States v. Wong Kim Ark,* at the U.S. Supreme Court. Similar to Chae Chan Ping, Wong Kim Ark returned to the United States from a trip to China after the Scott Act was enacted. Immigration authorities denied his entry, and he turns to the court. Unlike Chae Chan Ping, who is an immigrant, Wong's birthplace is in the United States. The high court rules that anyone born in the United States is a citizen and that that right cannot be taken away. This landmark case allows U.S.-born Chinese to leave and return freely.

PUBL. The first Japanese-language newspaper in the mainland United States, the *Nichibei Shimbun,* is published in San Francisco (*nichi* is for "Japan" and *bei* for "America"). The founder of the paper, Abiko Kyutaro (1865–1936), arrived in San Francisco in 1885 at age 20. As an advocate for farming and landownership, he encouraged fellow Japanese immigrants to settle permanently. To create a model of his ideal Japanese farming community, Abiko will establish a Japanese farming community in the San Joaquin Valley in 1906.

SOCI. Japanese farmers in the United States form *kenjinkai,* which are prefecture-based social organizations. The farmers rely on kenjinkai for social activities such as annual picnics, as well as network support for employment, housing, and credit. Through rotating credit groups within their kenjinkai, individual immigrants can pool their resources together for initial business investment. Like the district associations organized by Chinese immigrants, kenjinkai provide services crucial to the survival of Japanese immigrants. Different organizations under the kenjinkai assist members in leasing and purchasing land, settling disputes, obtaining supplies, disseminating information about agricultural techniques and produce prices, and selling crops in the city markets.

TREA. The Treaty of Paris between the United States and Spain concludes the Spanish-American War. Spain vacates its colony in Cuba, recognizing America's influence in the area. Spain also cedes Puerto Rico, Guam, and the Philippines to the United States. These islands become America's first foreign colonies. American occupation of the Philippines will lead to brutal warfare against native insurgency forces.

WARS. American commander of the Pacific fleet Admiral George Dewey sinks the Spanish squadron in Manila Bay (his crew includes a few Japanese immigrants). Emilio Aguinaldo is brought from exile in Hong Kong back to Manila by the Americans. He declares independence for the Philippines in June. His force helps the Americans defeat the Spaniards in the Philippines. The Spanish-American War ends, and the United States acquires the Philippines through the Treaty of Paris.

WARS. The United States officially annexes Hawaii under President William McKinley's administration. A joint resolution of Congress approves the annexation on July 7. The flag of the United States is raised over Iolani Palace in Honolulu on August 12.

WARS. The Boxer Rebellion (1898–1901), a Chinese nationalist uprising against foreigners, Christians, and the Qing government, begins when a secret society of Chinese, Yihetuan (the Boxers United in Righteousness), emerges in the northwest Shangdong Province. The Boxers are mostly poor peasants and laborers, including several female groups. They consider the introduction of foreign goods disruptive to the traditional Chinese economy and foreign constructions harmful to the natural harmony. This sentiment is shared by many Chinese, including some Qing government officials. After the Opium Wars, China signed many humiliating treaties with western powers. Many Chinese fear their country will be carved up like a melon. The Boxers attack Christian missionaries and converts in China's northeastern provinces. They occupy the Chinese capital, Beijing, seizing foreign legations in both Beijing and Tianjin. An army of 2,000 sent by western powers to protect their citizens is defeated. On June 21 the Chinese dowager empress declares war against foreign powers. On July 14, an international expedition of nearly 20,000 soldiers under a joint command structure of 8 western nations, including the United States, occupies Tianjin. Beijing falls on August 14. The Qing government will sign the Boxer Protocol on September 7, 1901.

1899

PUBL. Chinese American Ng Poon Chew starts *Hua Mei Sun Bo* (Chinese American Morning Paper), a Chinese-language weekly in Los Angeles. Born in Guangdong Province in China, Chew came to the United States in 1881. He studied English in a Sunday school in the San Jose area of California and was converted to Christianity in 1883. He would later attend the San Francisco Theological Seminary and become America's first Chinese Presbyterian minister on the Pacific coast. *Hua Mei Sun Bo* is circulated among Chew's friends in California. This experience prepares Chew to eventually launch a daily newspaper.

RELI. The North American Buddhist Mission in San Francisco is incorporated under the laws of California by Japanese missionaries.

WARS. The Philippine-American War (1899–1901) breaks out as American military forces begin their occupation of the islands under the provisions of the Treaty of Paris. Emilio Aguinaldo's guerrillas fight against American colonialism. This bloody war will last for 41 months, taking as many as 20,000 Filipino lives and some 4,200 Americans in the guerrilla warfare. Anti-imperialism sentiment begins to emerge at home, criticizing U.S. military actions in the Philippines.

TWENTIETH CENTURY

1900

HEAL. The coroner in San Francisco suspects a case of bubonic plague after an autopsy of a Chinese corpse in March. City officials immediately conduct a house-to-house inspection and forbid Chinese and Japanese to travel to outside of California without certificates from the U.S. Marine Hospital Service. Houses in Chinatown are washed with lime, sulfur dioxide, and mercury bichloride. A court order will later declare the city's action discriminatory.

LAWS. President William McKinley signs the Organic Act into law on August 30 to establish a U.S. territorial government in Hawaii. The islands become a U.S. territory on July 14, and all islanders become U.S. citizens. Chinese laborers can no longer migrate to the islands once American laws become applicable there.

LAWS. In *United States v. Mrs. Gun Lim,* a federal circuit court opens the door for immigration of the wives of Chinese merchants. The court decides that wives and minor children of Chinese merchants domiciled in the United States should be allowed to enter the country without the certificates required by the 1884 act.

POPU. The U.S. Census records 89,863 Chinese on the mainland, including 4,522 women. Due to the enforcement of exclusion legislation, the Chinese population in the United States starts to decline.

POPU. The census counts 24,326 Japanese living in the mainland United States. An additional 60,000 Japanese are residing in Hawaii.

PUBL. Ng Poon Chew and several Chinese Christians publish the first independent community newspaper, the *Chinese-Western Daily* (*Chung Sai Yat Po,* 1900–1950), in San Francisco. This paper is not affiliated with any parties or political groups in China. It enjoys a large circulation among the Chinese in the western part of the United States and Mexico.

SETT. Japanese enclaves are formed in San Francisco, Sacramento, Fresno, Portland, Seattle, Tacoma, Salt Lake City, and Vancouver, British Columbia.

1901

ASIA. The United States establishes a civilian government in the Philippines after the Philippine-American War, under the governorship of William Howard Taft. Many Americans will serve in the territorial government and work as teachers to westernize the Filipinos.

LAWS. California's anti-miscegenation law is amended to prohibit marriages between whites and "Mongolians." This restriction will not be lifted until 1948.

MIGR. Peter Rye becomes the first recorded Korean immigrant to Hawaii on January 9.

SOCI. A group of Chinese residents in Philadelphia is organized to obtain civil rights in the United States. In a public statement, the organization declares that its main goal is to abolish laws that deprive Chinese of the right to naturalize. Recognizing the importance of political participation, this organization calls Chinese American citizens to vote in elections.

SPOR. A group of boarding school students in Hawaii organizes perhaps the first Japanese American baseball team, under the supervision of Takie Okumura.

TREA. The Boxer Protocol is imposed on China by western nations on September 7, ending the Boxer Rebellion. The protocol forces China to pay an enormous indemnity, allow armed foreign guards to protect the legation quarter in perpetuity, and execute leading Boxer supporters. Fearing the Boxer incident will lead to China's partition, the United States declares its determination to preserve China's safety, peace, and administrative entity. Russia expands its sphere of influence in Manchuria during the rebellion. The Boxers' defeat further weakens the Qing dynasty and accelerates political development toward revolution. The United States will later turn part of the Boxer indemnity into scholarships for Chinese students to study in America.

1902

ECON. Several Japanese businessmen found the Japanese American Industrial Corporation. One of the largest labor contracting firms in California, the corporation supplies Japanese labor to agriculture, mining, and railroads.

LAWS. The Philippines Organic Act is passed, setting up terms for the civil government established in the previous year. Some level of self-governance is allowed under U.S. rule.

LAWS. Another amendment of the Chinese Exclusion Act is enacted, extending Chinese exclusion for 10 more years. Immigration of Chinese to the U.S. territories is also restricted.

LAWS. In *Tsoi Sim v. United States,* Chinese Americans successfully establish a case in the U.S. Circuit Court of Appeals for the Ninth Circuit that allows an alien Chinese wife of an American citizen the right to reside with her husband. Tsoi Sim was three when she came to the United States with her father in 1882, before the Chinese Exclusion Act. Because she does not carry an alien registration card—a violation of the Geary Act—she is arrested and put on

deportation proceedings. However, Tsoi Sim is married at the time, and her husband is a U.S.-born Chinese. Delivering the opinion of the court, District Judge Thomas Porter Hawley declares that 1) a citizen of the United States should be entitled to greater rights and privileges than an alien merchant; 2) upon marriage, Tsoi Sim's husband's domicile became hers, and she should be entitled to live with her husband; and 3) if she is to be deported for violating the Geary Act, she will also have the right to immediately return, upon the sole ground that she is the wife of an American citizen. This case is extremely important to the Chinese immigrant community. Up to this point only wives of Chinese merchants have been allowed entry. The ruling implies that any American citizen of Chinese ancestry can go to China, get married, and then bring his wife back to the United States. Only 44 Chinese women are admitted to the United States in 1902; in 1924, 938 will be admitted. A total of 2,848 Chinese women will enter as wives of American citizens between 1906 and 1924. *Tsoi Sim v. United States* will stand for more than 20 years until the 1924 Immigration Act bars all aliens ineligible to citizenship.

1903

CIVI. Japanese and Mexican farm workers strike jointly for higher wages in Oxnard, California. For years, Oxnard beet-growers have hired Japanese and Mexican laborers through their own co-ethnic labor contractors. The creation of a new Western Agricultural Contracting Company (WACC), however, forces independent Japanese labor contractors to work as subcontractors, making the farm workers pay double commission. A Japanese-Mexican Labor Association (JMLA) is formed to protest the WACC. The association elects a Japanese president and vice president and a Mexican secretary. About 1,200 Japanese and Mexican workers strike in March. During a demonstration, one Mexican worker is shot to death and several others are injured. A few JMLA officials are arrested. Through mediation by an American Federation of Labor (AFL) representative, the WACC agrees to the JMLA's demands and allows the workers to bargain directly with the growers under their own contractors. The growers agree to

The Japanese-owned Oakland Noodle Co. advertises its products as Chinese to appeal to American consumers:

Chop Suey Noodles: Housewife's Aid

Why bother to make noodles when we may buy the Chop Suey Brand? These delicious products are made by expert chefs, according to a special formula that has been handed down from generation to generation in the family of Jitsuji Aoki, owner of the Oakland Noodle Co.

The wise housewife keeps half a dozen packages of them on her pantry shelf so that she is never without the makings of a main dish, an entrée or a garnish. They lend themselves to every meal in the day, and may be blended with all shell fish, eggs, tomatoes, meats, chicken, cheese, etc. Try Chop Suey Brand Noodles and see how superior they are. Your grocer has them, or phone the Oakland Noodle Co., Lakeside 1633.

Also ask your grocer for Chop Suey Brand Soy Sauce, mild and mellow. It will add a pleasing flavor to many dishes.

Source: Oakland Tribune, June 1, 1930.

raise wages as well. The victory of the strike encourages J. M. Lizarras, the JMLA secretary, to apply for a charter from the AFL. The AFL president, Samuel Gompers, agrees to the request only if Lizarras withholds union membership from Chinese or Japanese. Lizarras rejects the offer from Gompers.

ECON. Japanese immigrant Jitsuji Aoki opens the Oakland Noodle Co. in California, selling plain and egg noodles. Although the noodle recipes are said to be passed down through Aoki's family for generations, the company decides to market its products as "chop suey" noodles. This is probably done out of two concerns: most American consumers do not seem to be able to differentiate Japanese from Chinese, and these consumers are more familiar with Chinese food products than Japanese. This marketing strategy apparently works well. By the 1930s, Chop Suey noodles and other products of the company will be sold at mainstream grocery stores in the San Francisco Bay area.

Letter of J. M. Lizarras, the Mexican Secretary of the Japanese-Mexican Labor Association, to Samuel Gompers, the President of the American Federation of Labor, after the Latter Refuses to Accept Membership of Any Chinese or Japanese

"We beg to say in reply that our Japanese brothers here were the first to recognize the importance of cooperating and unity in demanding a fair wage scale . . . . In the past we have counseled, fought and lived on very short rations with our Japanese brothers, and toiled with them in the fields, and they have been uniformly kind and considerate. We would be false to them and to ourselves and to the cause of unionism if we now accepted privileges for ourselves which are not accorded to them . . . . We will refuse any other kind of charter, except one which will wipe out race prejudice and recognize our fellow workers as being as good as ourselves. I am ordered by the Mexican union to write this letter to you and they fully approve its words."

Source: Karl Yoneda, "100 Years of Japanese Labor History in the USA," in Amy Tachiki et al., *Roots: An Asian American Reader* (Los Angeles: University of California, Los Angeles, Asian American Studies Center, 1971), 152.

EDUC. The *pensionado* program starts in the Philippines, sponsored by the U.S. government. The program provides aid to young students to study in the United States. More than 200 Filipino students will receive American education under the program by 1912.

MIGR. Contract laborers from Korea begin to arrive in Hawaii. Knowing the influence that diplomat Horace N. Allen has in Korea, the Hawaiian Sugar Planters Association invites him to visit Hawaii. The planters are concerned about the growing number of Japanese workers on the islands since the barring of the Chinese, and the Korean workers are recruited to tip the balance. Returning to Korea, Allen persuades King Kojong to allow his people to work in Hawaii. An emigration franchise is set up, and Allen passes this business opportunity to his friend David W. Deshler. By then Hawaii is already a U.S. territory, and the contract labor system is prohibited. Deshler's office assists prospective emigrants in bypassing legal restrictions. It establishes a special bank that lends $50 cash to each laborer in addition to transportation fares. Upon arrival, the laborers show the money in their possession to immigration inspectors as proof that they are not contract laborers. Like the Chinese and Japanese before them, most Koreans are contracted to work in the sugar plantations. About 7,000 Koreans will migrate to Hawaii before 1905. Japan forces Korea to end the outflow in 1905. An additional 1,000 Koreans will immigrate to the U.S. mainland.

RELI. Christians make up 40 percent of Korean emigrants to Hawaii.

SOCI. Ahn Chang-ho establishes the Chinmokho (Friendship Society), the first Korean immigrant community organization on the U.S. mainland. An intellectual and influential member of the community, Ahn arrived in the United States in 1899. He will later found the Hung Sa Dang (Young Koreans Academy) and play a leadership role in the Korean independence movement. He will also serve as secretary of the interior and then as secretary of labor in the Korean provincial government-in-exile in Shanghai. Ahn will die in 1938, after being jailed by Japanese occupants in Shanghai in 1935.

Filling, weighing, and sewing sacks of raw sugar at a plantation mill, Hawaii Islands (1910–1920). [National Photo Company Collection, Library of Congress Prints and Photographs Division, LC-DIG-npcc-30938]

1904

CIVI. About 1,200 Japanese plantation workers in Hawaii strike in Waialua during the harvest season for higher wages. Their demand is ignored at first, and the workers refuse to load the harvested sugarcane lying on the ground. Suffering severe losses, the planters give in and make some concessions. The workers return to work after the victory.

CIVI. Japanese workers on the Lahaina plantation on the island of Maui stage a strike. The strike is triggered by a conflict between a luna (overseer) and the workers. One Japanese worker is injured by the luna and becomes blind, but a local judge decides to fine the luna only $25. In protest, 900 Japanese plantation workers stop work. The police and militia are called in, killing one striker and wounding a few more. The strike ends when the luna in question is fired and the planters promise better housing for the workers.

ECON. An American-educated Japanese, Jo Sakai, founds a farming colony near Boca Raton, Florida. The colony declines four years later due to natural disasters and competition from Cuban pineapple growers.

LAWS. Another amendment to the Chinese Exclusion Act is passed, making exclusion of the Chinese permanent.

SOCI. The Chinese American Citizens Alliance (CACA) is established based on the United Parlor of the Native Sons of the Golden State, led by Walter U. Lum, Joseph K. Lum, and Ng Gunn. This organization of U.S.-born Chinese speaks out against Chinese exclusion and experiences significant growth. The CACA will have nine local lodges by 1920. By 1925, membership in its San Francisco lodge will reach 2,000. Working closely with other community organizations, the CACA will take the lead in lobby activities of the community to amend immigration laws.

WARS. The Russo-Japanese War (1904–1905) is fought in Korea. Japan defeats a western colonial power and emerges with military might in Asia.

1905

ASIA. People in China boycott American goods in response to unfair treatment of their emigrants in the United States. The Chinese are angry at the exclusion laws, especially the Geary Act, which forces merchants to carry registration cards or risk arrest and deportation. Since 1904, the United States has been on its way to imposing tougher restrictions on Chinese immigrants through a new treaty negotiation with China, and the *Ju Toy* decision of 1905 adds another blow to the immigrants. Chinese in the United States, Hawaii, and the Philippines call for the support of the Chinese government as well as their people in China. A movement of boycotting American goods spreads out in port cities along the central and south China coast in August, organized and carried out by Chinese merchants, students, and other individuals. Business deals with American companies are cancelled, and the sale of American goods drops. The boycott slows down two months later, when the Chinese government interferes under pressure from the United States.

EDUC. Ting Chia Chen and Ying Shing Wen become the first Chinese to attend the U.S. Military Academy at West Point.

FAMI. Japanese women come to America in much larger numbers than Chinese women. They constitute over 22 percent of the Japanese population Hawaii and 7 percent on the mainland.

LAWS. *United States v. Ju Toy,* a U.S. Supreme Court decision, affirms that the bureau of immigration has final jurisdiction over entry and deportation issues of Chinese immigrants. The ruling denies Chinese the right to judiciary review, giving immigration authorities a freer hand in dealing with Chinese arrivals.

RACE. The Asiatic Exclusion League, the first anti-Japanese pressure group, is created in San Francisco. The league has branches in Nevada, Colorado, and the Canadian province of British Columbia. It plays an important role in the anti-Japanese and anti-Asian movement in U.S. politics.

RELI. The Korean Evangelical Society is organized in San Francisco. Some 40 percent of Korean immigrants are Christians before coming to the United States, largely due to the work of American Protestant missionaries. Some migrants are converted to Christianity on their way to Hawaii and the mainland.

SOCI. Korean immigrants establish the Mutual Assistance Society in San Francisco and will soon publish a Korean-language newspaper.

WARS. After a military attack on Manchuria in northern China in 1904, Japan declares Korea its protectorate. Korea is under the rule of Japan, and its subjects are prohibited from leaving for the United States.

1906

AGRI. Abiko Kyutaro (1865–1936), the founder of the *Nichibei Shimbun* newspaper, establishes the American Land and Produce Company in the San Joaquin Valley of California to encourage more permanent Japanese settlement in the United States. Born in 1865, Abiko was converted to Christianity as a teenager and came to the United States at age 20. He was educated at the University of California at Berkeley. An entrepreneur, newspaperman, and labor contractor, Abiko is concerned about the future of the Japanese in America. The early immigrants came to America to make quick money, planning to return to their homeland. Because of this sojourner mentality, they are not interested in improving their living conditions or contributing to the American society. Abiko believes this is the main problem with his community. He argues that the *issei* (immigrants) should plant roots in America by bringing their wives and families and that they should become naturalized citizens. Abiko thinks that the best way for Japanese immigrants to become settlers in the United States is through farming. He uses his newspaper to advocate permanent settlement on tracts of land. Abiko's American Land and Produce Company is built on 3,200 acres of desert land near Livingston, California. It is divided into 40-acre parcels sold to individual farming families. The settlement model established by Abiko is called the Yamato Colony. The farmers grow a variety of fruit trees and grapes, and they plant eucalyptus trees around their residences. They also choose a site for a cemetery. This farming community will become home for 42 issei families by 1917.

EDUC. The San Francisco school board denies children of Japanese descent the right to attend regular public schools, creating a diplomatic crisis between the United States and Japan. Earlier, in 1893, the board passed a resolution ordering all Japanese students to enter the segregated Oriental School, which was established for children of Chinese or Mongolian descent. However, the Japanese consul general, Sutemi Chinda, quickly registered his protest and won support from many white students, clergymen, educators, and businessmen. Although anti-Japanese sentiment was strong, the Japanese population in the United States was small at the time. After the turn of the century, however, anti-Japanese agitation gains momentum, and the school board again resolves to send Japanese pupils to the Oriental School. On October 11 the board formally orders all Japanese pupils to attend the Oriental School with the Chinese. News of this decision causes outrage in Tokyo, adding pressure on the U.S. government. Fully aware of Japan's rising military power in Asia, the U.S. government has no intention of offending the Tokyo government. President Theodore Roosevelt has promised the government of Japan that its immigrants in the United States will be treated fairly. He tries to draw a distinction between Chinese and Japanese and even hints that he intends to extend naturalization to the Japanese. The president sends his Secretary of Commerce Victor H. Metcalf to San Francisco to investigate the situation, and he promises Japan that its immigrants will be protected. Finally, the government files suits in both state and federal courts to force the school board to admit the 41 Japanese school-age students. Recognizing that the incident is not simply about education, the president communicates to the Japanese ambassador that stopping immigration of Japanese laborers is the only effective way to solve the problem. The Japanese government is willing to compromise, agreeing to issue no more passports to Japanese laborers. The school board reverses its decision and allows Japanese students to attend regular public schools.

EDUC. Most Filipino migrants to Hawaii and the United States are graduates of schools established by Americans in the Philippines. These schools teach American history and ideologies using English-language textbooks. Western education makes it relatively easier for Filipino workers to adjust to new lives in Hawaii and the United States.

LANG. About 60 percent of the Filipino immigrants in Hawaii are from the Ilocano-speaking provinces of Ilocos Norte, Ilocos Sur, La Union, Abra, and Pangasinan. Another 30 percent of the recruited workers are from the Cebuano-speaking provinces of Cebu, Bohol, and Negros Oriental. Most educated Filipino migrants can also speak English.

MIGR. Recruitment of Filipino workers begins. The Hawaiian Sugar Planters Association sends Albert F. Judd, a lawyer, to Manila to recruit contract laborers. Judd is commissioned to bring 300 Filipino families to Hawaii, but he succeeds in getting only 15 the first year and another 150 a year later, in 1907. The recruitment effort will resume in 1909 after Japanese laborers are excluded. Hawaiian planters are especially interested in Filipino workers for two reasons. First, because the Filipinos are U.S. "nationals," they are not restricted by exclusion legislation. Second, alarmed by the growing dominance of Japanese workers, the planters are searching for a new source of labor to undermine organized labor activities. Some 122,100 Filipinos will arrive in Hawaii between 1907 and 1935.

MIGR. The San Francisco earthquake creates an opportunity for Chinese to circumvent exclusion laws. Chinatown is destroyed in the earthquake and fire, and so are many of the city's municipal records, including birth certificates. Some Chinese now claim they were born in the city and are in fact U.S. citizens. Using their newly-claimed citizenship status and evoking the principle established in *United States v. Wong Kim Ark* and *Tsoi Sim v. United States,* they can leave and return freely and become eligible to bring their wives and children to the Unites States. A few thousand young Chinese will pose as children (mostly sons) of these citizens, creating the "paper sons" phenomenon.

RELI. Ninety percent of the Filipino migrants are Catholic, as a result of the presence of the Catholic Church in the Philippines during the centuries of Spanish colonization.

SOCI. Japanese Americans in San Francisco and Berkeley organize the Social Revolutionary Party. Founded and heavily influenced by Kotoku Shusui, the most outspoken leader of the Japan Socialist Party, the Social Revolutionary Party advocates class solidarity and racial equality. It also publishes a journal, the *Kakumei* (Revolution).

1907

EDUC. The U.S. colonial government establishes its first nursing school in the Philippines. A year before the founding of this government institution, a small number of Filipino women began training in the Iloilo Mission Hospital School of Nursing founded by the Baptist Foreign Mission Society. Some Philippine-trained nurses will travel to the United States for advanced professional education. Some also will receive education through the pensionado program. These women will return to the islands and assume teaching and administrative responsibilities in Filipino nursing schools.

LAWS. The United States restricts the immigration of Japanese laborers. In order to help Japan save face, no law is passed to prohibit Japanese immigration. Instead, this is accomplished

---

Open Letter from the Japanese Socialist Party to the American Socialist Party on Exclusion

"Comrades: We believe that the expulsion question of the Japanese laborers in California is much due to racial prejudice. The Japanese Socialist Party, therefore, hopes that the American Socialist Party will endeavor to bring the question to a satisfactory issue in accordance with the spirit of international unity among workingmen. We also ask the American Socialist Party to acquaint us with its opinion as to this question."

Source: Oakland Socialist Voice, January 19, 1907.

through the so-called Gentlemen's Agreement. Japan agrees to register its emigrants in the United States and stop issuing passports to laborers. President Roosevelt will also issue Executive Order 589, prohibiting Japanese in Hawaii, Mexico, or Canada from re-migrating to the U.S. mainland. These restrictions apply to Koreans as well.

LAWS. The Expatriation Act stipulates that any American woman who marries a foreigner shall take the nationality of her husband. This woman may resume her American citizenship only upon the termination of the marital relationship. The U.S. Supreme Court will uphold the law in 1915, declaring that a female citizen becomes an alien upon marriage to an alien even if the couple weds and resides in the United States.

MIGR. Large groups of Asian Indians begin to immigrate to the United States instead of Canada. Most of the early immigrants from India are from the Punjab region, where many farmers are losing their land due to heavy taxation by the colonial government. British colonization of India has a big impact on Indian diaspora. Many Punjabi Sikhs have served in the colonial army and police force, which has given them opportunity to travel to different areas within the British empire. The Indians began their journeys to Canada in the early years of the twentieth century. The Canadian railroad companies welcomed the newcomers at first and hired many of them as section hands, and the number of Indians has increased from 258 in 1904 to more than 2,000 in 1907. The Indian influx to British Columbia will stop later in the midst of overwhelming hostility against them. Because both India and Canada are part of the British empire, the Canadian government will not be able to exclude Indians easily. Exclusion will be achieved by two orders-in-council of 1908. One of them will require each newcomer to show $200 in his possession upon arrival, a sum few labors will be able to accumulate. Another will grant entry only to individuals who come by "continuous journey" from their homeland. Without direct transportation available between India and Canada it will be almost impossible for anyone to come by continuous journey. When Indians are no longer welcomed

by Canada, the United States becomes the destination for those who decide to come to North America.

PUBL. The United Korean Society publishes its newspaper, the *United Korean News,* in Hawaii.

RACE. In September, several hundred white workers march to the Asian Indian community in Bellingham, Washington, and force 700 Asian Indians across the border into Canada. A similar incident takes place two months later in Everett, where all Indian workers are forced to leave the town.

RELI. Most immigrants from India in the early twentieth century adhere to Sikhism, a reform religion representing a syncretism of Islam and Hinduism. Based on a doctrine of egalitarianism, Sikhism challenges the Hindu caste system. Sikh men do not shave their beards or cut their hair, and they wear turbans because they are required to cover their heads in the temple. In Hong Kong, the Sikhs builds a *gurdwara* (temple) that provides travelers with temporary board and lodging. This gurdwara becomes a stopover place for Indian immigrants to North America, since many have to wait for at least a month before getting on a steamship. Some Asian Indian immigrants are Hindus. One of the world's oldest religions and the most popular religion on the Indian subcontinent, Hinduism is based on a distinctive caste system. The caste system prescribes occupations for each group and determines social relations among these groups. There are also small groups of Muslims among the early Indian immigrants.

SOCI. Korean immigrants in Hawaii create the United Korean Society. The organization, with headquarters in Honolulu and branches on different islands, provides leadership for all Korean organizations and village councils in Hawaii. The United Korean Society and California's Mutual Assistance Society will later merge into the Korean National Association.

1908

ECON. Most Asian Indian immigrants are farmers from Punjab. In the United States, about 700 of them are hired to construct the Three-Mile Spring Garden Tunnel of the Western Pacific Railroad. The railroad company uses Indians to replace Italian strikers in Tacoma, Washington. Along the Columbia River, some immigrants find work in the lumber mills. When these jobs are no longer available, they move south to California. The arrival of Asian Indian workers allows farmers there to keep wages down: these workers' daily pay is $0.25 to $0.50 lower than that of Japanese laborers. The farm laborers organize into gangs. Like the Japanese farm laborers, these groups of men travel together from field to field, sleeping in tents, bunkhouses, barns, and sheds. The gangs find work through their own labor contractors.

FOOD. The diet of Asian Indians is often determined by their religion. The Muslims do not eat pork, and they consume poultry and lamb butchered by themselves. The Hindus are vegetarians. The Sikhs consume a lot of milk products and use a lot of butter with their tortilla-shaped bread. Asian Indian dishes are often heavily seasoned. Curry, coriander seed, cumin seed, cayenne, and black pepper are commonly used for cooking.

SOCI. The Korean Women's Association is established in San Francisco.

1909

CIVI. Japanese plantation workers strike for four months on the island of Oahu, Hawaii. The monthly wages for Japanese workers are $18.00, which is $4.50 less than what the Portuguese and Puerto Rican workers are paid. Some local Japanese newspapermen and professionals formed the Higher Wages Association (HWA) in 1908, but the Hawaiian Sugar Planters Association refused to negotiate workers' wages with them. In late May, workers on several plantations on Oahu stop working, and their strike receives financial support from workers from other islands and from business owners. Chinese merchants also let the strikers purchase food on credit. But the Japanese immigrant community is divided, with some newspapers and church groups opposing militant actions. The Hawaiian Planters' Association hires spies from within the immigrant group. Key members of the HWA and newspapermen are arrested and jailed one after another. The strikers and their family members are evicted from plantation housing when scabs are hired to replace them. Meanwhile, a local English-language press accuses Japan of organizing the strike in order to take over the sugar industry and all of Hawaii. The strike ends in August when the workers exhaust all of their resources. But this collective action has a long-lasting impact. The planters later will agree to end the racially discriminatory wage scales. A bonus system proposed by the workers during the strike will also be established.

COMM. Koreans in the United States are strongly committed to the independence movement in their homeland. They organize against Japanese colonization in Korea and donate their hard-earned money to the patriotic cause. Leaders of Korea's independence movement are most influential in the community.

LAWS. The Payne-Aldrich Tariff Act, also known as the Philippine Tariff Act, is enacted, setting terms for imports from the islands.

POLI. Park Yong-man trains Korean cadets for the Korean independence movement. After his graduation from the University of Nebraska in 1909, Park sets up five military academies in Nebraska, California, Kansas, and Wyoming. He will move to Hawaii in 1912 to head the military training centers under the Korean National Association and organize 300 members into a single Korean National Brigade. Park will later serve briefly as minister of foreign affairs in the Korean provincial government-in-exile in Shanghai in 1919. He will also train young Koreans in northern China until his assassination in 1928.

PUBL. The *New Korea,* a Korean immigrant newspaper, is published by the Korean National Association.

PUBL. Yung Wing, the very first U.S.-educated Chinese scholar, publishes his autobiography, *My Life in China and America.* Written in English, the book is translated into both Chinese and Japanese; it will be reprinted in 1978.

PUBL. Sui Sin Far (Edith Maude Eaton, 1865–1914), the first Chinese woman writer in North America, publishes "Leaves from the Mental Portfolio of an Eurasian," an autobiographic essay. A daughter of an English entrepreneur and a Chinese mother, the author was born in England, where as a child she observed various forms of British bigotry against Asians. Immigrating to the United States with her family at age 6, Sui was shocked to see how Chinese children were treated by the Americans. She writes about the lives of Chinese in the United States with a strong ethnic consciousness, and she deals with issues of cultural conflicts, racial relations, and interracial marriages. As an accomplished freelance journalist and writer, Sui has published articles in many mainstream literary journals and newspapers, including *The Century, The Independent,* the *New England,* the *Overland Monthly,* and the *New York Evening Post.* Among her other well-known publications are "Chinese Workmen in America," and *Mrs. Spring Fragrance.* A collection of her writings, under the title of *Mrs. Spring Fragrance and Other Stories,* will be reprinted in 1995.

SOCI. The Japanese Association of America is founded in San Francisco, initiated by the Japanese consulate general. It is the most important Japanese American community organization prior to World War II, with branches established in different parts of the United States. For various reasons, not all Japanese in America belong to the association. The association charges an annual membership fee of one to three dollars. It maintains a close tie with Japan and functions as an organ of the imperial government. It is authorized by the Japanese consular service to issue traveling documents to Japanese in America. It also determines which individuals are eligible to bring wives or other family members. The association hires lawyers to help fight discriminatory legislation. Most leaders of the association are successful entrepreneurs or farmers. George Shima, who will later become a millionaire known as the "Potato King," is the first president of the association.

SOCI. The Korean National Association is established. Combining membership from the Mutual Assistance Society in California and the United Korean Society in Hawaii, this new organization will assume leadership for bringing about Korea's independence from Japan.

1910

CRIM. A group of Korean immigrants hired to pick oranges in Upland, California, is attacked by white workers with rocks and stones. The mob orders the Koreans to leave town immediately. The Koreans are able to stay only because their employer, Mary Steward, purchases guns to arm them.

ECON. The vast majority of Japanese, Korean, Filipino, and Asian Indian immigrants on the U.S. mainland work as migratory farm laborers. Ethnic labor contractors, individuals who can communicate in both English and their native language, operate as intermediaries between laborers and growers. Japanese labor contractors, for example, function as employment agents. They recruit laborers from the port cities and transport them to the fields in the country, and they negotiate wages with the growers on behalf of the laborers. Some contractors have as many as 1,000 laborers under them. The commissions they receive allow some of them to emerge as successful businessmen and community leaders. Many Japanese laborers also rise to become independent farmers. To obtain land, they use four methods: contract, share, lease, and ownership. The farmers under contract work for wages, while those under the share system receive a portion of the crop. Land lease is more desirable, because the farmers have more control over the land. Once they can afford it, the farmers purchase land. Like the Chinese before them, Japanese farmers concentrate on short-term crops like berries and truck vegetables. By 1910 they produce 70 percent of California's strawberries.

ECON. In urban areas, Chinese in segregated ethnic communities build a distinctive and largely self-sufficient ethnic economy. Ethnic entrepreneurs establish small businesses that cater mainly to co-ethnic customers. Many Chinese also operate hand laundry business. These entrepreneurs create employment opportunities for fellow immigrants.

ECON. Japanese in urban America build an ethnic economy featuring hotels, boarding houses, restaurants, shops, stores, and pool halls, catering mainly to Japanese immigrants. Their hotels provide lodging for newcomers, and some hotel owners are also labor contractors. According to data released by the immigration commission a year earlier, there are between 3,000 and 3,500 Japanese-owned businesses in the western states, most of them in San Francisco, Seattle, Los Angeles, and Sacramento. Within the 2,277 businesses surveyed, there are 337 hotels and boarding houses, 381 restaurants, 187 barbershops, 136 poolrooms, 136 tailor and dye shops, 124 provision and supply stores, 97 laundries, and 105 shoe shops. These businesses create jobs for the owners as well as for 1,200 immigrant laborers. Most of the businesses are small in scale. Japanese farmers also sell their produce to urban dwellers. In the Los Angeles City Market, 67 percent of the produce stalls are owned by Japanese. A sizable number of Japanese find employment in domestic service. Nearly one-third of the 10,000 Japanese living in San Francisco in 1904, for example, were domestic service workers.

ECON. Though most Korean immigrants are agricultural laborers, some settle in the cities, where they find jobs as restaurant workers, gardeners, janitors, and domestic workers. Outside the cities, Koreans are employed by railroads and in the salmon fisheries in Alaska. Small in population, the Koreans do not build an ethnic economy; relatively few of them are business operators.

EDUC. The number of Asian children attending public schools in the United States increases to 4,048 from 2,019 a decade earlier.

EDUC. Hawaii-born Arthur K. Ozawa, the first Japanese American lawyer, is admitted to the bar in Michigan and Hawaii. Ozawa receives his law degree from the University of Michigan.

FAMI. The immigration of "picture brides" changes the sex ratio of the Japanese American community and allows the growth of families. In 1900 there were 850 Japanese women among 18,000 men on the U.S. mainland; 400 were married. In 1910, about 5,600 married women are found among a total female population of 8,000. And a decade later, the number of married women will increase to 22,000, out of a total female population of 38,000. The female population in Hawaii in 1920 will be 48,000.

FAMI. The Koreans on the U.S. mainland are mostly bachelors. Of the 1,029 Koreans who migrated to the mainland from Hawaii between 1905 and 1910, only 45 were female. After 1910, 115 picture brides will arrive, but the imbalanced sex ratio will continue for many more decades.

MIGR. Japanese picture brides begin to arrive. Although the Gentlemen's Agreement restricts the immigration of Japanese laborers to the United States, the Japanese government strategically retains a loophole for the outflow of Japanese women. Accordingly, parents, wives, and children of laborers already in America can still obtain passports. This loophole gives rise to "picture brides," based on a traditional Japanese custom of arranged marriage. In many traditional Asian societies, marriage is not considered an individual matter, but rather a family concern. Parents often help their sons and daughters select marriage partners, and prospective brides and grooms sometimes exchange photographs before meeting each other. After the Gentlemen's Agreement, many Japanese laborers in Hawaii and on the mainland utilize the traditional marriage system to form families. They select prospective brides through picture exchanges. To save the cost of passage, weddings are performed in Japan without the presence of the grooms, and the brides officially enter the grooms' family registers to be eligible to come to America. Initially the Japanese consuls in the United States, through the Japanese Association of America, decide that an individual has to prove assets of $1,400 to $2,200 to qualify for bringing a picture bride. The qualification will be lowered in 1915 to $800, making it relatively easier for groups of laborers to pool their resources. The majority of the 66,926 Japanese women who arrive in Hawaii between 1908 and 1924 are picture brides.

MIGR. An immigration detention center is established on Angel Island near San Francisco. Thousands of Asian immigrants, especially the

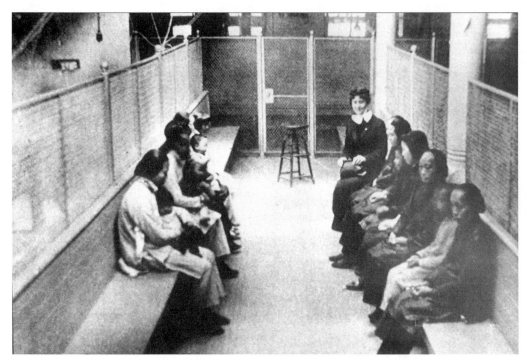

A group of Chinese and Japanese women and children wait to be processed, as they are held in a wire mesh enclosure at the Angel Island internment barracks in San Francisco Bay in the late 1920s. The Angel Island Immigration Station processed one million immigrants from 1910 to 1940, mostly from China and Japan. [AP Photo]

Chinese, will be detained and interrogated in the facility for extended periods of time. Those who fail to prove their claims and papers are genuine will be deported. (Also see entry in 1979)

POPU. The U.S. Census records 94,414 Chinese residing in the United States.

POPU. The census counts 2,767 Filipinos in the United States.

POPU. The Japanese have replaced the Chinese as the largest Asian group. The 1910 census counts 152,745 Japanese living in the United States.

POPU. The census counts 5,008 Koreans in the United States.

SETT. Most Asian immigrant laborers have no permanent camps in which to live. As migratory farm workers, they move constantly from field to field, carrying clothes, blankets, and cooking pots with them. Living arrangements as such make it difficult for these Asian groups to form stable communities.

Poem Carved on the Wall of the Angel Island Immigration Station by an Anonymous Chinese Detainee

Imprisoned in the wooden building day after day,
My freedom withheld; how can I bear to talk about it?

Source: Him Mark Lai, Genny Lim, Judy Yung, eds., *Island: Poetry and History of Chinese Immigrants on Angel Island, 1910–1940* (San Francisco: HOC DOI, 1980), 68.

SETT. The development of an ethnic economy contributes to the rise of Little Tokyos (*Nihonmachi*). These ethnic business sections are filled with boarding houses, hotels, restaurants, shops, and stores, which provide comfort to fellow immigrants. These urban communities of entrepreneurs and service workers also channel new immigrants to agricultural jobs, as many hotel or boarding house owners are also labor contractors.

SOCI. To finance their business endeavors, Asian immigrants establish rotating credit systems. They organize into groups to pool financial resources to lease or purchase land or to start businesses. This type of organization is called *hui* in Chinese, *tanomoshi* in Japanese, and *kae* in Korean. Each individual in a group will contribute the same amount of money. The one with the highest bid of interest will become the first to borrow from the fund. After this person returns the money to the group, the second-highest bidder will have his turn. The amount of interest charged will be decreased, and the last person to utilize the fund has no obligation to pay interest.

SPOR. Prostitution and gambling are the most popular forms of recreation for the lonely male Asian immigrants. One Japanese survey of overseas Japanese prostitutes reports 913 in Honolulu and 371 in San Francisco in 1910. After a long day of work, Japanese laborers often retreat to pool halls. In 1912 there will be 41 Japanese-operated pool halls in San Francisco, 21 in Sacramento, 19 in Fresno, and 35 in Los Angeles.

SPOR. Gambling and dancing are important forms of entertainment for Filipino immigrants. They gather for cockfights, and some also gamble in Chinatowns. The dance hall is one of the most popular gathering places for the Filipino workers. Dressed in their best suits, Filipino men spend their hard-earned money to dance with American girls in dance halls filled with loud music. Each dance costs $0.10, and some men will spend a whole day's wage for 10 dances. In the dance halls, Filipino men have their chance to meet women and find love.

WARS. Japan annexes Korea. Korean people will be under Japan's colonial rule until the end of World War II.

1910–1924

MIGR. About 500 Korean nationalists flee their country after Japanese annexation and settle in the United States. More than 1,000 Koreans also migrate to the mainland from Hawaii.

1911

SOCI. The Filipino Federation of Labor is founded.

WARS. Sun Yat-sen (1866–1925) founds the Republic of China. Following his brother to Hawaii in the 1880s, Sun attended missionary school on the islands before going to Hong Kong for medical school. Back in Hawaii, he is able to mobilize support and raise money from the Chinese immigrant community, which enables him to organize the nationalist revolutionary movement in China. Dynastic history in China ends.

1912

ECON. Kinji Ushijima, better known as George Shima, gains fame as the "Potato King"—a Japanese Horatio Alger. Arriving in the United States in 1887, Shima started as a potato picker in San Joaquin Valley. After a brief career as a labor contractor, he leased and bought undeveloped swamplands in the delta and converted them into fertile farmland. His potato farm covers 10,000 acres of land. Shima will die in 1926 with an estate worth $15 million.

RELI. The Sikhs build their first gurdwara in the United States in Stockton, California. This elaborate temple is the spiritual and social center for Sikhs along the Pacific coast. Religion is important in holding the Asian Indians together, as most of them are followers of Sikhism. Eventually each town with a few dozen Sikhs will build a temple and select a priest of its own.

SOCI. The Punjabi Sikhs on the Pacific coast form the Khalsa Diwan near Holt, a small town in the Sacramento Delta. This registered corporation becomes the stopover place for newly arrived laborers and students. It is also a public gathering center for Sikh intellectuals who are involved in political activities for India's independence from Britain.

SPOR. Hawaiian native swimmer Duke Kahanamoku ties the world record and wins the gold medal in the 100-meter freestyle event at the Olympic Games in Stockholm, Sweden. Kahanamoku first broke the world record at an amateur athletic union swim meet in Hawaii. With the support of funds raised by Hawaiians, he was able to come to the mainland for the Olympic trials. He will break his own world record for the same event in the 1920 Olympics in Antwerp, Belgium.

1913

AGRI. The California Alien Land Law is enacted on May 19, prohibiting aliens ineligible for citizenship from purchasing or leasing land for more than three years for agricultural purposes. The law will be amended in 1920 and 1923, setting stricter terms. Similar laws are passed in Washington, Oregon, Idaho, Montana, Arizona, New Mexico, Nebraska, Texas, Kansas, Louisiana, Missouri, and Minnesota. The law targets mainly Japanese immigrants because of their success in farming.

Duke Kahanamoku, Hawaiian Olympic swimmer, poses in a swimming pool in Los Angeles, California, 1933. [AP Photo]

ECON. Korean immigrant Kim Hyung-soon forms a business partnership with Kim Ho in Reedley, California. The original Kim Brothers Company is a fruit wholesaler; it expands into a large operation of orchards, nurseries, and fruit-packing. Kim Hyung-soon and an employee named Anderson will experiment with a variety of peaches, including the nectarine—a hybrid of peaches and plums.

POLI. Syngman Rhee (1875–1965), the first president of the Republic of Korea, begins to organize his followers for Korea's independence. Arriving in the United States in 1904, Rhee received a bachelor's degree from George Washington University and a master's degree from Harvard University. He was the first Korean to earn a Ph.D. in the United States, which he received from Princeton University in the field of international law. After a brief return to Korea, Rhee fled to Hawaii in 1912 after Japan colonized his homeland. He is the principal of the Korean Community School, as well as the founder of the Korean Methodist Church and the Korean Christian Institute. He also establishes a newspaper and organizes the Tongji-hoe (Comrade Society), and he emerges as the most powerful figure in the immigrant community. As the first president of the Korean provincial government-in-exile, he will spend much time not in Shanghai, China but in Hawaii and Washington, D.C., collecting funds and lobbying for support from Americans. He will be the president of the Republic of Korea between 1948 and 1960.

PUBL. *Ghadar* (sometimes translated as *Gadar* or *Ghadr*), a newspaper by the Hindustan Association of the Pacific Coast, is published. The word *ghadar* means "revolution," and the first editor of the radical newspaper is Har Dayal, a Hindu intellectual and the founder of the Ghadar Party. The newspaper is printed in Urdu, Grumulki, and several other languages, and it is distributed to many areas of Indian diaspora, including the United States, Canada, Hong Kong, Japan, the Philippines, British Malaya, Singapore, British Guiana, Trinidad, Honduras, South Africa, and East Africa.

SOCI. Punjabi Sikhs in Oregon and Washington start the Hindustan Association, with centers in

Portland and Astoria. The association is funded by a well-to-do labor contractor for the lumber mills in the Pacific Northwest.

1914

ECON. To circumvent the 1913 Alien Land Law, Japanese farmers use the names of their American-born children to own and lease land. Some also operate their farms through land corporations in which they hold shares. Regardless of the legal restrictions, the land leased by farmers will increase from 155,488 acres in 1913 to 192,150 acres in 1920. Land owned by Japanese will increase from 26,707 acres to 74,767 acres during the same time period.

FAMI. Very few Asian Indian immigrants come with families. According to one study, women represent only 0.24 percent of the 5,000 Asian Indians in California. Quite a number of Asian Indian men marry Mexican immigrant women. In these interracial households, both Indian food and Mexican food are served. The couples try to learn each other's language, but their children usually speak English. The children are mostly raised as Catholics, although some are also exposed to Indian religion through the networks of their fathers.

MED. Sessue Hayakawa, a Japanese stage actor, enters Hollywood, appearing in two movies during his first year in the United States: *The Wrath of the Gods* and *The Typhoon*. Hayakawa will gain fame as the star of Cecil B. DeMille's *The Cheat* a year later. His film roles are controversial and subject to resentful criticism from the Japanese American community, but Hayakawa will become the romantic idol of female American moviegoers in the late 1910s. He will star or costar in many films, including *Alien Souls* (1916), *The Call of the East* (1917), *Forbidden Paths* (1917), *The Secret Game* (1917), *The White Man's Law* (1918), and *The Bravest Way* (1918). Hayakawa will start his own production company in 1918. His production company, Howarth Pictures, will produce a number of films, including *His Birthright* (1918), *The Dragon Painter* (1919), and *The Tong Man* (1919). His wife, Tsuru Aoki, will often costar in his films. Hayakawa will also star in several French and Japanese films, as well as Hollywood features such as *Daughter of the Dragon* (1931, with Anna May Wong), *Tokyo Joe* (1949, with Humphrey Bogart), and *Three Came Home* (1950, with Claudette Colbert). His role in *The Bridge on the River Kwai* (1951) will be nominated for an Academy Award. Known as the first Asian male star of Hollywood, Hayakawa will receive a star on the Hollywood Walk of Fame. He will pass away in 1973.

PUBL. Wu Tingfang (1842–1922), a prominent Chinese scholar and diplomat, publishes *America Through the Spectacles of an Oriental Diplomat*. Wu received education in Singapore, Hong Kong, and England. He was the Chinese minister to the United States between 1896 and 1902. A contributor to American mainstream magazines such as *Harper's,* the *Independent,* and *North American Review,* Wu offers subtle comments and satire in his observations of American society.

RACE. Fifteen Korean farm laborers hired to pick fruit for a local grower in Riverside, California are captured by a crowd of angry, unemployed workers. The mob takes the Koreans to the local train station and forces them to leave the area.

TREA. The Underwood-Simmons Act is signed on October 3 in place of the Payne-Aldrich Tariff Act. The new treaty sets terms for free trade between the United States and its Philippine territory.

1915

WARS. The Ghadar movement takes place. Led by the Ghadar Party, a radical Asian Indian diaspora group organized with the ultimate goal of overthrowing British rule in India, more than 400 immigrants from the United States travel to their homeland to start a revolution. The revolutionaries receive arms from the Germans, but their actions are detected by British intelligence. Many Ghadarites are arrested and executed. The party will fall apart in 1917.

1917

LAWS. The 1917 Immigration Act creates an Asiatic Barred Zone, excluding Asian Indians using a geographic criterion. Because the Indian subcontinent is under the British empire, prohibiting inhabitants from there becomes a complicated matter. Drawing an imaginary line from the Red to the Mediterranean, Aegean, and Black seas, and then through the Ural Mountains, the law stipulates that all people living in the area east of the line, including the Indian subcontinent, are excluded.

MILI. During World War I, about 29,000 Japanese Americans, both issei (immigrants) and *nisei* (American-born Japanese) are registered for the Selective Service in the Territory of Hawaii.

SOCI. The Japanese Boys Club and Japanese Girls Club are organized.

1918

AGRI. Abiko Kyutaro builds a second Japanese farming colony in Cressey, California. This new colony is closely associated with Abiko's first farming colony in Livingston.

LAWS. The Act of May 9 permits native-born Filipinos or Puerto Ricans who have served in the U.S. military to gain citizenship without the required declaration of intention and proof of five years' residence within the United States. The law does not mention servicemen from other Asian groups.

SOCI. To overcome their differences in religion and culture, Asian Indians establish the Hindustani Welfare Reform Society in California's Imperial Valley. "Hindustani" is an adjective that means Indian.

1919

AGRI. Abiko Kyutaro establishes a third Japanese farming colony in Cortez, California, 13 miles northwest of his Livingston Colony.

ASIA. A Korean provincial government-in-exile is established in Shanghai, China to lead the Korean independence movement. In Korea, a nationwide demonstration protesting Japan's colonial rule meets with Japanese police brutality; many are killed. Immigrants in Hawaii and on the U.S. mainland start a fund-raising campaign for independence. This effort will continue

in the following decades until the end of the World War II.

LAWS. The Act of July 19, 1919 allows "any person" of foreign birth who has served in the U.S. military to petition for naturalization without providing declaration of intention and proof of five years' residence. Similar to the Act of May 9 in 1918, this law facilitates the naturalization of servicemen, including Filipinos, but it fails to specify whether excluded Asian groups are entitled to such benefits.

POLI. About 150 Koreans attend the first Korean Liberty Congress in Philadelphia to support the nationalist movement in their homeland against Japan's colonial rule.

SOCI. Second-generation Japanese Americans organize the American Loyalty Club in San Francisco. This club aims to demonstrate its members' loyalty to the United States. It is a response to anti-Japanese sentiment.

1919–1920

CIVI. A large-scale strike organized by both Japanese and Filipino plantation workers in Hawaii takes place. Japanese labor organizations on the different islands are united under the Federation of Japanese Labor in Hawaii. This association draws up several demands, including a daily wage of $1.25, a new bonus system, eight-hour workdays, double pay for overtime, and paid maternity leave for women. Pablo Manlapit, the founder of the Filipino Federation of Labor in 1911 and the Filipino Unemployment Association in 1913, is the head of a Higher Wages Association for Filipino workers. The coordinators face great challenges because the strike involves organizations of two ethnic groups. Communicating with workers scattered on different plantations on different islands is also difficult. About 2,600 Filipinos and 300 Spaniards and Puerto Ricans start the strike on January 17. The total number of strikers reaches 8,000 with the participation of Japanese workers. About 12,000 Filipinos and 10,500 Japanese strikers and their families are evicted from plantation housing; many children and women are forced to camp out. Lack of funds adds additional pressure. When influenza hits Hawaii, more than 2,000 people become ill, and the death toll reaches at least 100. The strike is nonetheless very successful; only 166 Japanese workers remain on the job. Despite efforts of local church and community leaders in mediating the situation, the Hawaiian Sugar Planters Association refuses to negotiate.

Under pressure of anti-Japanese sentiment, the Federation of Japanese Labor changes its name to the Hawaii Laborers' Association and applies for membership in the American Federation of Labor, but the national union ignores the request. To win public support, 3,000 Japanese and Filipino strikers and their families hold a "77 Cents Parade." Carrying American flags and pictures of Abraham Lincoln, participants march through the streets of Honolulu, carrying signs with statements such as "We are not Reds, God Forbid, But are Brown Workers Who Produce White Sugar"; "We Want to Live Like Americans"; and "How Can We Live Like Americans on 77 Cents?" The strike lasts for six months and ends with many workers leaving their jobs. Housing, sanitation, and recreational facilities are improved after the strike and wages are increased. The Hawaiian Sugar Planters Association also tightens its control over the workers with the backing of the territorial government, making union activities almost impossible.

1920

AGRI. Korean farmers in the Sacramento Valley and Willows, California, enjoy great success in rice cultivating, while their fellow immigrants in Stockton, California make a substantial profit in potato farming. Korean farmers in the San Joaquin Valley specialize in commercial fruit, and they ship a variety of fresh fruits to Korean wholesale markets in Los Angeles.

AGRI. Some Asian Indian farm workers become tenant farmers or landowners. Small groups of two to eight men form partnerships in farming and become equal shareholders. They also form groups to lease land. In California, as many as 90,000 acres of land are leased or owned by Asian Indian farmers. Because they are in high demand, Asian Indian farm workers now receive the same wages paid to Japanese and white workers. The situation will change after the 1923 *Thind* decision, which makes Asian Indian aliens ineligible

for citizenship. Many Indians will become laborers again.

AGRI. The California Alien Land Law is amended to prohibit aliens ineligible for citizenship from serving as guardians of land under the names of their American-born children. The new law also prohibits these individuals from leasing land.

ECON. Korean entrepreneurs operate more than 20 hotels in Dinuba, San Francisco, Stockton, Los Angeles, Manteca, Riverside, and Lompoc, California; Yakima, Washington; and Chicago, Illinois. The hotel owners often serve as labor contractors. They provide room and board for the immigrants and find work for them. There are also 30 barbershops and 25 laundries operated by Koreans in the Pacific coast states. Other businesses established by Korean entrepreneurs include restaurants, grocery stores, bakeries, and photo studios.

POLI. The Korean American community establishes the School of Aviation in Willows, California. This is made possible when Kim Chong-nim, a farmer known as the "Rice King," purchases three airplanes for the school. Young Korean Americans are trained in the school in preparation for fighting against Japanese rule in Korea.

POPU. The census records 85,202 Chinese in the United States. The effectiveness of exclusion is quite clear, as the Chinese population continues to decline. It is extremely difficult for Chinese women to gain entry, although the population of female Chinese is on the rise, largely due to the birth of the second generation.

POPU. The presence of large numbers of women and families has allowed the Japanese population in the United States to grow steadily between 1910 and 1920, although Japanese laborers are excluded. The 1920 census shows a total of 220,596 Japanese residing in the United States.

POPU. The census records 26,634 Filipinos residing in the United States and Hawaii.

POPU. The census counts 6,181 Koreans on the U.S. mainland; 75 percent of them are male.

POPU. By 1920, some 6,400 Asian Indians have entered the United States.

1920–1930

EDUC. School segregation policies are no longer enforced. Large numbers of Asian American children are gaining access to public education in integrated schools; some are attending college.

1921

AGRI. Japanese immigrants establish a sugar plantation in Texas. It will enjoy brief success.

LAWS. The 1921 Immigration Act introduces a quota system to limit the number of immigrants. National quotas are calculated based on a small percentage of the population of that country. A new national quota system will replace this one in mid-1924.

LAWS. A federal district court denies the petition of Easurk Emsen Charr, a Korean immigrant, for U.S. citizenship. Charr believes he is qualified for citizenship because of his service in the U.S. Army during World War I. But the court declares that Koreans should be categorized as part of the Mongol family and therefore are ineligible for citizenship. The court also concludes that existing laws regarding servicemen and citizenship do not include aliens ineligible for citizenship.

MIGR. Picture brides from Japan and Korea can no longer come to the United States. Under pressure from the United States, Japan agrees in the so-called Ladies Agreement not to issue passports to prospective picture brides. This agreement makes it more difficult for male Japanese laborers to form families in the United States.

PUBL. The first Filipino American newspaper, the *Philippine Independent News,* is published in Salinas, California.

RACE. Fifty-eight Japanese immigrant laborers in Turlock, California are forced by a local mob to leave the area.

SOCI. Filipinos in San Francisco form the Caballeros de Dimas-Alang, a fraternal organization.

SOCI. Second-generation Japanese Americans form the Seattle Progressive Citizens League.

SOCI. Korean immigrants organize the Comrade Society under the leadership of Syngman Rhee.

1922

AGRI. In *Estate of Tetsubumi Yano,* Japanese Americans win the right to serve as guardians of their American-born children in the California supreme court. Two-year-old Tetsubumi Yano was born in the United States to immigrant parents. Her family has 14 acres of land under her name. The state court decides that Yano's parents should be allowed to serve as her guardians. California alien land laws have deprived aliens ineligible for citizenship the right to own land. But according to this court ruling Japanese immigrants can farm their own land if the land is under the name of their U.S.-born children. This victory is short-lived, however. In 1923 a new California law will forbid aliens ineligible for citizenship from serving as guardians of any estate.

EDUC. The Filipino Nurses Association (FNA) is formed with 150 members. Rosario Montenegro Delgado, a graduate of the Philippine General Hospital nursing class of 1912, is elected as the first president. The FNA will gain membership in the International Council of Nurses in 1929, indicating the transformation of the field of nursing in the Philippines into an international profession.

LAWS. The Cable Act makes an American woman's citizenship independent of that of her husband, contingent upon her husband's eligibility for naturalization. Since American women won the right to vote, the issue of independent citizenship for married women can no longer be ignored. Under pressure from suffrage groups, Congress amends the 1907 Expatriation Act, honoring the principle of gender equality by making a woman's citizenship independent of that of her husband. This significant reform measure is nonetheless racially discriminatory. According to the new law, a woman who marries a person ineligible for citizenship will still forfeit her American citizenship. This law will remain effective until 1930.

LAWS. In *Takao Ozawa v. United States,* the U.S. Supreme Court denies alien Japanese the right to U.S. citizenship. Having immigrated to the United States at a young age, Takao Ozawa attended high school and college in Berkeley, California before settling in Honolulu and working for an American company. Ozawa informs the court that he is honest and industrious, and he does not drink liquor, smoke, or gamble. His wife was educated in America, his children attend an American school, and his family speaks English at home. As a true American and a Christian, Ozawa says he does not have any connection with Japan and is loyal to the United States. But his petition for naturalization is rejected. The U.S. Supreme Court declares that Ozawa is not entitled to naturalization because he is clearly not Caucasian. This landmark case adds Japanese immigrants into the category of aliens ineligible for citizenship. A few previously naturalized Japanese immigrants will have their citizenship revoked due to this court decision.

MED. Seventeen-year-old Chinese American Anna May Wong (1907–1961) stars as Lotus Flower in the film *The Toll of the Sea,* after appearing in *The Red Lantern* three years earlier. The Los Angeles-born Wong will gain more fame as the Mongol slave in *The Thief of Bagdad* (1924). But during the era of Chinese exclusion she can only get roles that portray stereotypical Chinese women. Frustrated, Wong will leave the United States for Europe, appearing in films such as *Song, Big City Butterfly, Tai-Tang,* and *Piccadilly.* She also performs on stage in London and New York. After returning to Hollywood, Wong will appear in *Daughter of the Dragon* (1931) and costar with Marlene Dietrich in *Shanghai Express* (1932). She will also be featured in *Daughters of Shanghai* (1937). During World War II, Wong will devote much of her energy to the war relief effort in China against Japan. In the 1950s, she will take a few television roles and run her own series, *The Gallery of Madame Liu-Tsong.* The first Chinese American actress to gain prominence in films, Wong's life and career will be the subject of several books and documentaries. (Also see entry in 1961)

1923

AGRI. Japanese Americans lose four cases against alien land laws in the U.S. Supreme Court. In *Terrace v. Thompson,* the high court upholds a 1921 alien land law of the state of Washington, declaring that the plaintiff does not have the right to lease his land to a Japanese alien; in *Porterfield v. Webb,* the court decides that the 1920 California Alien Land Law is constitutional; in *Webb v. O'Brien,* the court rules that sharecropping agreements involving alien Japanese are illegal; in *Frick v. Webb,* the court decides that aliens ineligible for citizenship have no right to own stock in corporations formed for the purpose of farming.

LAWS. In *United States v. Bhagat Singh Thind,* the U.S. Supreme Court denaturalizes an Asian Indian based on the color of his skin. An immigrant having arrived from India in 1913, Thind is a World War I veteran. Anthropologists classify Indians as Aryans, and Thind is one of the few dozens of Asian Indians naturalized in the United States. His advocacy for Indian independence from the British empire drew the attention of the U.S. government, and immigration authorities challenged his naturalization right in court. The U.S. Supreme Court backs the government, arguing that although Asian Indians might indeed be Aryans ethnographically, they are not the same as white persons. The physical group characteristics of the Hindus, the court declares, are distinguishable from the various groups of persons commonly recognized as white. Moreover, the court concludes, since immigration from India is barred, Indians should be treated the same as other Asians on issues concerning naturalization. In other words, based on the fact that Indians' skin color is not white and that they are excluded, the court declares that Asian Indians are not entitled to naturalization rights. Many of Thind's fellow Indians are denaturalized following this landmark case.

1924

AGRI. Under restrictions of alien land laws, Japanese develop new methods to stay in agriculture. One method is called middleman arrangement, in which a Japanese farmer gets help from a U.S. citizen. The farmer has the citizen lease the land for him to farm. To avoid legal complication, the two parties enter an employment agreement that indicates the farmer is hired by the citizen as a manager or foreman. The second method is for a farmer to enter into two separate agreements with a landowner. With a written agreement the landowner hires the Japanese as an employee, but the two agree verbally that the Japanese will cultivate the land as a cash or share tenant. The third method is to have land companies lease land for the farmers.

ASIA. Japan changes its rule regarding nationality so that children born in the United States of Japanese parents are not necessarily Japanese nationals. Japanese nationality laws previously granted citizenship to anyone born of a Japanese father, regardless of where the birth took place. U.S. law, on the other hand, grants citizenship status to anyone born on American soil, regardless of ethnicity or the citizenship of the parents. Such discrepancies automatically gave dual citizenship status for Japanese children born in the United States. Anti-Japanese groups thus questioned the loyalty of these children to the U.S. government. Under this pressure, Japanese community leaders urged the Japanese government to change its existing regulations. A 1916 law enabled young nisei under age 17 to renounce their Japanese citizenship. Otherwise they would have to fulfill military service obligations. This new amendment abolishes the old rules. A child born in the United States of a Japanese father is no longer entitled to Japanese citizenship unless the parents register him or her at a Japanese consulate within 14 days of the birth. All children born prior to 1924 can also renounce their Japanese nationality.

ASIA. The Mongolian People's Republic, set up as a Chinese province between 1691 and 1911, as an autonomous state under Russian protection between 1912 and 1919, and again as a Chinese province after 1919, is established.

CIVI. Filipino plantation workers in Hawaii strike to demand higher wages, an eight-hour working day, and better housing. The strike lasts for eight months, carried out by 2,000 workers on 23 plantations. In a fight involving two factions of Filipinos, 16 workers are killed and 161

are arrested. Pablo Manlapit, the leader of the Filipino Federation of Labor, is arrested during the strike. He is tried, convicted, and sentenced to 10 years of labor, but he is later freed and forced to leave Hawaii. He will be caught organizing in Hawaii again and forced to go to the Philippines in 1932.

LAWS. President Calvin Coolidge signs into law the Immigration Act of 1924, which implements a racially biased quota system to limit the number of immigrants from less-desired eastern and southern European countries. The number of immigrants to be admitted annually per the quota is calculated as 2 percent of the foreign-born population of each nationality residing in the United States in 1890. The new legislation has a grave impact on immigration from Asian countries. Although Asian nations are not named, Section 13(c) provides that no alien ineligible for citizenship shall be admitted to the United States. Because Chinese and Asian Indians are already barred from obtaining citizenship, this provision is added to satisfy the anti-Japanese forces in western states. Immigration from Japan is cut off completely. This law provides legal grounds for immigration authorities to turn down any immigration applicants from China, Japan, Korea, and India. Wives of U.S. citizens are also affected.

LAWS. In *Cheung Sum Shee et al. v. John Nagle*, the U.S. Circuit Court of Appeals for the Ninth Circuit rules that alien Chinese wives of merchants should be allowed to live with their husbands in the United States. According to the court, an alien who comes to the United States solely to carry on trade under existing treaties should not be considered an immigrant and therefore should not be excluded under the 1924 act. Although wives of resident Chinese merchants do not come to carry on trade, the court reasons that by necessary implication they should be admitted with their husbands.

LAWS. In *Chang Chan et al. v. John Nagle,* the U.S. Circuit Court of Appeals for the Ninth Circuit denies entry to Chinese wives of American citizens. Although the petitioners are all citizens of the United States, the court declares that their wives do not become citizens, being ineligible for naturalization, and that no alien ineligible for citizenship shall be admitted to the United States. Between 1925 and 1930, not a single woman will gain entry as the wife of an American citizen.

MIGR. Thirty-five Chinese wives of U.S. citizens are denied entry in San Francisco and Seattle in July. They will not be admitted until 1930.

PUBL. The *Chinese Times* (1924–), the newspaper of the Chinese American Citizens Alliance, begins publication in San Francisco. Although the founders of the papers are fluent in both English and Chinese, they decide to use the Chinese language to reach both the immigrant and American-born Chinese audience. The newspaper will soon enjoy the largest circulation of Chinese newspapers published in San Francisco. Between 1942 and 1943, its circulation will reach almost 10,000. The newspaper will be a leading advocate for immigration reform and civil rights for several decades, and it will be the only non-party-affiliated Chinese American newspaper to survive the Great Depression, World War II, and the Cold War.

SOCI. Chinese Americans form a Boli Ju (Committee to Challenge the 1924 Immigration Act) to lead the protest against new immigration restrictions. It raises $7,000 within a few months and uses the funds to hire three prominent attorneys to challenge the law and secure admission for the wives of citizens.

1925

LAWS. In *Hidemitsu Toyota v. United States,* the U.S. Supreme Court denies foreign-born Japanese who have served in the U.S. military the right to naturalization by separating them from Filipinos. Born in Japan, Hidemitsu Toyota arrived in the United States in 1913. He is a World War I veteran honorably discharged from the military. A U.S. district court for the district of Massachusetts at first granted his petition for naturalization and issued him a certificate of citizenship in 1921, but it later changed its decision and canceled his certificate. A circuit court of appeals inquires of the U.S. Supreme Court whether a U.S. serviceman of the Japanese race,

born in Japan, may legally be naturalized under the Act of May 9, 1918 and under the 1919 law, which allow American servicemen of Filipino descent born outside the United States to become citizens of the United States. The high court, however, holds that the limitations based on color and race remain as part of the naturalization laws, but such restrictions no longer apply to Filipinos because they are not aliens. The court concludes that Toyota cannot be naturalized because of his race and color, regardless of his military service. This court ruling is significant to Filipino immigrants in the United States. By implication, the Filipinos are not subject to limitations of naturalization laws based on color and race because they are not aliens.

POLI. The Chinese American Citizens Alliance, an organization of American-born Chinese who are entitled to vote, takes the public spotlight lobbying Congress, requesting that American citizens of Chinese ancestry be accorded the same rights as alien merchants regarding the entry of their wives. The Chinese American Citizens Alliance writes to prominent American citizens and organizations for support and circulates its pamphlet to members of Congress. The 69th Congress receives a senate bill and a house bill to amend the 1924 Immigration Act. It forms the Committee on Immigration and Naturalization and holds hearings. Trying to reestablish the principle in *Tsoi Sim v. United States,* the Chinese argue that an American citizen should have the right to his wife's companionship, that his domicile should be hers, and that a Chinese American citizen should be entitled to no less protection than an alien Chinese merchant. If Chinese merchants can bring their wives to live with them in America under the treaty between China and the United States, the same should be allowed to American citizens of Chinese ancestry. Members of the house committee ignore the rights of American citizens. No action is taken.

PUBL. Etsu Inagaki Sugimoto publishes *A Daughter of the Samurai.* A daughter of a samurai in feudal Japan, Sugimoto dedicates her book to Japan and America, which she addresses as her "two mothers."

1927

RACE. The American Federation of Labor resolves at its annual convention to urge Congress to prohibit Filipino immigration.

SPOR. James Sakamoto (1903–1955) becomes the first nisei boxer to fight professionally at the Madison Square Garden Coliseum in New York City. Sakamoto will later become an active member of the Japanese American Citizens League.

1928

POLI. The Chinese American community introduces two bills to the 70th Congress to amend the 1924 Immigration Act, requesting again that American citizens of Chinese ancestry be accorded the same rights as alien merchants regarding the entry of their wives. Again, Congress refuses to act.

PUBL. James Sakamoto publishes the *Japanese American Courier* in Seattle, Washington.

PUBL. Korean immigrant New Il-Han publishes *When I Was a Boy in Korea*, which offers detailed descriptions of Korean manners and customs, as well as holidays, sports, housing, food, and silk worm culture. A young immigrant to the United States, the author graduated from Michigan College, formed a family with an American-born Chinese woman, and makes a living managing an Asian food product store. His book, however, contains nothing about the experiences of Asians in the United States.

1930

ECON. About 25 percent of the 45,200 Filipinos on the U.S. mainland are service workers. They work as janitors, valets, kitchen helpers, and dishwashers, as well as service boys in hotels, restaurants, and private households. Another 9 percent of the Filipinos work in the Alaska salmon fisheries; they represent 15 percent of the Alaskan fishery work force. Most Filipinos, about 60 percent of them, find work in agriculture. After the exclusion of Chinese, Japanese, Koreans, and Asian Indians, Filipino farmer laborers are in high demand. The workers are organized into gangs or crews. They are represented by their own labor contractors to deal with the growers.

Very few Filipinos are engaged in business activities. Filipino women usually work as maids, cooks, and farm laborers.

FAMI. Filipinos migrating to the United States are predominantly young men. In 1930, only 10,484 or 16.6 percent of the 63,052 Filipinos in Hawaii are female. On the U.S. mainland, only 2,941 or 6.5 percent of the 45,208 Filipinos are female. A Filipino laborer is more likely to take his wife with him to Hawaii than to the mainland because the plantations provide opportunities to work as well as housing for married couples. The Hawaiian planters also encourage Asian laborers to have families, because they believe that family responsibilities will make the workers more reliable. On the U.S. mainland, Filipinos are mostly migratory farm laborers. It is difficult to have families when the workers have to move from field to field and find temporary shelter on the job sites. The relatively few Filipino women are well respected and well treated in a community of bachelors.

FAMI. Because Filipinas are few in the United States, many Filipino men marry women outside of their ethnic community. They form families with Mexican, Chinese, Japanese, and white women. Most interracial couples are Filipino-Mexican.

LAWS. An amendment of Section 13(c) of the 1924 Immigration Act is signed into law by President Herbert Hoover on June 13, 1930. The amendment grants entry to alien Chinese wives of U.S. citizens married prior to May 26, 1924, but such privileges are not extended to alien Japanese, Korean, and Indian wives. Citizen members of Chinese American couples married after 1924 will still be separated from their alien Chinese wives.

LAWS. In February, Los Angeles Superior Court Judge J. K. Smith rules that Filipinos are members of the "Mongolian" race. This ruling will make interracial marriage difficult for Filipinos.

POLI. The Chinese American community introduces to the 71st Congress a senate bill and two house bills, requesting yet again that American citizens of Chinese ancestry be accorded the same rights as alien merchants regarding the entry of

Observation of Carlos Bulosan, a Filipino American Writer Who Arrives in the United States in 1930

"I came to a building which brightly dressed white women were entering, lifting their diaphanous gowns as they climbed the stairs. I looked up and saw the huge sign:

MANILA DANCE HALL

The orchestra upstairs was playing; Filipinos were entering. I put my hands in my pockets and followed them, beginning to feel lonely for the sound of home.

The dance hall was crowded with Filipino cannery workers and domestic servants. But the girls were very few, and the Filipinos fought over them. When a boy liked a girl he bought a roll of tickets from the hawker on the floor and kept dancing with her. But the other boys who also liked the same girl shouted at him to stop, cursing him in the dialects and sometimes throwing rolled wet papers at him. At the bar the glasses were tinkling, the bottles popping loudly, and the girls in the back room were smoking marijuana. It was almost impossible to breathe."

Source: Carlos Bulosan, *America Is in the Heart,* 1943 (Reprint, Seattle: University of Washington Press, 1973, 105).

their wives. The Chinese American Citizens Alliance urges American-born Chinese to exercise their political power by participating in local and state elections and endorsing candidates who are more sympathetic to Chinese immigration issues. During the Great Depression, however, Congress focuses on restricting further immigration, and demand for the liberalization of immigration policies faces more obstacles. Eager to achieve at least some positive results, the petitioners modify the requests. Recognizing that the overriding concerns of Congress are the possible influx of Chinese women and the probability that Japanese Americans will take advantage of the proposed amendment, they request only the admission of Chinese wives—instead of all alien wives—of citizens. The senate bill is finally passed by both houses and signed into law.

POPU. There are 102,159 Chinese, 108,424 Filipinos, 278,734 Japanese, and 8,332 Koreans in the United States and Hawaii.

PUBL. Korean immigrant writer Kang Younghill (1903–1972) publishes *The Grass Roof.* Kang will later publish a fictionalized autobiography, *East Goes West,* in 1937.

RACE. A racial riot breaks out in Watsonville, California. In December 1929, the police arrested a Filipino because he was seen with a white teenage girl. He was released only after the girl's mother said that her daughter was engaged to the man. A month later, the Northern Monterrey Chamber of Commerce in Pajaro (near Watsonville) passes an anti-Filipino resolution to make it difficult for Filipino workers to find employment. Filipinos in the Watsonville area circulate pamphlets and newspaper articles in protest. Tension mounts at a Filipino dance hall for several days, as an increasing number of white workers gathers outside. Fermin Tober is killed in the midst of an anti-Filipino riot in Watsonville on January 22, as a crowd of more than 500 men try violently to force Filipinos out of the area. Seven mob members are arrested, but no one is convicted of any crime.

SOCI. The Japanese American Citizens League (JACL), the most influential Japanese community organization formed by American-born children of immigrants, is established on August 29. Most members of the JACL have been educated in the United States, and they have the right to vote. At its first national convention in Seattle, the JACL discusses education and civil rights issues. The organization gains support from Japanese American communities throughout the west coast. The original 8 chapters will expand to 38 in six years. The JACL will play more important roles during and after World War II.

1930–1940

ECON. Racial discrimination in the job market compels educated Asian Americans to seek self-employment in their ethnic communities. Many second-generation Asian American men and women work in garment shops, hotels, laundries, canneries, restaurants, and fruit stands, following in the footsteps of their immigrant parents.

EDUC. An increasing number of Asian Americans are enrolled in high schools and colleges. The educational opportunities available differentiate Asian American children from their immigrant parents. American educational institutions provide them with not only academic knowledge but also experiences that encourage their desire for more equitable race and gender relations. In the classroom, Asian students can compete with their non-Asian peers, and some are able to excel academically. They learn that they have rights as individuals and deserve respect from others. The rewards of education help young Asian Americans realize and value their own strength, but they still face difficulties assessing their future after graduation. Asian students are excluded from most extracurricular activities in high schools. They cannot dance with their white peers, and they are not invited to social activities.

FAMI. An increasing number of Chinese women work in the garment industry. Most Chinese garment factory workers were male in 1920. But by 1930, female workers are dominant. Women have to combine work with their domestic responsibilities.

PUBL. The Chinese American press flourishes in the 1930s. Most of the newspapers published by the Chinese in the United States are in Chinese instead of English. To increase its influence overseas, the Chinese nationalist government funds a few newspapers in North America, including the *Young China Morning Paper* and the *Chinese National* in San Francisco, the *San Min Morning Post* in Chicago, the *Chinese Nationalist Daily* and the *Meizhou Ribao* in New York, and the *United Chinese News* in Honolulu. These newspapers serve as propaganda machines of the Chinese Nationalist Party. Marxist sympathizers in the community publish the *Chinese Vanguard* and the *Chinese Journal;* both are suppressed by the community establishment in the 1930s. The first all-English news weekly, the *Chinese Digest,* is founded in 1935 by a group of second-generation Chinese Americans in San Francisco's Chinatown, but the paper folds in 1940 due to insufficient subscribers.

RACE. Anti-Asian agitation intensifies during the Great Depression, especially against Filipino agricultural workers. Asian Americans are used as scapegoats for the nation's economic crisis.

RELI. Although most Chinese Christian churches in the United States are still supervised by American denominations, some begin to gain financial independence. An increasing number of church ministers are born in China.

SPOR. Chinatowns in the cities provide various forms of recreation for Chinese bachelors. Other patrons include Filipinos. On weekends Filipino migratory workers often congregate in Chinatowns, where they find ways to escape loneliness in restaurants, brothels, and gambling houses.

SPOR. Male and female Asian high school and college students organize their own basketball and volleyball teams. Some travel to different schools to compete with other Asian sport teams, but few have the opportunity to play or compete with their non-Asian peers.

1931

COMM. Chinese in America begin to train pilots for the Chinese air force after the Japanese occupation of Manchuria in northeastern China. Several Chinese American aviation schools and clubs are established with money solicited from community members, and some accept female trainees. Instruction programs are available in San Francisco, New York, Portland, Los Angeles, Chicago, Pittsburgh, Boston, Tucson, Phoenix, and Honolulu. About 200 community-trained pilots who have no chance to apply their skills in the United States will be sent to China.

PUBL. Pearl Sydenstricker Buck (1892–1973) publishes *The Good Earth*. Born Pearl Comfort Sydenstricker on June 26, 1892 in West Virginia of Presbyterian missionary parents, Buck spent most of her childhood and teen years in China, speaking both English and Chinese. A graduate of Randolph-Macon Woman's College in Virginia, she returned to China in 1914 and married John Lossing Buck, an agricultural economist from Cornell University. The Bucks spent many years in an impoverished rural community in Anhui Province before settling down in Nanjing, with Pearl Buck teaching at the Nanjing University. The couple will eventually get a divorce.

Buck has been interested in writing since her childhood and published short stories in major American literary journals in the 1920s. Her first novel, *East Wind, West Wind,* was published in 1930. *The Good Earth,* her second novel, is a best-seller, and it will bring Buck the Pulitzer Prize and the Howells Medal in 1935. The novel will later be adapted into an MGM film. In 1938, Buck will become the first American woman to receive the Nobel Prize. *The Good Earth* offers a humane portrayal of a Chinese peasant and his family in impoverished and war-torn China. It helps improve the image of Chinese people in the United States. The commercial success of the novel reflects a growing interest among American audiences in China and Chinese people. The publisher of John Day Company, Richard Walsh, is Buck's second husband. Returning to the United States in 1934, Buck will become an advocate for civil rights and women's rights. She and her husband will found the East and West Association in 1942 to promote transpacific cultural exchange and the Welcome House in 1949 to facilitate international interracial adoption. She will be instrumental in the movement to repeal Chinese exclusion legislation during World War II. Buck will author more than 70 books, including novels, poetry, drama, children's literature, and translations from Chinese. She will pass away in 1973 at age 79.

SOCI. Hari G. Govil founds the India Society of America in New York.

WARS. Japan invades Manchuria in northeastern China on September 18, 1931.

1932

FAMI. Katherine Sui Fun Cheung becomes the first Chinese American woman to receive a commercial flying license in the United States. Trained with the Chinese Aeronautical Association in Los Angeles, she will later join Amelia Earhart's Ninety-Nine Club for women pilots and begin entering air races. The Chinese American community will raise money in 1937 to buy a Ryan ST-A plane for her to fly to China to teach Chinese volunteers. Because of an accident before her scheduled takeoff, in which her airplane will crash and her cousin die, Katherine will not be able to make the trip to China.

1933

SOCI. The Filipino Labor Union is founded in November, with a number of branch offices in central California.

SOCI. In New York, more than 1,000 Chinese laundrymen form the Chinese Hand Laundry Alliance (CHLA) on April 23. The Council of Aldermen of the City of New York proposes an ordinance to impose a security bond of $1,000 and an annual license fee of $25 on all public laundries. It also requires U.S. citizenship for every public laundry owner. Most Chinese laundrymen are not able to pay these exorbitant fees. The immigrants do not have citizenship either, since Chinese aliens are ineligible for citizenship. Because the Chinese Consolidated Benevolent Association in New York refuses to take their case seriously, the CHLA launches its own campaign against the proposed ordinance and hires its own lawyers. The city is compelled to reduce the bond from $1,000 to $100 and the license fee from $25 to $10. The CHLA will emerge as a leading radical community organization in New York in the 1940s.

1933–1934

CIVI. Filipino lettuce pickers in the Salinas Valley of California under the Filipino Labor Union (FLU) mobilize 700 workers for a one-day walkout in August 1933. A year later the union's 2,000 members join a strike of the Vegetable Packers Association (an American Federation of Labor affiliate). It demands that the growers negotiate with union representatives and double the wages of their workers. Two Filipinos are shot by the growers during the strike, and several leading union members are arrested. Violence also erupts between the strikers and the picket-line crossers. The strike ends when a camp of several hundred Filipino farm workers is burned down. Two years after the failed strike, Filipino and Mexican farm workers will officially join the American Federation of Labor and become part of the Field Workers Union, Local 30326.

1933–1936

CIVI. Chinese sailors in New York join a strike organized by the National Maritime Union (NMU). During the Great Depression, a large number of foreign workers are employed by U.S. shipping companies. The Chinese are singled out for unusually harsh treatment: each worker is required to post a $500 bond, and 50 percent of his wages is withheld until he is discharged by the company. In addition, Chinese sailors are the only foreign workers who do not have the privilege of going ashore at American ports. The NMU is an anti-discrimination organization that accepts minority workers. The NMU invites Chinese sailors to join a strike in 1936, agreeing to address special concerns of Chinese workers, including equal treatment and the right of alien Chinese sailors to shore leave. About 3,000 Chinese sailors join the strike.

1934

CIVI. Garment shop workers in San Francisco's Chinatown organize to take collective action. The Chinese branch of the Trade Union Unity League's Needle Trade Workers Industrial Union leads a series of strikes and work stoppages, but the employers of the factories refuse to negotiate. In November, the workers form a Chinese branch of the International Ladies' Garment Workers Union. A year later, this branch will lead workers at the National Dollar Stores factory, the largest garment factory in San Francisco's Chinatown, to strike. The factory will close in 1936. These strikes allow Chinese garment workers to join the activities of mainstream American unions.

COMM. Leaders of the Japanese American Citizens League organize the first Nisei Week festival in Los Angeles. Through spectacles, performances, contests, speeches, street decorations, and costumes, the festival aims to use traditional Japanese rituals to showcase the loyalty of second-generation Japanese Americans to the United States.

LAWS. President Franklin D. Roosevelt signs the Tydings-McDuffie Act, restricting immigration from the Philippines. After the Spanish-American War the Philippines became a U.S. territory, and Filipinos were American "nationals." Attempts were made by the government in the early 1930s to repatriate Filipinos, with little success. Finally, the exclusionists joined forces with those who supported independence of the Philippines. The result is the Tydings-McDuffie Act. The law changes the status of the Philippines from a U.S. territory to a commonwealth, under the condition that the islands will be granted independence in 10 years. Filipinos are now aliens instead of nationals, and Filipino immigration is limited to a quota of 50 persons each year.

MUSI. At the first Nisei Week festival in Los Angeles, 1,000 young Japanese women dance in traditional Japanese kimonos.

SPOR. In central California, eight second-generation Japanese baseball teams form the nisei Central Japanese League.

1935

ASIA. The Philippine Commonwealth is established with Manuel Luis Quezon y Molina (1878–1944) as its president.

LAWS. A special act is passed to grant U.S. citizenship to about 500 Asian immigrant World War I veterans. Among them is Tokutaro Nishimura Slocum, a sergeant major who was severely wounded during the war. Though Tokutaro was made a naturalized citizen after the war, his citizenship papers were revoked in 1921. This new law allows him to reestablish his citizenship status.

LAWS. The Filipino Repatriation Act is enacted on July 10, offering Filipinos in the United States the opportunity to return to the Philippines at the expense of the U.S. government. More than 2,190 Filipinos are repatriated. Those returned are subject to quota restrictions for reentry.

MED. The Grandview Film Company is founded in San Francisco by Chinese Americans. This is the only company that produces Chinese motion pictures in the United States. Most members of the film crew, from the director to actors and actresses, have other jobs.

1936

LAWS. A bill is introduced to the 74th Congress requesting that the privilege of citizens to bring their wives into the country be extended to all races ineligible for citizenship. The bill passes the house but fails in the senate. This result will be repeated in the next Congress.

MUSI. Ahn Ik-t'ae (1906–1965), a Korean immigrant living in Philadelphia, completes his composition of the Korean national anthem.

POLI. Second-generation Japanese Americans become active in the electoral politics of Hawaii. Of the 39 elected officials for the territorial government, 9 are nisei.

1937

PUBL. One of the first sociological studies on Koreans in Hawaii is completed by Bernice B. H. Kim at the University of Hawaii.

SOCI. A group of Chinese workers returning from their summer jobs in Alaskan salmon canneries organizes the Chinese Workers Mutual Aid Association in San Francisco in September. The association is formed without the permission of the Chinese Consolidated Benevolent Association. It maintains strong ties with American labor unions as well as with the American Communist Party, and it supports the Chinese Communist revolution.

WARS. Japanese military aggressors attack Chinese troops near Beijing on July 7. Chinese resistance against Japanese invasion becomes a nationwide effort, supported by Chinese overseas from most parts of the world.

1938

COMM. After the Japanese launch a full-scale military invasion of China, Chinese Americans mobilize to support the resistance effort in their ancestral land. They hold many rallies and organize fund-raising events.

ECON. There are a small number of Filipino business establishments in the 1930s. Los Angeles has 16 Filipino restaurants and 12 barbershops, but there are no Filipino enclaves or neighborhoods. The Filipino districts in cities like Stockton and Los Angeles are merely gathering centers for migratory workers.

POLI. Hawaii-born Chinese Hiram Fong begins his service in the house of representatives of the territorial legislature. A 1935 Harvard University law school graduate, Fong will become the speaker of the house in 1949 and the first U.S. senator from the state of Hawaii in 1959.

SOCI. The Chinese Youth Club, the largest Chinese youth organization in New York, is established. The club has close ties to the Chinese Hand Laundry Alliance.

1939

CIVI. Korean Americans picket in Los Angeles against U.S. shipment of scrap iron and airplane fuel to Japan.

FOOD. The expansion of the Chinese American food industry into the non-Chinese market becomes apparent. Beginning in the late 1920s, a few Chinese-run full-service restaurants have appeared outside San Francisco's Chinatown. To attract non-Chinese customers, some entrepreneurs distribute coupons in department stores, and quite a few of them combine dining with stage performances. These restaurants transform the traditional chop suey-style dishes into Americanized Cantonese food, and many serve western-style food and drink.

HEAL. An epidemic of tuberculosis strikes the city of San Francisco. About 25 percent of the cases are found in Chinatown. The city's health officer, Dr. Jacob Casson Geiger, blames the deplorable housing conditions in Chinatown for the health problem. Health officials, Chinese and non-Chinese business leaders, social workers, and civic activists join forces to urge the city government to provide adequate public housing, clinics, and social welfare services in Chinatown.

SPOR. Chinese American Charlie Low, a native of Nevada, opens the Forbidden City, a nightclub on the outskirts of San Francisco's Chinatown. The club advertises food with shows performed by an all-Chinese cast (though some performers are actually of Japanese and Filipino ancestries). It also advertises American-style drink and western food, as well as the opportunity to dance with Chinese girls of great beauty and skill. There are several Chinese-run nightclubs in San Francisco in the late 1930s, catering mainly to non-Chinese customers.

SPOR. The Japanese American 3YSC (Three-Year Swim Club) in Hawaii wins its first national team swim title in Detroit, Michigan. On the team is Kiyoshi "Keo" Nakama, the winner of the 200-meter freestyle event. Nakama will win a total of 27 NCAA, Big Ten (college), and AAU (Amateur Athletic Union) titles. He will also coach the U.S. Olympic and University of Hawaii swim teams.

1940

AGRI. Japanese farmers make great contributions to agriculture in western states. In California, for example, they produce 5 percent of the state's fresh snap beans, 67 percent of its fresh tomatoes, 95 percent of its spring and summer celery, 44 percent of its onions, and 40 percent of its fresh green peas.

ECON. Most Chinese Americans are either self-employed or working for small co-ethnic entrepreneurs. The 1940 census reveals that out of a gainfully employed population of 36,000, only about 1,000 Chinese hold professional and technical jobs; an additional 750 individuals are white-collar clerical workers. This situation will change significantly during World War II. By 1950, of 48,000 gainfully employed Chinese, 3,500 will hold professional and technical jobs.

The number of clerical workers will increase to 3,200.

ECON. Though their numbers are relatively small, Asian American women make great contributions to their family and ethnic economies. Most Asian-owned businesses cannot make ends meet without the free labor provided by their wives and children. Wives of Chinese laborers find work sewing, canning fruit, or shelling shrimp. Many Japanese women work in the fields, and they find work as domestics in urban areas. Asian immigrant women often combine wage earning with family obligations. Without the support of extended family members, women have to watch their children while at work. In Chinatown garment shops, babies sleep in little cribs next to their mothers' sewing machines, and children of Japanese farm laborers on the U.S. mainland and in Hawaii are often taken to the fields by their mothers. These arrangements are important in maintaining the traditional order of the family and community.

LAWS. The government enacts the Alien Registration Act in June, requiring all aliens age 14 and older to register with the Justice Department.

POPU. An estimated 2,400 Asian Indians live in the United States; more than half of this population resides in California. The census counts 106,334 Chinese in the United States and Hawaii. The imbalanced sex ratio continues, as there are 285 Chinese males for every 100 females on the U.S. mainland. This rate, however, shows a significant improvement from earlier decades due to the birth of the second generation. About 98,535 Filipinos reside in the United States and Hawaii. The Japanese population has increased to 285,115, and the majority of Japanese Americans are born in the United States. The Korean American population remains small; the census counts 8,568 Koreans residing in the United States and Hawaii.

PUBL. The *Chinese Press* (1940–1952), an English newspaper published by second-generation Chinese Americans, is established in San Francisco.

PUBL. In New York, members of the Chinese Hand Laundry Alliance publish the *China Daily News* to voice their own concerns. Many laundrymen will purchase a few shares each.

The paper openly expresses its resentment at the merchants' controlled community establishments, and it shows great sympathy toward the Communist-led revolution in China.

RACE. In two separate meetings, leaders of the Japanese American Citizens League assure the Los Angeles city council and the U.S. Army and Navy Intelligence Service of their loyalty to the United States, in the midst of increasing Japanese aggression in Asia.

RACE. Hann Kil-soo, leader of the Sino-Korean People's League, urges Koreans in Hawaii to differentiate themselves from Japanese subjects by registering as Koreans. Hann also asserts that the Japanese in Hawaii are prepared to assist Japan if Japan launches a war against the United States.

SETT. The majority of Chinese are urban dwellers. Many of them reside and work in racially segregated ghettos. Chinatowns are established in San Francisco, Oakland, Los Angeles, New York, Chicago, Boston, and other cities.

SETT. A large proportion of the Japanese American population is still in agriculture, although the number of urban dwellers is increasing. Little Tokyo in Los Angeles serves as the economic and cultural center for a population dispersed in a number of communities throughout southern California.

TREA. Germany, Japan, and Italy enter the Tripartite Pact in September, committing to one another to wage war against any nation that attacks any one of them.

1941

ASIA. In mid-October, Japan's civilian government of Prince Fumimaro Jonoye is taken over by a military cabinet led by General Hideki Tojo.

RACE. The Japanese American Citizens League sends a telegram to President Franklin D. Roosevelt, pledging the loyalty and cooperation of the nisei. The Japanese American Creed, written by Mike Masaoka, the president of the Japanese American Citizens League, appears in the *Congressional Record* on May 9.

RACE. The United States freezes the assets of Japanese immigrants on July 26.

RACE. Two days after the Pearl Harbor incident, 160 Japanese immigrant community leaders in Hawaii are detained in Honolulu. Based on unconfirmed rumors, Secretary of the Navy Frank Knox suggests that Japanese Americans in Hawaii are collaborating with the enemy. General John L. DeWitt, head of the Western Defense Command, is not convinced that all Japanese Americans should be interned at first. He argues that an American citizen is different from an alien. But he will change his position a few months later.

WARS. France signs an agreement with Japan in July, permitting Japanese troops to move freely through its Indochinese colonies. During World War II France has very limited control in the colonies. Efforts of General Charles De Gaulle to reestablish French presence in Laos in 1944 will be suppressed decisively by the Japanese.

WARS. Japan occupies Indonesia.

WARS. The United States places an embargo on the shipment of petroleum products to Japan. Similar sanctions are taken by the British and Dutch.

WARS. The Japanese air force attacks Pearl Harbor, a U.S. naval base in Hawaii, on December 7. The next day, the United States declares war on Japan. Germany and Italy declare war on the United States on December 11, forcing the United States to officially enter the war.

1942

CIVI. The first large-scale protest by Japanese internees occurs at the Poston War Relocation Center in Arizona on November 18. The protest and strike take place after two internees are detained.

CIVI. Mass demonstrations erupt at the Manzanar detention camp in California on December 6. Although more than two-thirds of the internees were born in the United States, they are not trusted by the government. *Kibei*—second-generation Japanese Americans who grew up in Japan—are the main suspects. The incident begins after

---

How to Tell Your Friends from the JAPS

"Virtually all Japanese are short. Japanese are likely to be stockier and broader-hipped than short Chinese. Japanese are seldom fat; they often dry up and grow lean as they age. Although both have the typical epicanthic fold of the upper eyelid, Japanese eyes are usually set closer together. The Chinese expression is likely to be more placid, kindly, open; the Japanese more positive, dogmatic, arrogant. Japanese are hesitant, nervous in conversation, laugh loudly at the wrong time. Japanese walk stiffly erect, hard heeled. Chinese, more relaxed, have an easy gait, sometimes shuffle."

Source: *Time*, December 22, 1941.

Fred Tayama, a young leader of the Japanese American Citizens League, is beaten up and hospitalized because some internees believe that he turned in names of some issei and kibei to the FBI. Harry Ueno, a kibei who has challenged camp authority by trying to organize a kitchen workers' union, is arrested. Three thousand internees gather to request the immediate release of Ueno. Two protesters, James Ito and James Kanagawa, are killed by armed military police; at least 10 others are injured. Several leaders of the protest are arrested and transferred to an isolated camp.

COMM. About 120,000 Japanese in the United States, including 94,000 in California, where anti-Japanese sentiment is strong, are evacuated. Almost a month after Pearl Harbor, on January 5, the War Department classifies Japanese American men of draft age as 4C—enemy aliens. This classification will remain until January 1943. An investigation report on Pearl Harbor by the Roberts Commission implies that Japanese Americans in Hawaii are involved in espionage activates. The report intensifies public fear of possible sabotage on the west coast, leading to media attacks against Japanese Americans.

After Executive Order 9066, the secretary of war is authorized to evacuate civilians from designated military areas. The army divides the west coast states into 108 districts. Residents of Japanese ancestry on Terminal Island in Los Angeles Harbor are given 48 hours to evacuate in February. A few thousand individuals are able to relocate to territory east of the defense zone, which includes California, western Washington

and Oregon, and a small part of Arizona, before March. The majority—more than 110,000—are evacuated from their homes and sent to internment camps. On March 2, General John L. DeWitt, Western Defense commander, issues Public Proclamation No. 1, ordering the removal of persons of Japanese ancestry from Bainbridge Island, Washington, signifying the beginning of the mass evacuation. The Japanese are told to bring only what they can carry; most families will lose the bulk of their personal and real property. The internees are first sent to 16 assembly centers, quickly set up by the government at fairgrounds, race tracks, and other public facilities. At Puyallup, Washington; Portland, Oregon; Marysville, Sacramento, Tanforan, Stockton, Turlock, Salinas, Merced, Pinedale, Fresno, Tulare, Santa Anita, Manzanar, and Pomona, California; and Mayer, Arizona, the assembly centers provide temporary accommodation for the interned Japanese families. Because these facilities are usually not too far away from the homes of the internees, occasional visits by friends and neighbors are possible. Meanwhile, permanent relocation centers are built by the Army Corps of Engineers on federal land in desolate places—in Tule Lake and Manzanar, California; Minidoka, Idaho; Heart Mountain, Wyoming; Topez, Utah; Poston and Gila River, Arizona; Amache, Colorado; and Rohwer and Jerome, Arkansas. The smallest camp houses 8,000 individuals; the largest 20,000. By early November, all the detainees are transferred from assembly centers to relocation centers. About 200 Japanese in Alaska are also removed and

This 1942 photo shows the evacuation of American-born Japanese civilians during World War II, as they leave their homes for internment, in Los Angeles, California. The sidewalks are piled high with indispensable personal possessions, while cars and buses wait to transport the evacuees to the war relocation camps. [AP Photo]

interned. A total of 1,037 Japanese are sent from Hawaii to mainland internment camps. In addition, 2,100 persons of Japanese ancestry from South America, mostly from Peru, are also interned in the United States.

Most Japanese Americans follow the recommendations of their community and comply with the successive government orders.

FAMI. Chinese American Ah Ying (Hazel) Lee Joins the Women's Flying Training Detachment. A year later, she will enter the first class of the Women Airforce Service Pilots. The daughter of immigrant parents, she graduated from Portland's Chinese Aeronautical School in 1932 with plans to serve in the Chinese air force, but both she and her classmate Virginia Wong (Huang Guiyan) were rejected by the Chinese military because of their gender. World War II gives Lee

an opportunity to fly for the United States. She will be killed while on duty in 1944.

LAWS. Executive Order 9066, drafted by the War Department, is signed by President Roosevelt on February 19. The order does not mention any specific groups or individuals, but it empowers Secretary of War Henry L. Stimson to exclude anyone from areas he might designate and to provide these persons with transportation, food, shelter, and other accommodations. The order is phrased in the way of a relief measure, but Japanese Americans are clearly the target.

LAWS. Public Law 503 is enacted on March 24, making it a misdemeanor to violate an order by the secretary of war to leave a "military area."

LAWS. President Roosevelt issues Executive Order 9102 on March 18, establishing the civilian

The Army's Seven-Day Timetable for Evacuation

A. Posting of the Exclusion Order throughout the area: From 12:00 noon of the first day to 5:00 A.M. the second.

B. Registration of all persons of Japanese ancestry within the area: From 8:00 A.M. to 5:00 P.M. on the second and third days.

C. Processing, or preparing evacuees for evacuation: From 8:00 A.M. to 5:00 P.M. on the fourth and fifth days.

D. Movement of evacuees in increments of approximately 500: On the six and seventh days.

Source: U.S. War Department, *Final Report: Japanese Evacuation from the West Coast, 1942* (Washington, D.C., 1943), 100.

War Relocation Authority to take charge of the evacuation and internment under Executive Order 9066.

LAWS. Japanese American Minoru Yasui is arrested in Portland, Oregon on March 28, for violation of a curfew order imposed by the military authority, which prohibits German, Italian, and Japanese nationals, as well as all children of Japanese immigrants, from going out between 8:00 P.M. and 6:00 A.M. Born in Oregon, Yasui graduated from the University of Oregon with a law degree. He violates the curfew order deliberately to challenge its constitutionality. He is jailed and convicted, and his appeal will eventually reach the U.S. Supreme Court. The high court, however, will uphold the constitutionality of the curfew and of evacuation in 1944.

LAWS. Gordon Hirabayashi, a student at the University of Washington in Seattle, refuses to follow curfew and internment orders in order to test their constitutionality. In June 1943, the U.S. Supreme Court will declare unanimously in *Hirabayashi v. United States* that an American citizen of Japanese ancestry has to obey a curfew order. The court avoids issues concerning the internment.

LAWS. Fred Korematsu is arrested in Oakland, California for failing to report to the evacuation center. He is getting married at the time and has a plan to move east. In *Korematsu v. United States* (1944), the court's 6–3 decision will uphold the evacuation order.

LAWS. American-born Mitsuye Endo files a writ of habeas corpus challenging the government's right to hold her in the internment camp. This test case is backed by the Japanese American Citizens League. A Methodist, Endo speaks no Japanese and has never been to Japan, and her brother is serving in the U.S. Army at the time. Her case is not resolved for more than three years, during which time she remains in the Tule Lake camp. In the *Ex Parte Endo* decision (1945), the court will decide unanimously that a citizen of undoubted loyalty to the U.S. government should not be held in camp, and that she should be set free unconditionally.

MUSI. The Chinese Youth Club in New York has a chorus, and so does Min Qing in San Francisco. Both organizations offer their members opportunities to work together and perform on stage. Their dance and drama groups will be quite active in the 1940s.

RACE. Partly because of Japanese military aggression in Asia, many Asian American groups do not show public sympathy regarding the discriminatory treatment of Japanese Americans. Instead, they try to distance themselves from the Japanese. Many Chinese and Koreans wear badges identifying them as non-Japanese. But some community leaders question the actions of the government. Chinese American newspaper editor Gilbert Woo points out that innocent Japanese Americans should not be treated as military aggressors and that the internment of Japanese Americans will not help win the war.

Minoru Yasui of Portland on His Decision to Challenge the Curfew Law

"It is my belief that no military authority has the right to subject any United States citizen to any requirement that does not equally apply to all other U.S. citizens. If the government curtails the rights of any person, the damage is done not only to that individual but to the whole social structure.

   If we believe in America, if we believe in equal democracy, if we believe in law and justice, then each of us, when we see or believe such errors are being made, have an obligation to make every effort to correct such mistakes."

Source: Lauren Kessler, *Stubborn Twig: Three Generations in the Life of a Japanese American Family* (New York: Penguin Books, 1994), 177.

SOCI. Several youth groups in San Francisco form the Chinese Youth League, later known as Min Qing (Chinese American Democratic Youth League). The group will sponsor a variety of social and cultural programs. Its library provides reading materials in classical Chinese literature, history, and Marxist theory. Many members are encouraged to write essays for the group's own publications.

1942–1944

COMM. Inside the internment camps, Japanese Americans cope with their lives behind the barbed wire, the watchtowers, and the armed guards. They are assigned to barracks, and each 20- by 120-foot barrack is divided into four or six rooms. Each room is usually for one family and is equipped with a stove and an electric light, and each individual is provided with an army cot. Families do not cook for themselves. They eat together in large mess halls. The internees cultivate little gardens and organize classes of singing, dancing, and flower arranging to fill their time. Internees are not allowed to leave the camps unless special permits are granted. They are able to leave for work, education, and military service.

ECON. Japanese internees find work inside the camps. Unskilled workers receive $12 a month, while $16 is paid for skilled work. Professionals are paid $19 a month. Many teenagers and adults are able to work.

ECON. Due to wartime shortages of labor, many Asian American men and women are allowed to enter the armed forces and defense industries regardless of their citizenship status or English skills. There are many incentives for Asian Americans to take these jobs. Military service qualifies Asian immigrants for U.S. citizenship, breaking through the restrictions of existing naturalization laws. Employees in defense industries receive much higher wages than jobs pay elsewhere, and they can apply for government-subsidized housing. Thousands of Asian Americans will participate in the war effort.

EDUC. The National Japanese American Student Relocation Council is established to help interned nisei to continue their college

Chinese American Luella Louie, a defense industry worker in World War II. [Courtesy of Luella Louie]

educations outside the camps. The council will assist several thousand Japanese Americans to go to midwestern and east coast universities. Many young nisei are able to leave the camps through the program.

MILI. A total of 15,998 Chinese Americans are recruited to the U.S. military, including 1,621 in the navy, between 1940 and 1946. About 40 percent of these military personnel are foreign-born. Two hundred fourteen Chinese American servicemen and women give their lives to their country.

MILI. Thousands of Filipinos are inducted into the U.S. armed forces. The First Filipino Infantry Regiment is activated in California in April 1942; the Second Filipino Infantry Regiment is formed later that year. Both units are racially segregated. Many Filipinos continue to serve as stewards in the U.S. Navy throughout the war.

MILI. Some 3,600 young Japanese Americans enter the U.S. Army directly from camps. An all-nisei infantry battalion is formed in Hawaii in May 1942 and sent for training at Camp McCoy, Wisconsin. The unit is organized as the 100th Infantry Battalion. The all-Japanese American 442nd Regimental Combat Team assembles for training at Camp Shelby, Mississippi in May 1943. On September 2, 1943 the 100th Infantry Battalion is incorporated into the 442nd Regimental Combat Team in Italy.

MILI. The Army Intelligence School is moved from San Francisco's Presidio to Camp Savage, Minnesota to become the Military Intelligence Service Language School in 1942. Trained bilingual Japanese Americans are often used as interrogators during World War II.

PUBL. The *Chinese American Weekly* (1942–1965) starts publication in New York. The newspaper sets a moderate tone on China politics and is popular in the 1950s and early 1960s.

RACE. The war brings unanticipated changes to the lives of Asian Americans. While Japanese Americans are seen as enemy aliens and sent to internment camps, Chinese are portrayed positively by the American media. The image of Filipino Americans in the United States also improves as American troops fight side by side with Filipino forces in the Philippines.

1943

CIVI. Japanese Americans interned at the Heart Mountain internment camp organize to protest the loyalty questionnaire they are obligated to answer, claiming that imprisonment without due process conflicts with the constitutional guarantee of fairness in the administration of justice.

CIVI. A mass demonstration takes place at the Tule Lake internment camp in California to protest the death of a farm worker. The government responds by sending military forces equipped with tanks.

LAWS. The repeal of Chinese exclusion legislation is signed into law by President Franklin D. Roosevelt on December 17, ending 61 years of Chinese exclusion. During World War II Congress has been under pressure to end Chinese exclusion, partly because Japanese propaganda has been seeking ways to weaken the Sino-American alliance. Tokyo has broadcast U.S. policies against the Chinese to Chinese audiences in an effort to discredit America's influence in Asia. Pressure has also come from American's own allies. The Citizens Committee to Repeal Chinese Exclusion has seized the momentum and launched an effective lobbying campaign. As a goodwill gesture to its wartime ally, the repeal act opens the door to Chinese immigration and makes the Chinese eligible for naturalization. The annual quota for Chinese immigrants is limited to 105, which includes all people of Chinese origin, regardless of their place of birth, even though the 1924 Immigration Act classifies quota immigrants based on place of birth rather than ethnicity or nationality. A deduction will be taken from the Chinese quota for a Chinese born in Hong Kong with a British passport, and no Chinese born in a western hemisphere country can enter as a free immigrant. The repeal act casts a new shadow on the immigration of Chinese women and children. Existing laws allow Chinese children of American citizens and Chinese wives of American citizens married before 1924 to be admitted; under the new law every

Chinese person entering the United States (except for the exempted groups) is subject to quota deduction. The new law is significant nevertheless, because it changes the status of Chinese from inadmissible to admissible and therefore entitles them to general immigration regulations. Chinese American war veterans will become the first Asians to send for their families under the War Brides Act.

POLI. The Citizens Committee to Repeal Chinese Exclusion (CCRCE) is formed by a group of Americans who are sympathetic to China. Some Chinese American organizations urge Congress to end exclusion, but they are advised by the CCRCE to keep a low profile during the campaign. The committee intentionally limits its membership to non-Asian citizens to convince Congress that it is the white Americans rather than the Chinese who want the exclusion to end. This tactic by the CCRCE appears to be effective; Chinese exclusion acts are repealed on December 17.

PUBL. Second-generation Chinese American Pardee Lowe publishes *Father and Glorious Descendant,* an autobiographic account of his own experiences. Born in San Francisco in 1905, Lowe grew up outside Chinatown in East Bay, in a predominantly white neighborhood. His family was well to do and eager to become Americanized, and Lowe had bright dreams as a child. The autobiography presents the author's painful discovery of the harsh realities that the Chinese have to encounter in the United States, regardless of their levels of acculturation.

RACE. Except for Japanese Americans, circumstances for Asian Americans continue to improve. In California, Attorney General Robert W. Kenny makes it clear that nationals of the United States and citizens of the Philippines are allowed to hold real property in the state. Koreans in the United States are also exempted from enemy alien status.

RACE. In February, the U.S. government administers a loyalty questionnaire at all 10 detention camps to men and women over age 17. The main purpose is to identify and register nisei men for the draft, but the questions are worded in such a way that Japanese Americans find them impossible to answer. No other ethnic group has had its loyalty challenged in this way during World War II. Many internees respond "no" to questions number 27 and 28 (see sidebar). The War Relocation Authority later will designate Tule Lake, California as a segregation center for those detainees who refuse to sign the loyalty oath or say "yes" to question 27 or 28.

RACE. General John DeWitt testifies before the House Naval Affairs Subcommittee in San Francisco: "A Jap's a Jap. You can't change him by giving a piece of paper."

1944

ASIA. Ho Chi Minh forms Viet Minh, a Communist group, and prepares for the seizure of power in Vietnam. Agents are sent to neighboring Laos and Cambodia to work with nationalists there to forestall French reoccupation.

Excerpt from the Loyalty Questionnaire

Question 27 (to draft age males): Are you willing to serve in the armed forces of the United States on combat duty, wherever ordered?
Question 28: Will you swear unqualified allegiance to the United States of America and faithfully defend the United States from any or all attack by foreign or domestic sources, and forswear any form of allegiance or obedience to the Japanese emperor, or any other foreign government, power or organization?

Source: Commission on Wartime Relocation, *Personal Justice Denied: Report of the Commission on Wartime Relocation and Internment of Civilians* (Washington, D.C., 1982), 192.

EDUC. The Servicemen's Readjustment Act of June 1944, commonly known as the GI Bill of Rights, is passed to allow the government to spend federal funds for veterans' education in colleges and vocational schools. This bill allows about half of the Japanese, Chinese, and Filipino American World War II veterans and some Korean War veterans to enter college. The number of Asian American college graduates will increase significantly after the war.

FAMI. Maggie Gee becomes the second Chinese American woman, after Ah Ying (Hazel) Lee, to join the Women Airforce Service Pilots (WASPs). Born in Berkeley, California, Gee graduated from the University of California. She worked in two shipyards after Pearl Harbor, before joining the WASPs. She will later serve at the WASP squadron at the Las Vegas Army Air Force Base, giving flying lessons and ferrying military aircraft. After the war Gee will enter graduate school in Berkeley and become a physicist at the Lawrence Livermore National Laboratory.

Chinese American Maggie Gee, a member of the Women Airforce Service Pilots during World War II. [Courtesy of Maggie Gee]

LAWS. President Franklin D. Roosevelt signs Public Law 405, allowing U.S. citizens to renounce their citizenship in time of war.

MILI. About 1,000 Filipino Americans are selected to go to the Philippines by submarine for a secret mission. Landing in various spots throughout the archipelago, they work with anti-Japanese underground groups and gather intelligence for General Douglas MacArthur's headquarters in Australia.

MILI. Internees at the Heart Mountain camp in Wyoming organize the Fair Play Committee (FPC) to protest the drafting of detainees. The committee holds a mass meeting; about 400 nisei vote unanimously to resist the draft until their constitutional rights are restored. Sixty-three young nisei will be convicted for refusing to report for induction, and 267 men will be convicted of draft resistance. Seven leaders of the Heart Mountain FPC will be convicted of advising others to resist the draft.

MILI. In protest of continued incarceration of their families, 106 nisei soldiers at Fort McClellan, Alabama refuse to undergo combat training; 21 of them are sentenced to jail. Others are assigned to the 100th General Service Battalion.

MILI. The all-Japanese American 442nd Regimental Combat Team lands in Italy. It suffers 34 percent casualties in action and becomes the most decorated unit of its size during the war. Before it merged into the 442nd Regimental Combat Team in Italy in September 1943, the 100th Infantry Battalion sustained more than 900 casualties and became known as the "Purple Heart Battalion." The all-Japanese American 100th Battalion/442nd Regimental Combat Team will later rescue the Texas "Lost Battalion" in a battle that lasts for five days. The unit will rescue 211 Texans at a high cost: 184 Japanese American soldiers will be killed, and several hundred more injured.

SOCI. Korean Americans organize the Post-War Assistance Society to provide relief goods to Korea. A similar organization in Hawaii also collects donations for people in Korea after the war.

1945

ASIA. The Viet Minh liberates portions of North Vietnam from the Japanese and declares the establishment of the Democratic Republic of Vietnam. The government selects Hanoi as the capital and Ho Chi Minh as its president. Meanwhile, France tries to retake its colonies in Indochina after the Japanese defeat in World War II.

ASIA. Korea is separated at the 38th parallel, set by the United States. Mutual suspicion between the United States and the Soviet Union leads to the establishment of separate regimes in Korea. The Soviet Union accepts the surrender of the Japanese in Korea north of the 38th parallel. The United States occupies the part below that line.

COMM. Japanese Americans are allowed to leave the internment camps and return to their homes on the west coast in January.

FAMI. Thousands of Chinese women are reunited with their husbands in the United States. Unlike young war brides from other parts of the world, the Chinese war brides are much older, at an average age of 32.8. Most of them are not newlywed brides but longtime wives of Chinese immigrants in transnational families. Until now, these women have been prevented from joining their husbands in the United States because of exclusionary immigration laws against the Chinese. In a five-year period between 1945 and 1950, more than 6,000 Chinese women will immigrate to the United States under the War Brides Act, the Alien Fiancées and Fiancés of the War Veterans Act, and the Chinese Alien Wives of American Citizens Act, balancing the sex ratio of Chinese in America.

LAWS. The War Brides Act is enacted, granting admission to alien spouses of World War II veterans on a non-quota basis, except for groups excluded in immigration laws. Aimed at facilitating the immigration of European wives of American GIs, the law incidentally opens the door for Chinese wives. Because the Chinese are admissible after the 1943 repeal of exclusion, they are one of the first qualified Asian groups to bring in their spouses and children.

LAWS. The U.S. 10th Circuit Court of Appeals overturns the convictions of the seven Heart Mountain Fair Play Committee leaders in December.

MIGR. For the first time, women make up the majority of new immigrants from China due to postwar legislative changes.

WARS. The all-Japanese 100th Battalion/442nd Regimental Combat Team in the Po Valley campaign breaks the supposedly unbreakable Gothic Line in northern Italy on April 5. Three weeks later, the 522nd Artillery Battalion of the 442nd Regimental Combat Team is among the first U.S. troops to liberate the Dachau concentration camp in Germany.

WARS. Germany surrenders to the Allies on May 7, ending World War II in Europe.

WARS. The United States drops an atomic bomb on Hiroshima, Japan on August 6. This is the world's first use of nuclear weapons in warfare. The destruction wipes out 60 percent of the city. The Soviet Union enters the war against Japan and moves into Manchuria in China two days later. The United States drops the second atomic bomb the day after on the seaport of Nagasaki, Japan. The attacks on Hiroshima and Nagasaki take about 340,000 lives.

WARS. Japan surrenders to the United States on September 2.

1946

ASIA. Malaya and Singapore become separate British colonies, after the Straits Settlements are dissolved. Penang and Malacca are under the Malayan Union, while Singapore becomes a separate colony.

ASIA. The Philippines gain independence from the United States on July 4. The Tydings-McDuffie Act of 1934 had promised this independence in 1944, but World War II and Japanese occupation of the Philippines caused its delay.

EDUC. Nursing training recovers in the Philippines after World War II (many programs had been disrupted during the Japanese occupation). Nine universities and colleges will start to offer baccalaureate programs in nursing between 1946 and 1948. Some nursing graduates will win scholarships to study in the United States.

LAWS. The Act of July 2 ends exclusion of Filipinos and Asian Indians and grants both ethnic groups naturalization rights. The quota for Indian immigration is limited to 100 people per year.

LAWS. The Alien Fiancées and Fiancés of the War Veterans Act allows women who plan to marry World War II veterans to gain temporary admission to the United States.

LAWS. The Alien Chinese Wives of American Citizens Act amends a 1930 law and grants admission to all alien Chinese wives of U.S. citizens. This law ends a 20-year lobby of the Chinese American community to win admission for citizens' wives.

MILI. Pfc (private first class) Sadao S. Munemori, who was killed in action in Italy on April 5, 1945, becomes the first Japanese American to receive a Congressional Medal of Honor. This honor comes after an investigation initiated by the chair of the Military Affairs Committee, which finds that Japanese Americans have been treated unfairly in this regard.

MILI. The all-Japanese military unit, the 100th Battalion/442nd Regimental Combat Team, parades down Constitution Avenue in Washington, D.C., in mid-July and receives a Presidential Unit Citation from President Harry S. Truman.

POLI. Wing F. Ong, a Chinese immigrant, is elected to the Arizona house of representatives. He is the first Asian American on the mainland to win political office. Ong will serve two terms in this position.

PUBL. Filipino American writer Carlos Bulosan (1911–1956) publishes his autobiography, *America Is In the Heart.* The son of a farmer on the island of Luzon in the Philippines, Bulosan arrived in America in 1930 with only $0.20 in his pocket. He took menial jobs as a cannery worker, dishwasher, houseboy, and farm hand. Later, he became a union organizer. Bulosan is the author of many poems, articles, and novels. His work will be printed again after the 1970s.

PUBL. Chinese American Gilbert Woo founds the *Chinese Pacific Weekly* (1946–1979) in San Francisco. Financially independent, this newspaper enjoys a wide circulation for over three decades. The paper refuses to take a partisan position on China politics. At a time when the community is divided along the lines of political struggle between the nationalist government and Communist forces in China, the *Weekly* will become a major advocate for a united Chinese America.

RACE. A group of 432 persons of Japanese ancestry, labeled as "disloyals" to the United States, is repatriated to Japan.

RACE. The last of the detention camps, Tule Lake in California, is closed on March 20. The U.S. government provides the internees with train fare back home, but many of the Japanese Americans have no home to return to because they sold all their possessions during the evacuation. The War Relocation Authority program officially ends on June 30.

SPOR. After World War II, Japanese American athletic leagues are reorganized, starting with the Nisei Athletic Union in both northern and southern California.

WARS. A French cruiser shells Haiphong, the port of Hanoi, late in the year, killing 6,000 civilians and triggering a bitter war against Viet Minh forces during the following eight years.

1946–1948

MIGR. The government detains 3,838 Chinese immigrant applicants, most of them war brides. Fraud is suspected. The Chinese American community puts the Immigration and Naturalization Service under public scrutiny. Only a small fraction of the detainees are eventually deported.

1947

ASIA. Official diplomatic relations between the United States and Nepal are established. The United States will provide Nepal with economic assistance beginning in the 1950s and open its embassy in Kathmandu in 1959.

ASIA. Indian resistance to British rule gains momentum. The movement for independence progresses rapidly under the leadership of Mahmmad Jinnah and Jawaharlal Nehru, but it is Mohandas Gandhi (1869–1948), a man of charismatic and spiritual stature, and his mass-action techniques of nonviolent civil disobedience that eventually bring down British colonial rule. Long-standing religious and sectarian differences become the major obstacles for a united Indian nation. Muslim Pakistan will partition from the Hindu India shortly after and become an independent nation. Independent nations will later be established in Bangladesh, Bhutan, Nepal, and Sri Lanka.

LAWS. President Harry S. Truman grants full pardons to the 267 Japanese Americans who resisted the military draft during the war.

LAWS. The War Brides Act is amended, removing race restriction from the original law. Any alien spouses of American war veterans, including the excluded Asian groups, are now allowed to come to the United States without quota limits. This amendment opens the door to a small number of immigrants from Japan and Korea.

1948

ASIA. The new Republic of Korea (South Korea) is established, with Syngman Rhee as its founder and first president.

ASIA. Burma gains independence, ending 63 years of British colonial rule. Internal conflict and struggle will soon consume the nation's political energy. After 1958, the country will be controlled by military governments.

ECON. The Oasis Bookstore is opened in San Francisco's Chinatown by Chinese American war veteran Thick Hing Leong (1921–2003). Born in Guangdong, China, Leong immigrated to the United States at age 17. His first job was in a cannery. As the United States began its involvement in the war effort, Leong found work as a welder in a shipyard before entering the U.S. Army. A self-taught writer, Leong contributed regularly to community newspapers while in the military, publishing more than 100 essays in the *Chinese Times*'s especial column, "Informal Essays from the Military," under the pen name Liang Xiaomai. His Oasis Bookstore, which sells books published in the United States and China, serves as a gathering place for young Chinese Americans; several regular patrons of the bookstore will later become writers and community activists. The bookstore will be forced to close in 1957 during the Cold War.

EDUC. Many Filipino nurses begin to participate in the U.S. Exchange Visitor Program established under the Information and Education Act. The American Nurses Association and many hospitals are able to sponsor participants from foreign countries. The U.S. government issues visas to exchange visitors for a maximum stay of two years. The visitors are expected to return to their country of origin upon completion of the program. By the late 1960s, as many as 80 percent of the exchange participants in the United States will be from the Philippines.

LAWS. President Harry S. Truman signs into law the Displaced Persons Act, granting resident status to about 15,000 Chinese in the United States.

LAWS. President Truman signs into law the Japanese American Evacuation Claims Act on July 2, enabling World War II Japanese American internees to file claims for their financial losses. Many former internees fail to file claims because they have lost documents during the evacuation.

LAWS. In *The People v. Oyama,* the U.S. Supreme Court declares that California's escheat action, which allows the state to seize land of Japanese Americans, is unconstitutional.

LAWS. In *Shelly v. Kraemer,* the U.S. Supreme Court rules that race-restrictive housing agreements are not to be enforced. This decision lifts racial barriers in the real estate market, making it unlawful for landlords and real estate agents to refuse to rent or sell their houses to ethnic minorities.

LAWS. In *Takahashi v. California Fish and Game Commission,* the U.S. Supreme Court lifts racial restrictions on the issuing of commercial fishing licenses. It declares unconstitutional the Fish and Game Code of California, which has denied commercial fishing licenses to Japanese Americans.

LAWS. The California supreme court declares in *Perez v. Sharp* that the state's ban on interracial marriage is unconstitutional.

SPOR. Several Asian Americans win medals for the United States at the London Olympics. Filipino American Vicki Manolo Draves becomes the first woman in Olympic history to win both the high (platform) and low (springboard) diving gold medals. Another diver, Korean American Sammy Lee, wins a gold medal in the men's diving division. Lee will later win another gold medal at the 1952 games in Helsinki, Finland. Japanese American Harold Sakata, a Hawaiian native, wins the silver medal in weight lifting.

1949

ASIA. Communist Chairman Mao Zedong declares the founding of the People's Republic of China, ending a three-year civil war against Chiang Kai-shek's nationalist government forces. Chiang and his followers have fled to Taiwan on the island of Formosa. The United States will not recognize the new Chinese government until 30 years later.

ASIA. Indonesia gains independence, ending nearly two and a half centuries of Dutch rule. The movement for independence started at the beginning of the twentieth century. During World War II Indonesia was occupied by Japanese military aggressors. At the war's end, a small group of Indonesians proclaimed independence and established the Republic of Indonesia, but it has takenanother four years of warfare and negotiation for the Dutch to give up their colony. The United States supports the Indonesian independence movement; it will also appreciate the new nation's anti-Communist stand during the Cold War.

POLI. A political riot takes place in San Francisco's Chinatown. On the evening of October 9, 400 people gather at the Chinese American Citizens Alliance auditorium to celebrate the founding of the People's Republic of China. Among the participants are members of the Chinese Workers Mutual Aid Association, the Min Qing, students groups from colleges and universities in the bay area, and some other liberal individuals. Guests include members of the California Labor School and dockworkers from the International Longshoremen's Union. Half an hour into the program, a group of some 40 men, armed with lead pipes, eggs, and blue dye, rushes in to break up the meeting. They vandalize the meeting hall and throw eggs and dye at the participants. At least two men are injured. One college student is pushed to the floor and beaten by a group of five men. He is later treated at the hospital for scalp lacerations. Another wounded, a white worker, suffers a broken rib. The outbreak is believed to have been planned by community organizations that side with the nationalist government in Taiwan.

The Call for Community Unity

"We like to see many different ideas in the Chinese American community, leftist and rightist, opinions that conflicted with one another. Although we do not like to see newspapers fighting a war of words, a war of words is not a big problem. (There is no winner in a war of words. The ordinary readers are the wisest judges. They can tell from the words who is being deliberately provocative or which group is shifting the blame onto another.) But we are afraid now that a war of words is leading to unnecessarily ugly actions. Some forty or fifty years ago, the Chinese shed their blood fighting over prostitutes, opium, and gambling debts. If we let that tragedy repeat itself because of political disagreement, it will be dreadful to contemplate the future of our community."

Source: Chinese Pacific Weekly, September 3, 1949.

POLI. San Francisco's Chinatown is in terror on October 10, as posters calling for the "mop up of Chinatown's bandits" appear on buildings and walls. Fifteen Chinese Americans are named, and a $5,000 reward is offered for each one's death. Those on the list are either leaders of labor organizations or youth organizations or are newspapermen. Anonymous calls are made to independent newspapers warning them against covering the riot the night before.

PUBL. The *China Weekly* (1949–1950), a radical community newspaper, is published in San Francisco. The founder of the paper, Cai Fujiu (Henry Tsoi), is an immigrant who received a college education in Japan. Cai joined the Chinese Communist Party in Hong Kong in 1937, two years before his journey to the United States.

RACE. Iva Toguri, the so-called Tokyo Rose, is convicted as a traitor of the United States. The Los Angeles-born Toguri is a graduate of the University of California, Los Angeles. She was in Japan visiting a relative when Pearl Harbor was attacked. During the war she worked at a broadcast station in Tokyo. She did not denounce her American citizenship, even though there was great pressure from Japanese authorities for her to do so. Returning to the United States after being cleared by American occupation authorities, she faced charges filed by the Department of Justice for treason. Toguri is sentenced to 10 years in prison and will serve 6 years and 2 months. After her release, she will live with her family quietly until the early 1970s, when the Japanese American community will launch a campaign to win a presidential pardon for her. President Gerald R. Ford will grant the pardon on his last day in office.

1950

ECON. Lifted racial barriers in the job market allow many Asian American college graduates to become professionals in mainstream American society. Among 48,000 gainfully employed, 3,500 Chinese, for example, hold professional and technical jobs (only 1,000 Chinese out of a gainfully employed population of 36,000 held professional and technical jobs in 1940). This change makes the emergence of a middle class within the Asian American community possible.

ECON. Garment industry expands in San Francisco's Chinatown, with more than a hundred factories producing. Most of these factory owners are subcontractors. They will organize the Chinese Garment Contractors Association in 1951 to improve the bargaining position of association members. By 1965, about 3,500 Chinese women will be working in more than 150 garment factories in San Francisco.

MIGR. The government changes the screening procedure for Chinese immigration. Instead of determining an applicant's admissibility at the port of entry, the government requires the applicant to obtain travel documents from U.S. diplomatic agencies in China. This change brings the involvement of the State Department in handling Chinese immigration and enables the government to double-check the identity of each applicant. American diplomats in China now screen each prospective emigrant before issuing a visa or passport. Those emigrants who succeed in traveling to the United States then encounter immigration authorities at the ports of entry for final approvals. After the establishment of the People's Republic of China in 1949, U.S. diplomatic personnel in mainland China were called back. Chinese planning to emigrate now have to submit applications through the American consulate in Hong Kong, which is a British colony. The applicants are mostly young people who try to gain entry through derivative citizenship laws, as children of citizens born outside the United States.

POLI. The Federal Bureau of Investigation launches a large-scale investigation in the Chinese American community. Progressive youth and workers' groups are the main targets.

POPU. The census counts 150,005 Chinese, 122,707 Filipinos, 326,379 Japanese, and 7,030 Koreans in the United States. Many Asians who fought in World War II were eligible to send for their wives and children, allowing thousands of Asian women to gain entry in the late 1940s. These new immigrant women will help balance the sex ratio of Asian populations in the United States.

PUBL. San Francisco-born Jade Snow Wong publishes her first book, *Fifth Chinese Daughter,* a best-seller for several months. A second-generation Chinese American educated in San Francisco's public schools and at Mill's College in Oakland, Wong writes about her life, aspirations, and triumphs. The book is proof that with hard work and determination, a daughter of immigrant parents growing up in segregated Chinatown can achieve great recognition by the larger American society. But Wong's portrait is not all rosy; she painfully reveals the social realities of being Chinese and being a woman. For example, the book describes how she was advised by the replacement office of her college to find work in Chinatown, despite the fact that she received the highest honors in her class. In another example, although she did a great job working in a shipyard during World War II, she realizes there is no future for women in the male-dominated defense industry. Disillusioned, Wong returns to Chinatown after the war, where she works as a ceramic artist and writer. Her second book, *No Chinese Stranger,* is published following her trip to China, after the United States reestablishes its diplomatic relations with China.

RACE. President Harry S. Truman vetoes the McCarran Internal Security Act. If enacted, the law would have required registration of Communists and Communist organizations and would have allowed the government to intern any suspected individuals. Chinese Americans are believed to be the main targets.

SETT. Under the GI Bill, and as racial barriers in the real estate market are lifted gradually, many Asian American war veterans are able to purchase homes outside their ethnic neighborhoods.

WARS. Communist North Korea, backed by the Soviet Union, invades the U.S.-supported Republic of Korea in the south on June 25, triggering the Korean War. Two days later, President Truman sends American troops to aid South Korea. Through the Korean Augmentation to the U.S.

Army Program, General Douglas MacArthur, commanding general of the United Nations forces in Korea, makes plans to assign 20,000–30,000 Korean army recruits to U.S. Army units. Truman declares in late June that the United States is only committed to a limited war for the specific objective of restoring South Korea's frontier at the 38th parallel, but after North Korean forces are pushed back, MacArthur leads the UN troops across the dividing line and presses on toward the Yalu River on the Chinese border, ignoring warning of China's intervention. China responds by sending its own troops across the Yalu. Military confrontation between the United States and China in Korea sets the tone of U.S.-China relations for decades to come.

1950–1954
WARS. The United States begins its involvement in the Vietnam War. The establishment of a Communist government in China in 1949 and the U.S.-China conflict in Korea increases political and military concerns over the future of Vietnam and brings the United States to military conflict in Southeast Asia. During this period the United States sends a total of $2.6 billion worth of military supplies to French forces in Vietnam in the name of "containing" the spread of Communism.

1950–1959
MIGR. About 2,000–5,000 Japanese women immigrate to the United States annually in the 1950s, comprising 80 percent of all Japanese immigration.

1951
ASIA. The Communist government in China isolates itself from most of the world after the Korean War. Chinese in the United States can no longer send money to their families and relatives in mainland China. Communication with their families in China becomes difficult.

ECON. Chinese American scientist An Wang starts Wang Laboratories to commercialize the magnet core memory device that he has invented for computers. This business endeavor is immensely successful. In 1984, *Forbes* magazine will rank Wang the fifth-richest person in America.

MIGR. The United States allows about 5,000 Chinese college and graduate students studying in the states to obtain political asylum after the victory of the Communist Revolution in China. A few laws will pass in the 1950s and early 1960s to allow more Chinese intellectuals to come as refugees. A total of about 23,000 highly educated Chinese will be able to come and stay in the United States, changing class structures of the Chinese American community.

MIGR. The Immigration and Naturalization Service begins an effort to link Chinese immigration fraud to Communist activities in the Chinese American community. The agency works closely with the Federal Bureau of Investigation to raid living quarters and gathering places in Chinatowns, searching for illegal immigrants. It also checks immigration records of leftist Chinese Americans and makes plans to deport them.

MILI. *Go For Broke,* an MGM movie based on the all-Japanese American 100th Battalion/ 442nd Regimental Combat Team, is released.

TREA. The San Francisco Peace Treaty between Japan and 55 other nations is signed in September. Japan will gain its independence when U.S. occupation of Japan ends in April 1952. A security treaty between Japan and the United States allows the presence of U.S. military bases in Japan. In return, the United States promises to defend Japan in times of war.

1952

AGRI. The California supreme court declares that alien land laws violate the Fourteenth Amendment because they are racially discriminatory. According to the Fourteenth Amendment, no state is allowed to make or enforce any law which will deny to any person the equal protection of the law.

LAWS. The McCarran-Walter Act amends the 1924 Immigration Act, allocating 2,990 quota immigrants for Asia, 149,667 for Europe, and 1,400 for Africa. No quota limit is set for western hemisphere nations. The new law repeals the exclusion of Japanese and Koreans and makes them eligible for naturalization. Each Asian nation receives a quota of 105 immigrants per year. Since no ethnic group is labeled as alien ineligible for citizenship anymore, legislation based on this criterion, such as alien land laws, becomes groundless.

SPOR. Swimmers Ford Konno and Yoshinbu Oyakawa, both Japanese Americans, win Olympic gold medals at the summer games in Helsinki, Finland. Japanese American Tommy Kono wins the gold for weight lifting, and Korean American Sammy Lee wins two gold medals for diving.

1953

FAMI. The presence of U.S. military bases in Japan, Korea, and the Philippines facilitates many marriages between U.S. soldiers and Asian women. Most Japanese, Korean, and Filipino wives of American military personnel are married to non-Asian men. Though often called "war brides," they enter as non-quota immigrants as spouses of U.S. citizens under the 1952 McCarran-Walter Act. These brides follow their husbands to different parts of the country; some form social networks with other military wives.

LAWS. The Refugee Relief Act allows Chinese political refugees to gain entry and permanent resident status in the United States.

MIGR. Many of the 1.3 million Americans serving in the Korean War form families with local Korean residents. At the war's end, their wives immigrate to the United States as spouses of American citizens. About 500 Korean women arrive annually as GI wives in the 1950s.

PUBL. Japanese American Monica Sone publishes *Nisei Daughter,* an autobiographical account of the author's life growing up in a Japanese immigrant family in Seattle, Washington in the 1930s and of her family's experiences during World War II in an internment camp in Idaho. The book deals with the racial and cultural identities of second-generation Japanese Americans.

Writer Monica Sone on Her Issei Parents and Her Own Future after Her Family Is Finally Allowed to Leave the Internment Camp

"I gave a quick hug to Father and Mother and stepped inside the bus. As I looked out of the window, I saw them standing patiently, wrapped in heavy dark winter clothes, Father in his old navy pea jacket, Mother in black wool slacks and black coat. They looked like wistful immigrants. I wondered when they would be able to leave their no-man's land, pass through the legal barrier and become naturalized citizens. Then I thought, in America, many things are possible. When I caught Father and Mother's eyes, they smiled instantly.

I was returning to Wendell College with confidence and hope. I had discovered a deeper, stronger pulse in the American scene. I was going back into its main stream, still with my Oriental eyes, but with an entirely different outlook, for now I felt more like a whole person instead of a sadly split personality. The Japanese and the American parts of me were now blended into one."

Source: Monica Sone, *Nisei Daughter* (University of Washington, 1979), 237–238.

SPOR. Judo, a form of martial art, is formally recognized as a sport by the Amateur Athletic Union.

WARS. The armistice ending the Korean War is signed on June 23, restoring the prewar division at the 38th parallel. The United States backs South Korea and has no diplomatic relations with North Korea.

WARS. France grants independence to both Laos and Cambodia in December in the midst of the French-Vietnamese War.

1954

LAWS. In *Brown v. Board of Education,* the U.S. Supreme Court declares school segregation unconstitutional. By outlawing racial discrimination in public institutions, this landmark case provides ethnic minority groups legal ground for equal opportunity.

MIGR. Japanese Peruvians who are held in U.S. internment camps are allowed to apply for permanent resident status in the United States because Peru refuses to readmit them.

MILI. Japanese American Sergeant Hiroshi Miyamura, a veteran of World War II, receives the Congressional Medal of Honor from President Dwight D. Eisenhower for his service in the Korean War.

POLI. The All-American Overseas Chinese Anti-Communist League is established in New York. In the midst of the Cold War, Chinese Americans are pressured to distance themselves from China and assure the American public that they are not Communists.

TREA. The United States enters the Manila Pact with members of the Southeast Asia Treaty Organization (SEATO). One article of the treaty provides that in the event of war in the treaty area, each member will act to aid the others. This pact constitutes the basis of U.S. security commitments to key allies in Asia, including Japan, the Philippines, Thailand, and South Korea, as well as Australia.

WARS. Viet Minh forces defeat the French at Dien Bien Phu, ending eight years of the French-Vietnamese War and ending French colonial rule in Vietnam. The Geneva Agreement at the war's end partitions Vietnam at the 17th parallel, pending a political settlement through a nationwide election two years later. South Vietnam is backed by the United States; North Vietnam is close to Communist China and the Soviet Union. Prime Minister Ngo Dinh Diem proclaims South Vietnam a republic and will refuse to hold the national election. After the withdrawal of French forces, the United States increases its military involvement in Vietnam. It sends more military aid to and provides training for the South Vietnamese army to fight against the Viet Cong (South Vietnamese Communists). More than $1 billion in aid will be sent to South Vietnam between 1955 and 1961, and bombing raids on North Vietnam will begin in 1965.

1955

MED. Chinese American James Wong Howe wins an Oscar for cinematography for his work on *The Rose Tattoo*. A filmmaker for more than 50 years, Howe will film more than 125 movies in his career, including the popular *The Thin Man*. He will win a second Academy Award, for *Hud*, in 1963.

MIGR. About 1,000 Filipinas immigrate to the United States annually as dependents of American servicemen in the late 1950s.

POLI. Everett F. Drumright, the American consul general in Hong Kong, submits to the State Department a "Report on the Problem of Fraud at Hong Kong." The report alleges that China is planning criminal conspiracy to evade the laws of the United States through well-organized networks in Hong Kong, New York, and San Francisco, and it alleges that these networks are the main channel for youngsters educated in Communist schools or who served in the People's Liberation Army to emigrate to the United States. Beginning his career as a foreign service officer in 1930, Drumright spent many years in China before his post as the chief of the Office of Chinese Affairs at the State Department in 1945. During the McCarthy era, he works fervently to carry out the government's containment policy. He argues that current immigration laws are incapable of preventing Communist infiltration, and he wants authorization to crack down on immigration fraud.

1956

LAWS. California alien land laws are officially repealed.

MIGR. The government starts a grand jury probe in New York against Chinese immigration fraud in the name of investigating Communist activities. Through the media, the government tells the public that some young Chinese immigrants are probably Communists and that they can become a willing tool for espionage for Red China.

MIGR. American Harry Holt of Creswell, Oregon adopts eight Korean orphans and brings them to the United States. He will later found the Holt Adoption Agency, which facilitates the adoptions of thousands of Korean orphans by Americans.

POLI. Dalip Singh Saund (1899–1973), an Asian Indian immigrant, is elected to the U.S. House of Representatives and becomes the first Asian American to win a seat in Congress. Born in Punjab, India in 1899, Saund graduated from the University of Punjab in 1919. He came to the United States to study, earning a master's degree in mathematics in 1922 and a Ph.D. in 1924 from the University of California at Berkeley. For the next two decades, Saund enjoyed success as a farmer. His participation in politics began during World War II, when he campaigned to win naturalization rights for Asian Indians. Saund will serve as a member of Congress until 1962, when a severe stroke will leave him handicapped. (Also see entry in 1973)

SCIE. Chinese American physicist Chien-Shiung Wu proves the theory of the violation of parity law in weak interaction developed by Chen-Ning Yang and Tsung-dao Lee. Born in Liu Ho, China in 1912, Wu came to graduate school in the United States in 1936, earning a Ph.D. in physics from the University of California at Berkeley in 1940. During World War II, Wu became the first woman to join the Manhattan Project at Columbia University. Wu's discovery proves the theory proposed by Yang and Lee and helps them to win the 1957 Nobel Prize in physics. Wu will later receive an endowed professorship at Columbia University. She will become the first woman to receive the Comstock Award from the National Academy of Sciences, the first woman to receive the Research Corporation

Award, the first woman to become president of the American Physical Society, and the first woman and first American to win a Wolf Prize in physics.

1956–1965

POLI. The Justice Department launches the so-called Confession Program to destroy Chinese immigration networks. No official policy is issued. Through informal communications with leaders of the Chinese American community, the government encourages Chinese to confess their involvement in immigration fraud. The Chinese are told that they can adjust their status if they confess, giving the impression that by cooperating with the government, they have more to gain than to lose. Meanwhile, the Immigration and Naturalization Service presses Chinese to participate in the program or face criminal charges. The program exposes immigration networks and cripples many progressive organizations.

1957

ASIA. The Federation of Malaya, established in 1948, gains independence from Britain.

PUBL. Japanese American John Okada (1923–1971) publishes *No-No Boy.* The novel receives little attention from the Japanese American community until decades later. Born in 1923 in Seattle, Okada was a member of the U.S. Air Force during World War II. A graduate from the University of Washington, he earned a master's degree in English literature from Columbia University. His novel deals with the impact of the internment experience on Japanese Americans and the Japanese American community; it will later be recognized as the first Japanese American novel. (Also see entry in 1971)

PUBL. Chinese American Chin-Yang Lee publishes the best-selling *Flower Drum Song.* The book is later adapted into a Broadway musical.

SCIE. Chinese American Chen-Ning Yang shares the Nobel Prize in physics with Tsung-dao Lee for work on the violation of parity law in weak interaction.

Born in Hefei in China's Anhui Province in 1922, Yang received his bachelor's and master's degrees in science in war-torn China. With fellowship support, he came to study at the University of Chicago in 1946, receiving a Ph.D. in two years working under physicist Enrico Fermi. A researcher at the Harvard-affiliated Redcliffe's Institute for Advanced Study, he will later join the faculty at the State University of New York at Stony Brook. After his retirement in 1999, Yang will return to China to teach at Tsinghua University in Beijing, China, where he grew up as the son of a mathematics professor.

SCIE. Chinese American Tsung-dao Lee shares the Nobel Prize in physics with Chen-Ning Yang for work on the violation of parity law in weak interaction.

Born in Shanghai, China in 1926, Lee started college during the Chinese Civil War. Arriving at the University of Chicago in 1946, he and Yang became classmates under the supervision of Enrico Fermi. After receiving his Ph.D., he was a research scientist at the university and became a faculty member at Columbia University in 1953. He will earn the title of University Professor at Columbia in 1984. Beginning in the early 1980s, Lee and his wife, Hui-Chun Jeannette Chin, will be actively involved in bringing young Chinese students and scholars to study in the United States. He will organize the China-U.S. Physics Examination and Application and will later establish the Chun Tsung Endowment Fund in Beijing.

SOCI. The Korean Foundation is established to provide a fund promoting higher education among Koreans in the United States.

1959

ASIA. Singapore gains independence from Britain.

POLI. Daniel Ken Inouye—World War II veteran, majority leader in the territorial house from 1954 to 1958, and member of the territorial senate from 1958 to 1959—becomes the first Japanese American to serve in the U.S. Congress after Hawaii gains statehood. Inouye will become a member of the U.S. Senate in 1962.

Senator Daniel Inouye and Governor John Burns welcome President Kennedy to Hawaii. [Photo by Donald Uhrbrock//Time Life Pictures/Getty Images]

POLI. Hiram Fong (1906–2004), former speaker of the territorial house in Hawaii from 1949 to 1953, becomes the first Chinese American elected to the U.S. Senate. Born in Honolulu to immigrant parents, he was elected to the Hawaii territory legislature in 1938 and played an important role in achieving Hawaii's statehood.

1960

FAMI. A large number of Filipino nurses come to the United States through the U.S. Exchange Visitor Program. Between 1956 and 1969, more than 11,000 Filipino women participate in the program, as American hospitals recruit foreign-trained nurses. At least 25,000 Filipino nurses will migrate to the United States between 1966 and 1985.

MIGR. An average of 2,500 Japanese women, 1,500 Korean women, and 1,500 Filipino women arrive each year in the 1960s; many of them are wives of U.S. military personnel.

POPU. The census counts 237,292 Chinese, 176,310 Filipinos, and 464,332 Japanese in the United States. Asian Indians are included in the white category.

PUBL. Chinese American sociologist Rose Hum Lee publishes *The Chinese in the United States of America.* Lee is the chair of the Sociology Department at the University of Chicago and the first Chinese American woman to head a department in an American university.

SOCI. The Korean American Association of Greater New York is established. The organization will expand quickly after 1965, serving 500,000 Korean Americans in the New York area by the end of the century. It will also act as the umbrella organization over 200 regional, professional, educational, religious, and trade organizations.

1961

MUSI. Seiji Ozawa, a world-class music conductor from Japan, is appointed as assistant director of the New York Philharmonic. He will become artistic director of the Tanglewood Festival, summer home of the Boston Symphony Orchestra, in 1970 and will serve as the music director of the Boston Symphony Orchestra from 1973 to 2002.

OBIT. The first Chinese American movie star, Anna May Wong (1907–1961), dies at age 56. For many decades after her death, the actress will be remembered for the stereotypical "Dragon Lady" and demure "Butterfly" images that she was assigned to create in Hollywood films. Her life and career will generate great interest among scholars and filmmakers after the 1980s. (Also see entry in 1922)

1961–1970

MIGR. About 5,000 people from Thailand arrive in the United States. Many will eventually settle in this country.

1962

ARCH. Japanese American Minoru Yamasaki's Yamasaki Associates receives the commission to design the twin towers of the World Trade Center in New York City. The matching skyscrapers, the world's tallest building, will take 14 years to complete. This major U.S. landmark will be destroyed in a terrorist attack on September 11, 2001.

MIGR. A presidential directive by John F. Kennedy allows more than 15,000 refugees from the People's Republic of China to enter the United States.

MUSI. Zubin Mehta is appointed as the music director of the Los Angeles Philharmonic Orchestra. Born in 1936 in Bombay, India, Mehta received early music training in his hometown, where his father co-founded the Bombay Symphony. He began conducting the orchestra at age 16 and later gained international fame. He will become the music director for life of the Israel Philharmonic Orchestra.

POLI. Japanese American "Spark" Masayaki Matsunaga is elected to the U.S. House of Representatives from Hawaii. He will hold the post for seven terms before being elected to the U.S. Senate. (Also see entry in 1976)

POLI. Seiji Horiuchi of Brighton, Colorado becomes the first Japanese American elected to a state legislature in the continental United States.

1962–1973

POLI. Under the leadership of Democratic governor John Bruns, Japanese Americans, most of them veterans of World War II, occupy 55 percent of the leadership positions in the Hawaii territorial legislature. They serve important posts such as president of the senate, speaker of the house, and chairmen of key committees.

1963

ASIA. Malaysia is formed, consisting of the newly independent Federation of Malaya, Sabah, and Sarawak, as well as Singapore. As a major trading partner and investor, the United States maintains a good relationship with Malaysia.

POLI. Many Asian Americans participate in the March on Washington in Washington, D.C., on August 28. The Japanese American Citizens League sends 35 members to this demonstration of 200,000 people.

POLI. Japanese American Yuri Kochiyama begins her involvement in the civil rights movement in Harlem in New York, where she participates in several political activities of the African American community and will meet Malcolm X. A strong believer in interracial solidarity, Kochiyama will be at Malcolm's side when he is assassinated on February 12, 1965. The daughter of Japanese immigrant parents, Kochiyama and her family were sent to an internment camp in Jerome, Arkansas during World War II. This experience offered the then-20-year-old Kochiyama a lesson of social injustice. Not until the 1960s, however, does she devote herself fully to political activism. Kochiyama is known for her many decades of work for black liberation, Asian American equality, Puerto Rican independence, and political prisoner defense. She is the subject of several books and films.

SOCI. The Chinese Historical Society of America is established in San Francisco. The society will publish a journal, *Chinese America: History and Perspectives.*

1964

ARTS. Japanese American photographer Yoichi R. Okamoto becomes the head of the White House Photo Office for President Lyndon B. Johnson. For a term of four years, Okamoto captures many historical moments of Johnson's presidency and creates a candid style for future generations of political photographers.

POLI. Patsy Takemoto Mink, the first Hawaiian nisei woman to receive a law degree, is elected to the U.S. House of Representatives. Born in 1927 on the island of Maui in Hawaii, Mink graduated from law school at the University of Chicago and practiced law in Hawaii before serving in the territorial legislature. She is the first female representative from Hawaii and the first Asian American woman elected to Congress.

PUBL. Korean American Richard E. Kim publishes his first novel, *The Martyred,* a best-seller about the Korean War. The novel will be adapted into a play, an opera, and a film. Born in Korea, Kim received his college education in the United States. He will later publish *Innocent* (1968) and *Lost Names: Scenes from a Korean Boyhood* (1970).

PUBL. Chinese American author Bette Bao Lord publishes *Eighth Moon: The True Story of a Young Girl's Life in Communist China.* The story is based on the experience of Lord's younger sister, Sansan, who remained in China for more than a decade while the rest of her family migrated to the United States. Lord will later publish another book, *Spring Moon,* a best-seller and National Book Award nominee. The second book is a fictional account of the author's own journey to China, the place of her birth. Lord will later write a children's book, *In the Year of the Boar and Jackie Robinson,* based on her own experience as a child from China in America. Between 1985 and 1989, she will live with her husband, Winston Lord, in China, where he serves as the U.S. ambassador to China. She will publish *Legacies: A Chinese Mosaic* shortly after the journey.

SPOR. Japan hosts the 18th Summer Olympic Games in Tokyo. This is the first time the Olympic Games are held in Asia.

SPOR. Masanori "Mashi" Murakami, a Japanese baseball player, pitches for the San Francisco Giants. He is the first Japanese player to pitch for a Major League Baseball team in the United States. A member of the Nankai-Haws in Japan since 1962, Murakami came to the United States as an exchange student, but he stayed to play with the Giants. After two seasons Murakami will go back to Japan. He will come to the United States again in 1983 and become a batting practice pitcher for the Giants' home games. He will also work as a commentator, a sports writer, and a minor league coach.

1965

ARTS. A group of young Asian American actors founds the East West Players, the first Asian American theater company in the United States. The group is led by Japanese American Mako.

ASIA. Singapore separates from Malaysia and becomes an independent republic. It is immediately recognized by the United States.

LANG. Singapore is linguistically diverse due to its complex history, culture, and ethnic composition. Malay is the national language, but Chinese, English, and Tamil are all commonly used. Because English is the primary language taught at all levels of school systems, it is the official language of administration and within academia. This allows Singaporeans to settle in the United States without experiencing language difficulties.

LAWS. President Lyndon B. Johnson signs a new immigration law on October 3, in front of the Statue of Liberty in New York. The law abolishes the racially discriminatory quota system, setting a ceiling of 170,000 immigrants for the eastern hemisphere, with a maximum of 20,000 per country. The western hemisphere receives 120,000 per year without any country limit.

Family reunification provisions of the new law will impact the pattern of Asian immigration profoundly. Under the new law, spouses,

President Lyndon Johnson sits at his desk on Liberty Island in New York Harbor on October 3, 1965, as he signs an immigration bill abolishing the quota system. [AP Photo/stf]

unmarried minor children, and parents of U.S. citizens are entitled to enter outside the quota and without numerical limit. Within the quota, four out of seven preferences are given to family members, including unmarried children over age 21 of U.S. citizens, spouses and unmarried children of permanent residents, married children over age 21 of U.S. citizens, and siblings of U.S. citizens. Professionals, scientists, artists of exceptional talent, certain types of skilled and unskilled workers, and refugees are the other three preferences. A ceiling is set for each of the categories, and about 74 percent of the total quota immigrants are under the four family reunification preferences.

The 1965 Immigration Act will be amended several times. A 1976 amendment will restrict the number of professionals and other workers due to considerations of the domestic economy. This change will require professionals and workers to receive job offers in the United States before applying for visas. A reduced percentage quota for siblings of U.S. citizens will create a huge backlog for visa applicants in this category from countries such as the Philippines and China. A 1986 amendment will impose civil and criminal penalties on employers who knowingly hire illegal aliens. A 1990 amendment will increase the annual quota to 25,600 for each nation.

MIGR. Formal diplomatic relations between the United States and Singapore as well as the growth of U.S. investment in Singapore work to facilitate migration. An increasing number of Americans will reside in Singapore, and as a Visa Waiver Program country, Singaporeans can visit or settle in the United States with little difficulty. Under the International Visitor Program, the Fulbright Program, and many other scholarship programs, education and academic exchanges between the two countries are frequent.

RELI. The Malays from Singapore are mostly Muslim. Other Singaporeans are Buddhists, Taoists, Christians, Hindus, or Sikhs.

SOCI. The Filipino American Political Association is established in San Francisco.

1966

ASIA. The Great Proletarian Cultural Revolution is launched by Communist leader Mao Zedong in China. Although China is largely isolated from the western world, this political movement inspires grassroots activism in the United States.

TREA. The Treaty of Amity and Economic Relations facilitates economic exchange between the United States and Thailand. The United States will become Thailand's largest trading partner next to Japan.

1966–1976

COMM. Inspired by the Great Proletarian Cultural Revolution in China, many Asian American students return to their ethnic communities to organize grassroots activities. They challenge the leadership of traditional community organizations and raise issues regarding social problems. Their efforts to set up health clinics, legal aid services, and bilingual programs provide important assistance to the elderly, the poor, and new immigrants.

1967

LAWS. In *Loving v. Virginia,* the U.S. Supreme Court declares anti-miscegenation laws unconstitutional.

MED. Japanese American actor Mako, a Golden Globe Award winner for his role in *The Sand Pebbles,* is nominated for an Academy Award for best supporting actor. He will enter the Hollywood Walk of Fame in 1994.

SPOR. Japanese American boxer Paul Fujii wins the junior welterweight boxing championship.

WARS. The involvement of the United States in the Vietnam War deepens. Combat troops land in Vietnam in March. By the end of the year, half a million Americans are sent. The Communists

will launch the Tet (Lunar New Year) Offensive in 1968 and suffer an estimated 40,000 casualties.

1968

SCIE. Asian Indian American Har Gobind Khorana is awarded the Nobel Prize in physiology or medicine for his research on the cell's synthesis of protein control. Born in a village in Punjab, India, now a part of eastern Pakistan, in 1922, Khorana went to college in India before going to study at the University of Liverpool in England in 1945 with a Government of India Fellowship. After receiving a Ph.D., he worked in Vancouver, British Columbia for eight years before accepting a job at the Institute for Enzyme Research at the University of Wisconsin in 1960. He will become the Alfred P. Sloan Professor of Biology and Chemistry at the Massachusetts Institute of Technology in 1970.

1969

CIVI. The largest public protest against U.S. involvement in Vietnam takes place on October 15, as hundreds of thousands of students and others across the country observe Vietnam Moratorium Day. A month later, more than 250,000 protesters gather in Washington, D.C. Some 40,000 participants march to the White House, each holding a card with the name of an American killed in Vietnam.

COMM. Japanese Americans organize the first pilgrimage to the Tule Lake and Manzanar internment campsites. The Manzanar pilgrimage becomes an annual event in which community members and students participate. This campsite will be designated a California state historical landmark in 1973.

EDUC. Asian American Studies programs are established at San Francisco State University and the University of California at Berkeley. History classes on Chinese and Japanese Americans begin to be taught in American universities.

EDUC. The first Asian American Studies Center is established at the University of California, Los Angeles. This research unit enriches educational programs of the university by contributing new knowledge on a neglected ethnic group experience. The center establishes its own library and archives. It sponsors research programs and conferences and has its own publications. The center also develops student leadership programs and provides public educational services.

MUSI. Japanese American artist Yoko Ono marries John Lennon, the legendary musician and former Beatle. She collaborates with Lennon on many of his songs.

POLI. Students at San Francisco State University organize a demonstration to demand the establishment of ethnic studies programs. Similar demonstrations take place on the Berkeley campus of the University of California shortly after. Several colleges and universities on the Pacific coast have offered courses on ethnic minority studies in the late 1960s, but students now demand to have a curriculum that offers interdisciplinary analysis of the history of racism and class oppression. The Asian American Political Alliance is formed, with chapters at both universities. Student activists begin promoting the use of the term "Asian" in place of "Oriental." This turn of events sets the stage for the Asian American movement. Ethnic studies programs are established at San Francisco State University and the University of California at Berkeley as part of the settlement of student strikes.

PUBL. Him Mark Lai, together with Thomas W. Chinn and Philip P. Choy, publishes *A History of the Chinese in California: A Syllabus,* one of the very first books on Chinese American history. Born in San Francisco's Chinatown in 1925, Lai graduated from the University of California at Berkeley. Working as a mechanical engineer, he spent much of his leisure time reading books at the Oasis Bookstore in Chinatown, where he became acquainted with some community liberals and newspapermen. Due to many years of Chinese language school and tutoring from his mother, Lai achieved

complete bilingual ability. He volunteered for a liberal newspaper in San Francisco's Chinatown and was closely involved in Min Qing, serving as the president of the progressive youth club for many years. In the late 1960s, Lai began to contribute to newspapers with his own essays on Chinese American history. He will eventually quit his regular job to become a full-time researcher and writer. Lai will be one of the first scholars to offer Chinese American history classes at San Francisco State University. He will author several books and countless essays, including *Island: Poetry and History of Chinese Immigrants on Angel Island, 1910–1940* (with Genny Lim and Judy Yung), *Chinese American Voices: From the Gold Rush to the Present* (with Yudy Yung and Gordon Chang), *Chinese American Names: Tradition and Transition* (with Emma Woo Louie), and *A History Reclaimed: An Annotated Bibliography of Chinese Language Materials on the Chinese of America* (with Russell Leong and Jean P. Yip).

PUBL. The Chinese American Red Guard Party publishes a bilingual community newspaper, *Red Guard,* in San Francisco's Chinatown.

PUBL. Sociologist Harry Kitano publishes *Japanese Americans,* the first comprehensive account of the experiences of Japanese Americans after World War II.

SOCI. Chinese for Affirmative Action is founded in San Francisco to help Asian Americans in their fight for equal employment opportunities. Working with government agencies, Chinese for Affirmative Action provides bilingual materials to assist Asian Americans in finding jobs; its consulting services are designed for both job applicants and workers.

SPOR. Filipino American Roman Gabriel, a professional football player with the Los Angeles Rams, wins the Jim Thorpe Trophy.

Slogan of the Red Guard Party

DARE TO STRUGGLE AND DARE TO WIN!

Source: Red Guard 1, no. 3, June 25, 1969.

WARS. The United States begins a series of air raids in Cambodia, expanding its war effort in Indochina. Cambodia maintained its neutrality throughout the 1950s and 1960s.

WARS. In Laos, a growing American and North Vietnamese military presence makes neutrality impossible. U.S. bombs are dropped heavily on Laos in the late 1960s and early 1970s, aiming to destroy the Ho Chi Minh Trail there. The U.S. Central Intelligence Agency also launches a war against the Pathet Lao (Laotian Communists), arming 9,000 Hmong tribesmen under General Vang Pao. Many Hmong soldiers are killed during the war.

WARS. President Nixon announces his program for "Vietnamization," promising to bring 25,000 American combat troops home by August. Americans will train Vietnamese troops and let them assume the bulk of the fighting on the ground.

1970

FAMI. Interracial families are increasing significantly, largely due to the entry of thousands of Asian wives of American soldiers each year since the 1950s. The number of mixed-parentage Asian American children increases rapidly as a result.

MIGR. An average of 1,500 Japanese women, 2,300 Korean women, and 4,000 Filipinas arrive in the United States each year in the 1970s; many of these female newcomers are wives of U.S. military servicemen.

POLI. The Japanese American Citizens League resolves to seek redress for Japanese Americans interned during World War II, signifying the beginning of the redress movement. The league will seek $25,000 for each detainee and launch a national campaign. The redress movement will mobilize Japanese Americans and draw attention from politicians and the American public. The National Council for Japanese American Redress will form in Seattle, Washington in 1979, pushing for redress through the judicial system. The National Coalition for Redress/Reparations will form in Los Angeles and San Francisco, providing an activist workforce for the campaign. Bay Area Attorneys for Redress will also be organized in the San Francisco Bay area; it will later become the Committee to Reverse the Japanese American Wartime Cases, handling the petitions of Gordon Hirabayashi, Fred Korematsu, and Minoru Yasui. Other attorneys in the Pacific Northwest will also join the group.

POLI. Japanese American employees of the State of California are compensated with retirement credit for time spent in the internment camps. Similar credits will be granted to social security recipients.

POPU. The census counts 435,062 Chinese, 343,060 Filipinos, 69,150 Koreans, and 591,290 Japanese in the United States. All South Asians are included in the white category.

PUBL. Filipino American writer and illustrator Jose Aruego publishes *Juan and the Asuangs: A Tale of Philippine Ghosts and Spirits,* which is recognized as an outstanding picture book of the year by the *New York Times.* He will later be honored as the Outstanding Filipino Abroad in the Arts by the Philippine government.

1971

ARTS. Chinese American Frank Chin's *The Chickencoop Chinaman* is staged at the American Place Theatre in New York. Born in Berkeley, California, Chin grew up in Oakland's Chinatown and graduated from the University of California at Berkeley. A pioneer in Asian American theater, Chin is the author of several novels and many short stories. He will receive an American Book Award in 1989 for a collection of his short stories. Chin's 1974 play *The Year of the Dragon* will be adapted into a film. A controversial Asian American writer, Chin will be the subject of a biographical documentary film, *What's Wrong with Frank Chin,* which will be released in 2005.

ASIA. President Nixon's national security advisor, Henry Kissinger, secretly visits Beijing and meets with leaders of the Chinese Communist government. This historical trip paves the way for Nixon's visit to China a year later, which is the first step toward normalization of U.S.-China relations.

MED. Chinese American Connie Chung begins to work at CBS's Washington bureau, becoming the first Asian American and second female nightly news anchor for a major national television network. Born in Washington, D.C., Chung started her career broadcasting at a local television station. Her positions at CBS and later at NBC will allow her to establish a distinguished career in broadcast journalism, working together with prominent television news anchors such as Tom Brokaw and Dan Rather. She will win three Emmy Awards, as well as a Peabody Award.

OBIT. Japanese American writer John Okada dies of a heart attack at age 44. Several years after his death, his novel *No-No Boy* will be discovered and recognized by the Asian American community as the first Japanese American novel. Unfortunately, his other writings are not preserved. Stanford University will name its Asian American dorm after Okada, in memory of the author's contribution to the Asian American community. (Also see entry in 1957)

POLI. Korean American Herbert Choy is appointed by President Richard M. Nixon as judge to the U.S. Circuit Court of Appeals for the Ninth Circuit. He is the first Asian American to be appointed to a federal court.

PUBL. The *Amerasia Journal,* the first academic journal of Asian American studies, is published by the Asian American Studies Center at the University of California, Los Angeles. Russell C. Leong and Don Nakanishi are the co-founders of the journal, and Leong also serves as the editor. The *Amerasia Journal* is a leading interdisciplinary journal in Asian American studies.

1971–1980

MIGR. About 44,000 Thai immigrate to the United States.

RELI. Religion is of great importance in the Thai American community. Thai Buddhist churches serve as important networks, providing social services and support to newcomers.

1972

ARTS. Vietnam's Huynh Cong Ut, also known as "Nick" Ut, wins the Pulitzer Prize for photography for his picture of Phan Thi Kim Phuc, a naked nine-year-old girl running toward the camera escaping a napalm attack during the Vietnam War. This image, which captures the brutality and human trauma of the war, appears in major newspapers throughout the world. Huynh is a Los Angeles-based photographer for the Associated Press at the time.

MED. Thirteen-year-old Chinese American actress Rosalind Chao receives good reviews for her performance in a CBS sitcom, *Anna and the King.* Born in California, Chao began to perform with the California-based Peking Opera at age five. In her early teen years she will appear in television commercials and guest-star on television series. Her first acting role was in the CBS sitcom *Here Is Lucy.* Her role as a South Korean refugee in the final episodes of the television series *M*A*S*H* will help her establish herself in Hollywood. In *Star Trek: The Next Generation* and *Star Trek: Deep Space Nine,* Chao will play the Japanese exo-botanist Keiko O'Brien. Chao will also star in *Thousand Pieces of Gold* and a few other films. She will act in more than 25 films and more than 10 television series.

MILI. The United States ends a 27-year occupation of the Ryukyu Islands in Japan, of which Okinawa is a part.

POLI. Japanese Americans Ken Kawaichi and Dale Minami found the Asian Law Caucus. This legal advocacy group is organized to help Asian Americans deal with civil rights issues. Minami is a well-known community activist. Born in Los Angeles, California, he is a graduate of the School of Law at the University of California at Berkeley. He will later co-found the Asian American Bar Association of the Greater Bay Area, the Asian Pacific Bar of California, and the Coalition of Asian Pacific Americans.

1973

OBIT. Bruce Lee (1940–1973), Chinese American action film superstar and martial arts master, dies at age 32. The San Francisco-born Lee grew up in Hong Kong, where he became a dancer, a kung fu master, and a film star. Lee's version of martial arts gained him great popularity in the United States through his action films. He later started a martial arts school in Seattle and established an acting career in Hollywood as a martial arts fighter. But racial discrimination against Asian actors in Hollywood prevented Lee from getting important roles. When the television series *Kung Fu* selected a white actor over him for its cast, Lee returned to Hong Kong in protest.

OBIT. Asian Indian American Dalip Singh Saund (1899–1973), who served as a member of the U.S. House of Representatives from 1957 to 1962, passes away at age 74. Saund was the first Asian American and first Asian Indian American to serve Congress on the mainland. (Also see entry in 1956)

PUBL. Japanese American writer Jeanne Wakatsuki Houston, with her husband James Houston, publishes *Farewell to Manzanar,* a recollection of the Wakatsuki family's memories of their internment experiences during World War II.

SOCI. The Free Chol Soo Lee Defense Committee is formed in San Francisco to lead a movement to free Korean American immigrant Chol Soo Lee, who was convicted for the killing of a San Francisco Chinatown gang leader, Yip Yee Tak, and sentenced to life imprisonment. Born in Seoul, Korea in 1952, Lee immigrated to the United States at age 12. He was arrested and charged after Tak was shot to death. Supporters of Lee believe that Lee is innocent, and the committee is able to mobilize many members of the Asian American community. Lee's case will become more complicated in 1977, when he kills Morrison Needham in prison, in an act he claims to be self-defense, for which he faces the possibility of the death penalty. With the support of his community, Lee will be retried for the first incident and acquitted by the jury in 1982. Through plea bargain, he will also be able to use the time already served in jail as credit for the killing of Needham. Lee will be freed in 1983.

1974

EDUC. In *Lau v. Nichols,* the U.S. Supreme Court declares that failure to provide adequate education for non-English-speaking students is a violation of the equal protection clause of the U.S. Constitution. This decision brings about the establishment of English as a Second Language (ESL) programs in public schools. Immigrant children are entitled to English as a Second Language classes as well as special tutoring in language classes.

POLI. Norman Mineta wins a seat in the U.S. House of Representatives and becomes the first Japanese American from the continental United States to serve in Congress. Mineta previously served as the mayor of his hometown in San Jose, California. During World War II, Mineta's family was interned in Wyoming for three years. In the 100th Congress in 1987, Mineta and other Japanese American representatives in Congress will introduce a measure for redress, which will win Japanese American internees an official apology from the government and $1.2 billion in compensation. Mineta will be appointed by President Bill Clinton as the secretary of commerce of the United States in 2000, becoming the first Asian American to hold a post in the presidential cabinet. In 2001, he will be appointed as the secretary of transportation by President George W. Bush and serve the post until 2006.

POLI. Chinese American March Fong Eu is elected as California's secretary of state. Born in Oakland, California, Eu graduated from the University of California at Berkeley, and she earned an Ed.D. from Stanford University. Eu started her political career as a member of the California State Assembly in 1966. As secretary of state, she will be reelected four more times. She will be named by the *Ladies Home Journal* as one of America's "100 Most Important Women" in 1988. Serving her fifth term in 1994, she will be appointed by President Bill Clinton as the U.S. ambassador to Micronesia.

1975

ASIA. The Lao People's Democratic Republic, a Communist government, is established on December 2. Unlike in neighboring Vietnam and Cambodia, the transition of power is completed without military action. Diplomatic relations with the United States, which started in 1950, will deteriorate after the Vietnam War. Improvement will begin after 1982, and full diplomatic relations will resume in 1992.

ECON. Shahir Kadir, an Indonesian entrepreneur, wins a court case challenging a discriminatory law in Washington, D.C., that limits business ownership to U.S. citizens only.

ECON. The Refugee Cash Assistance program of the federal government provides financial assistance to Southeast Asian newcomers for up to 36 months. This program allows refugees time to receive training and seek employment in the United States.

FOOD. Many Korean restaurants appear in American cities, as the immigrant population grows. Rice, noodles, vegetables, tofu, fish, and meats are main ingredients in Korean cuisine. A typical Korean meal usually includes steamed white rice, a number of side dishes, and meat. Pickled vegetables, salt fish, and marinated seaweeds are the most common side dishes. These dishes are heavily seasoned with chili, sesame oil, soy sauce, fish sauces, garlic, and ginger. Pork, beef, and chicken are stir-fried, grilled, or stewed, and fish is served raw, dried, grilled, or steamed. The most famous Korean dish is *kimchi,* a pickled vegetable side dish served in every meal. There are many variations of kimchi, but the basic ones are made from Napa cabbage, daikon, or cucumber, fermented in chili pepper, garlic, ginger, and scallions. Korean barbecue is also well known. In traditional Korean restaurants, a charcoal grill is placed at the center of the dining table, and meats are barbecued after the diners are seated. Common Korean desserts are made from pounded rice or sweet rice, with sweetened red bean or sesame fillings. Tea, served hot, is the most common nonalcoholic beverage served in Korean restaurants. There are also Korean rice wine and beer.

LANG The Vietnamese language shows strong influences from Thai, Khmer, and Chinese. Chinese characters and indigenous phonetic script are both used. In the early twentieth century, the Vietnamese adopted a romanized script introduced by the French. Ethnic Chinese and other minority groups maintain their own cultures and speak their own languages and dialects.

LANG. Khmer is the official language in Cambodia, spoken by more than 95 percent of the population. Some ethnic Chinese, Vietnamese, Laotians, and others speak their own languages and dialects.

LANG. Lao is the official language spoken in Laos. It is very similar to Thai. French, English, Chinese, Vietnamese, Hmong, and other ethnic languages and dialects are used by various ethnic groups.

LAWS. The Indochina Migration and Refugee Assistance Act is enacted, providing federal funds to reimburse states for the expense of resettlement programs for Southeast Asian refugees.

MIGR. The United States begins to admit large numbers of Southeast Asians in response to the refugee crisis after the Vietnam War. On March 18, President Gerald Ford authorizes the attorney general to admit 130,000 Vietnamese and Cambodian refugees who left their homelands right before the Communist takeover. Among the first wave of refugees admitted are military and government officials, as well as the educated and well-to-do from urban areas, especially Saigon. Refugee camps are established in the Philippines, Guam, Thailand, Wake Island, and Hawaii. Agents of the Immigration and Naturalization Service process these people in Guam before sending them to receiving centers in the United States, where the refugees will register with one of the nine government-contracted voluntary agencies (the "volags") for resettlement through networks of individual sponsors.

MIGR. From 1975 to 1996, some 250,000 Lao refugees will be admitted to the United States, including 130,000 Hmong. The Wat Tham Krabok camp will be closed in 2004 as the United States admits about 15,000 Hmong refugees.

PUBL. Chinese American Laurence Yep publishes *Dragonwings,* an adventure story for young readers. The book receives a Newbery Honor Book award and is adapted for stage production. Born in San Francisco, Yep graduated from the University of California at Santa Cruz. He earned a Ph.D. from the State University of New York at Buffalo. He is the recipient of the Laura Ingalls Wilder Award and several other recognitions.

Yep's other published books include *Dragon's Gate, Sweetwater, When the Circus Came to Town, The Imp That Ate My Homework, The Magic Paintbrush, Tiger Magic,* and *The Earth Dragon Awakes.*

RELI. Although some refugees from Southeast Asia are Christians, most of them believe in Buddhism and follow Buddhist practices.

RELI. Hmong refugees bring their own religion with them to the United States. The Hmong people are known as "animists" who believe in the existence of spirits. These spirits are associated with their houses, nature, or ancestors. When a person is sick, a soul-calling ceremony is performed, in which a shaman is invited to communicate with the spiritual world. While many of the Hmong will be converted to Christianity after they settle in the United States, traditional religious rituals will still be performed within the community, especially when health problems occur.

SPOR. Ann Kiyomura, a Japanese American, and Kazuko Sawamatsu of Japan win a women's doubles title at the Wimbledon tennis championship in England.

WARS. Khmer Rouge, the Cambodian Communist force, overthrows the Phnom Penh's Khmer Republic and assumes power in Cambodia (renamed as Kampuchea) on April 17. The United States' diplomatic relations with the Khmer Republic end.

WARS. The Vietnam War ends with the fall of Saigon on April 30. Ho Chi Minh's Democratic Republic of Vietnam (north) will soon take over the former Republic of Vietnam (south). The Socialist Republic of Vietnam will be established in 1976.

1976

LAWS. President Gerald R. Ford issues Proclamation 4417, revoking Executive Order 9066, which authorized the internment of Japanese Americans during World War II.

MIGR. Small groups of refuge-seekers continue to escape from Cambodia, Laos, and Vietnam.

From Proclamation 4417

"February 19th is the anniversary of a sad day in American history. It was on that date in 1942, in the midst of the response to the hostilities that began on December 7, 1941, that Executive Order 9066 was issued, subsequently enforced by the criminal penalties of a statute enacted March 21, 1942, resulting in the uprooting of loyal Americans. Over one hundred thousand persons of Japanese ancestry were removed from their homes, detained in special camps, and eventually relocated.

We now know what we should have known then—not only was that evacuation wrong, but Japanese-Americans were and are loyal Americans. On the battlefield and at home, Japanese-Americans—names like Hamada, Mitsumori, Marimoto, Noguchi, Yamasaki, Kido, Munemori, and Miyamura—have been and continue to be written in our history for the sacrifices and the contributions they have made to the well-being and security of this, our common Nation.

NOW, THEREFORE, I, GERALD R. FORD, President of the United States of America, do hereby proclaim that all authority conferred by Executive Order 9066 terminated upon the issuance of Proclamation 2714, which formally proclaimed the cessation of hostilities of World War II on December 31, 1946.

I call upon the American people to affirm with me this American Promise—that we have learned from the tragedy of that long-ago experience forever to treasure liberty and justice for each individual American, and resolve that this kind of action shall never again be repeated."

President Gerald R. Ford, February 19, 1976.

These refugees are known as "boat people" from Vietnam who find their first asylum in Malaysia, Thailand, Indonesia, Singapore, or the Philippines and as "land people" from Laos and Kampuchea who enter Thailand. The refugee crisis will continue for many more years, compelling the United States to further open its doors. By 1978, an average of 1500 people a month will have left their homelands. About 450,000 Southeast Asian refugees will be admitted to the United States between 1979 and 1982. And from 1982 to 1992, between 40,000 and 80,000 will be admitted each year. About three-quarters of them come from Vietnam. California becomes home to the largest population of refugees, while Texas ranks second. Washington and Pennsylvania are two other major receiving states. About 40 percent of all the Hmong refugees will later resettle in Minnesota.

POLI. Japanese American S. I. Hayakawa, who was born in Canada, wins a U.S. Senate seat on the Republican ticket. Hayakawa is a former president of San Francisco State University. He will hold the senate post from 1977 to 1983.

POLI. Native Hawaiian Daniel K. Akaka is elected to the U.S. House of Representatives from Hawaii. He will serve for seven terms.

POLI. The Organization of PanAsian American Women is founded to provide a voice for the concerns of Asian Pacific American women. The organization seeks to develop Asian women's leadership skills and to maintain a national communication network.

POLI. "Spark" Masayaki Matsunaga wins a seat in the U.S. Senate, representing Hawaii, after seven consecutive terms in the U.S. House of Representatives. (Also see entry in 1962)

PUBL. Chinese American author Maxine Hong Kingston publishes *The Woman Warrior,* in which she portrays the conflicting cultural messages sent to her as she forged her identity as a Chinese American woman. Growing up in her parents' laundry business in Stockton, California, Kingston received her childhood education from her mother, Ying Lan Hong, whose legendary stories of Chinese people made a great impact on Kingston's written work. Kingston

graduated with an English degree from the University of California at Berkeley in 1962 before marrying her husband, Earl Kingston. Her second book, *China Men,* will be published in 1977. In 1989, she will publish her third book, *Tripmaster Monkey: His Fake Book.* Kingston will go on to write two other books, as well as many poems, short stories, and essays. Her work will be translated into more than 10 languages and read by people throughout the world. A recipient of the 1997 National Humanities Medal, Kingston will become a professor emerita at the University of California at Berkeley.

PUBL. *Years of Infamy: The Untold Story of America's Concentration Camps,* by Michiko Nisuira Weglyn, is published. The book exposes the hardships experienced by Japanese Americans inside the internment camps during World War II.

SCIE. Chinese American physicist Samuel Chao Chung Ting shares a Nobel Prize in physics with Burton Richter for the discovery of a new subatomic particle, the J particle. Born in Ann Arbor, Michigan in 1936, Ting spent his earlier years in China and Taiwan before immigrating to the United States at age 20. At the University of Michigan, Ann Arbor, Ting received his doctoral degree in 1962. After working briefly at Columbia University and in Hamburg, Germany, he joined the faculty of the Massachusetts Institute of Technology in 1967. He discovered the new J particle through an experiment at Brookhaven National Laboratory on Long Island, New York.

SETT. Settlement patterns of Southeast Asian refugees are shaped by their own social networks. Government policies and programs try to disperse the refugee population, but most newcomers, especially those with family members or relatives already residing in the United States, continue to move to areas of highly concentrated Southeast Asians in California. The largest Cambodian community is developed in the Long Beach area of Los Angeles. The largest Lao community is found in San Diego, although the Hmong people from Laos are especially concentrated in Fresno. The Vietnamese immigrants are highly concentrated in Orange County.

1977

POLI. President Jimmy Carter appoints Chinese American Thomas Tang to the U.S. Circuit Court of Appeals for the Ninth Circuit. The court presides over nine western states.

1978

ARCH. Chinese American architect I. M. Pei gains national and international fame as the East Building of the National Gallery of Art in Washington, D.C., is completed. Born in Guangzhou, China, Pei received his early education in Hong Kong and Shanghai. Coming to the United States in 1935 at age 18, Pei studied architecture at the University of Pennsylvania, the Massachusetts Institute of Technology, and Harvard University. One of the most prominent architects in modern history, Pei has designed landmark projects throughout the world. His work includes the John F. Kennedy Library in Cambridge, Massachusetts; the Bank of China Tower in Hong Kong; the Pyramids of the Louvre in Paris; the Rock and Roll Hall of Fame in Cleveland, Ohio; and the Miho Museum in Shiga, Japan.

MUSI. Chinese American cellist Yo-Yo Ma receives the prestigious Avery Fisher Prize. Born in Paris in 1955, Ma studied cello with his father at age four. A graduate of the Juilliard School of Music and Harvard University, Ma is considered the world's finest cellist. He made his appearance as a soloist with the Harvard Radcliffe Orchestra at age 15 and gained national and international recognition. As a soloist Ma will travel throughout the world, performing with major orchestras. Trained as a classical musician, Ma will constantly search for new ways to communicate with his audiences through his music and will become known for exploring new ideas and cultures. Ma will found the Silk Road Project to promote the study of traditions and cultures along the ancient Silk Road trade route, which links the Mediterranean Sea to the Pacific Ocean. Ma will become one of the world's best-selling classical music artists, making more than 50 albums. He will win 15 Grammy Awards and the 1997 Gramophone Award as artist of the year. He will

also receive an honorary doctorate degree from Princeton University in 2005.

MUSI. Japanese American jazz pianist Toshiko Akiyoshi, who also leads the Best Big Jazz Band, is named Best Arranger in the *Down Beat Readers' Poll.*

POLI. Japanese American Robert Matsui wins a seat in the U.S. House of Representatives after seven years of service as a city council member in Sacramento, California. He will be in office from 1979 to 2005, serving a total of 13 terms.

POLI. About 120 Asian American elected officials are serving in local, state, and federal offices. Most of them are Chinese or Japanese Americans.

POLI. A joint congressional resolution establishes the first 10 days of May as Asian/Pacific American Heritage Week. In 1992, Congress will expand the observance to a month-long celebration.

PUBL. Third-generation Japanese American poet Janice Mirikitani publishes her first volume of poetry, *Awake in the River.* She will publish two more volumes of poetry (*Shedding Silence,* 1986; and *We, the Dangerous: New and Selected Poems,* 1995) and edit several anthologies of poetry, prose, and essays. Mirikitani will receive more than 30 awards and honors, including the American Book Lifetime Achievement Award for literature.

WARS. Vietnam invades Cambodia, intensifying tensions with China. Beijing will interfere by launching a border war with Vietnam in early 1979.

1979

ASIA. The United States normalizes its diplomatic relationship with the People's Republic of China. Under the "one China" policy, recognition of China compels the United States to end official ties with the Republic of China in Taiwan.

EDUC. The Association for Asian American Studies is founded. This association works to advance professional standards in teaching and research in the field of Asian American studies. Through annual national conferences, workshops, journal publication, awards programs, and other professional activities, the Association for Asian American Studies promotes better understanding and communication among various subcomponents within Asian American studies and advocates education about Asian American experiences in colleges and universities.

FOOD. Normalization of diplomatic relations with China generates a growing interest in Chinese food in the United States. Some Chinese entrepreneurs will open new restaurants in American suburbs to suit the tastes of middle-class American diners. In addition to Cantonese cuisine, Sichuan, Hunan, and other Chinese regional cooking styles begin to gain popularity.

FOOD. A Korean fast food chain, Sorabol, starts business. Small restaurants from this chain will appear on the food court market, serving Korean barbecue, noodles, and soups.

MIGR. Normalization of U.S.-China relations creates a new pattern of Chinese immigration to the United States. Until this point Chinese from Taiwan have been the main beneficiaries of the 1965 Immigration Act, while those on the mainland have been completely shut out. Hong Kong, then a British colony, has received a small quota of its own. The establishment of diplomatic relations with China entitles the Chinese mainland an immigration quota equivalent to any other nation's. Large numbers of Chinese mainlanders will arrive in the decades to follow.

POLI. A monument is erected on the site of the administration building on Angel Island to commemorate the Chinese immigrants who were detained at the immigration station during exclusion. An exhibit recounting the experiences of early Chinese immigrants to the United States will be mounted at the site in 1984. Angel Island was a detention center for immigrants arriving through San Francisco from the other side of the Pacific from 1910 to 1940. Most of those detained were from China, but some were from other parts of Asia or the Pacific Islands. (Also see entry in 1910)

POLI. The Indochina Resource Action Center, later renamed the Southeast Asian Resource Action Center, is founded in Washington, D.C. The center provides assistance to Southeast Asian refugees. Its publications and workshops offer guidelines for sponsors and community organizations.

PUBL. Chinese American John Ta-Chuan Fang founds *AsianWeek,* an English-language weekly covering Asian American community activities.

PUBL. Korean American journalist K. W. Lee founds the English-language Korean American newspaper *Koreantown Weekly,* covering issues concerning Korean Americans in the United States. Arriving in the United States in 1950, the Korean-born Lee studied journalism at West Virginia University and at the University of Illinois. As a civil rights advocate, Lee has played an important role in Asian American political activism, including organizing the Free Chol Soo Lee Defense Committee in 1973. He will receive the Asian American Journalists Association's Lifetime Achievement Award in 1987, the Free Spirit Award from the Freedom Forum in 1994, and several other awards.

1980

COMM. The New York Chinatown History Project is launched, leading to the establishment of the Chinatown History Museum. The museum organizes exhibits, lecture series, symposia, book readings, and other social events. Located at 10 Mulberry Street, in the heart of New York's Chinatown, the museum also maintains a library.

ECON. Pakistani American Safi Qureshey, along with Thomas Yuen and Albert Wong, establishes AST Research Inc., a personal computer manufacturer. Qureshey later will become the head of the company when AST emerges as the fourth-largest producer of personal computers after IBM, Apple, and Compaq. The company will appear on the *Fortune* list of America's 500 leading companies in the early 1990s. Qureshey later will serve as CEO of Quartics, a wireless video technology company, and participate actively in several other high-tech ventures in southern California. He will also build a close relationship with the University of California, Irvine, serving as a regents' professor at its Graduate School of Management. A member of President Bill

Clinton's Export Council, Qureshey will also serve on California Governor Arnold Schwarzenegger's transition team.

FOOD. Next to Chinese cuisine, Japanese food gains popularity in the United States. Until the 1970s, Japanese restaurants could only be found in a few big cities and places with large Japanese American populations. As American diners begin to develop more sophisticated tastes for ethnic food, Japanese cuisine gains increasing popularity, especially among urban professionals. Unlike Chinese food, in which meats, fish, and most vegetables are fully cooked, raw fish is a key ingredient in Japanese cuisine, especially the popular sushi. To avoid health problems, Japanese chefs are highly skilled. Americanized forms of Japanese food will eventually be developed. The California roll, for example, will substitute raw fish with avocado, while the Philadelphia roll will use cream cheese instead. Japanese steakhouse and noodle variations will also be developed to suit the tastes of more diverse American diners. Some Japanese restaurants in the United States will include a few Chinese and Korean dishes in their menus. Japanese rice wine, sake, which is served warm, will be found in most restaurants, and teriyaki sauce will be commonly used in mainstream American cooking. Many food services and supermarkets will also carry packed sushi. A standard Japanese meal usually comprises a bowl of white rice or noodles, soup, pickles, and dishes made of fish, meat, vegetables, or tofu.

FOOD. With a significantly large South Asian population in the United States, Indian food also gains popularity, especially in the San Francisco Bay area, Los Angeles, Houston, Chicago, New York City, and Edison, New Jersey. Spices and herbs are heavily used in Indian cuisine, although there are many regional and cultural variations. Many Indian dishes are vegetarian, but chicken, lamb, fish, and meat dishes are also common. As a tradition, beef is not consumed by devoted Hindus, while pork is not eaten by Muslims. The most important grain staple ingredients are rice, wheat flour, and pulses. Chili pepper, black mustard seed, cumin, turmeric, fenugreek, asafetida, ginger, and garlic are the most frequently used spices, and most Indian curries are fried in vegetable oil. North Indian cooking uses dairy products heavily and bakes breads and meats in *tandoors*—large and cylindrical coal-fired ovens. Tandoor chicken, goat, and lamb meats are quite popular. East Indian cuisine has many variations of desserts, especially *rasagolla, chumchum, sandesh,* and *rasabli.* In the south, coconut and coconut oil, as well as curry leaves, are commonly used in cooking. Many Indian restaurants in the United States combine recipes from different regions and create standard and less-spiced dishes to suit the tastes of general American diners.

The main Indian beverage is tea, into which milk and spices such as cardamom, cloves, cinnamon, and ginger are added.

FOOD. Although Filipinos are the largest Asian population group in the United States, Filipino cuisine is not as noted as other Asian food because relatively few Filipinos are in the restaurant business. Spanish colonialism has had a long-lasting impact on Filipino cuisine, and the influences of Indian and Chinese cooking are apparent in Filipino food. Filipinos use fruits in cooking and consume large amounts of coconuts, tomatoes, mangos, pineapples, and bananas. Chicken, pork, beef, and fish are often pan-fried, deep-fried, or stewed. Filipino stewed dishes often combine a number of main ingredients and sweet, sour, and spicy flavors. There are many variations of rice-, fruit-, or dairy-based Filipino desserts and snacks, as well as alcoholic and nonalcoholic drinks.

LANG. The Thai and Lao languages are very similar, and so are the two cultures—allowing frequent interactions among people of these two ethnic groups. It is very common for refugees from Laos to work for Thai American entrepreneurs.

LANG. A significant number of newcomers from Southeast Asia are ethnic Chinese who can speak Cantonese. These immigrants often work in Chinese-run restaurants and garment shops; many later become entrepreneurs in these businesses as well.

LAWS. The 1980 Refugee Act is signed into law by President Jimmy Carter. The law adopts the

United Nations' definition of a refugee as anyone who, due to fear of being persecuted for reasons of race, religion, nationality, or membership of a particular social group or political opinion, seeks refuge outside of his or her own homeland. The law sets an annual quota for refugees at 50,000 and requires Congress to review refugee policies. The law also initiates the Office of Refugee Resettlement, to be established under the Department of Health and Human Services.

MIGR. The 1965 Immigration Act has had little impact on Japanese immigration. Between the 1960s and 1980s the Japanese economy has experienced the highest growth rates in the world. Japan's mature industrial economy is built upon advanced scientific research and a well-educated work force, high savings and investment rates, and well-balanced industrial development and foreign trade. Although the country has few natural resources, it has been able to obtain raw materials through foreign exchange. This economy has been able to absorb its own labor force, making emigration to the United States a less attractive alternative.

POLI. George R. Ariyoshi is elected as the third governor of Hawaii. He is the first Japanese American to win a governorship in the United States and will hold the governorship from 1974 to 1986.

POPU. The U.S. Census Bureau announces that the Asian/Pacific population in the United States reaches 3.5 million, making up 1.5 percent of the U.S. population. The Chinese are the largest Asian ethnic group, with a population of 806,040. The Filipinos rank next, with a population of 774,652. There are 700,974 Japanese, 361,531 Asian Indians, 354,593 Koreans, 261,729 Vietnamese, and 16,044 Cambodians. In addition, the census counts about 260,000 Native Hawaiians and Pacific Islanders.

POPU. Asian Indians are counted in the census as Asians for the first time; so are Guamanians and Samoans.

1981

ARCH. Twenty-one-year-old Chinese American architect and sculptor Maya Ying Lin's design

for the Vietnam Veterans Memorial in Washington, D.C., emerges as the winner from a national contest of 1,420 entries. The design, which features a simple V-shape formed by two black granite walls, is inscribed with the names of about 58,000 Americans killed or missing in action during the Vietnam War. The memorial will be completed and dedicated on November 11, 1982. Born in 1959 in Athens, Ohio, where her immigrant parents teach at Ohio State University, Lin is an undergraduate senior at Yale University when she submits the contest entry. After graduation she will receive a master's degree in architecture from Yale in 1985, and an honorary doctorate degree a year later. In New York City, Lin will establish her own design studio for architecture and sculpture in 1987. Her other important designs will include the 1988 Civil Rights Memorial in Montgomery, Alabama. Inspired by a quote from a Martin Luther King speech, "We will not be satisfied until justice rolls down like waters and righteousness like a mighty stream," Lin will create a memorial with polished black granite walls and a conical table; a time line of major civil rights events will be covered with a thin layer of water that visitors can touch. She will also design *TOPO,* an environmental landscape sculpture in the Charlotte Coliseum in North Carolina; the *Women's Table* at Yale University; and the Museum of African Art; as well as a huge clock at Pennsylvanian Station in New York City. Her sculptures and other art pieces will be displayed throughout the United States.

ARTS. Chinese American David Henry Hwang's first play, *FOB,* which deals with established Asian Americans and immigrant newcomers, premiers at Joseph Papp's Public Theater. The play wins Hwang an Obie Award. Born in Los Angeles, California, Hwang received his education at Stanford University and the Yale School of Drama. A prolific writer, he will produce many highly acclaimed plays. *The Dance and the Railroad* will be a finalist for the Pulitzer Prize for drama. In 1988, his *M. Butterfly* will premiere on Broadway, bringing Hwang a Tony Award for best play, as well as the Drama Desk Award, the John Gassner Award, and the Outer Critics Circle Award for best play. Hwang's other plays and adapted works will include *Family Devotions,*

Maya Ying Lin, on the site of the proposed Vietnam memorial, 1981. [AP Photo/Scott Applewhite]

Sound and Beauty, The House of Sleeping Beauties, The Sound of a Voice, As the Crow Flies, Face Value, Bang Kok, Bondage, Rich Relations, Trying to Find Chinatown, Golden Child, Peer Gynt, Tibet Through the Red Box, and *Jade Flowerpots and Bound Feet.* His *Golden Child* will win the 1997 Obie Award. Hwang will also create several musicals, adapt C. Y. Lee's *Flower Drum Song* into a musical, and write scripts for dance pieces. In 1999, he will star in a short film by Greg Pak, *Asian Pride Porn.*

CRIM. Hate crime against Southeast Asian immigrants begins to surface as more and more refugees enter local communities. In Texas, the Ku Klux Klan burns boats of Vietnamese immigrants, blaming the latter for competing against local fishermen.

MIGR. Although Taiwan is no longer received as a nation-state by the United States, the two maintain a friendly relationship with each other. To allow immigrants from the island, the United States grants Taiwan a separate quota from that of mainland China. The Chinese immigrant population will grow at a rapid pace because China, Taiwan, and Hong Kong each are given a separate quota.

MIGR. An increasing number of "parachute children" from Taiwan and Hong Kong begin to appear in the United States, especially in southern California. These children are parachuted by their parents to the United States to live by themselves or board in the houses of relatives or strangers. Their parents, meanwhile, stay in their native homeland to work and make money. Most of these children are between 8 and 17. They come with student visas to attend public or private schools. The parents believe their children will have better educational opportunities in the United States; they also hope to spare them military service in Taiwan, which male students have to go abroad before high school to avoid. By the mid-1990s, families in mainland China will also begin to parachute their children to the United States. Some of the parachute children are from wealthy families. Although financially secure, they lack parental supervision and protection. Quite a number of wealthy parachute children from Hong Kong and Taiwan become targets of kidnap or robberies.

POLI. Hearings held across the United States by the Commission on Wartime Relocation and Internment of Civilians, commencing in Washington, D.C., begin in July. The committee will hear from over 750 witnesses on issues relating to the legitimacy of detaining Japanese Americans during World War II.

PUBL. Ruthanne Lum McCunn, of Chinese and Scottish descent, publishes *Thousand Pieces of Gold,* a novel based on the real life story of a Chinese immigrant woman, Polly Bemis (Lalu Nathoy, 1853–1933). The book will be adapted into a Hollywood film. A prolific writer whose fiction works are filled with historically realistic details, McCunn will receive many awards and much recognition. She is the author of *An Illustrated History of the Chinese in America, Chinese American Portraits, The Chinese Proverbs* (with You Shan), *Sole Survivor: A Story of Record Endurance at Sea, The Moon Pearl, Wooden Fish Songs,* and *God of Luck.* Her writing will be translated into 11 languages and published in more than 20 countries.

SOCI. The Asian American Journalists Association is founded by Tritia Toyota, television journalist, and Bill Sing, a reporter with the *Los Angeles Times.*

1981–1990

MIGR. About 64,400 Thai immigrate to the United States.

1982

ARTS. Isamu Noguchi (1904–1988), a Japanese American sculptor and architect, receives the Edward MacDowell Medal for outstanding lifetime contribution to the arts. The son of a Japanese father and American mother, the Los Angeles-born Noguchi spent much of his childhood in Japan. Returning to the United States as a teenager, he apprenticed with Gutzon Borglum, the creator of Mount Rushmore National Memorial in South Dakota, although the well-known Borglum told him that he had no talent in sculpture. While studying medicine at Columbia University, however, Noguchi continued to take art classes at the Leonardo d' Vinci Art School and eventually decided to become an artist. After establishing himself as a stone sculpture artist in Paris and New York, he expanded his artistic boundaries by studying brush painting, pottery, and sculpture garden design in China and Japan. His work includes a large array of stone, metal, and wood sculptures as well as paintings, gardens, and playgrounds; many of them are displayed in museums as well as public spaces around the world. More than 200 pieces of Noguchi's artwork will be preserved in the Isamu Noguchi Garden Museum in Long Island, New York, which will be founded by the artist himself in 1985.

CRIM. Vincent Chin, a 27-year-old Chinese immigrant in Detroit, is killed in June by two white auto workers after a fight with the pair in a nightclub. The incident takes place at a time when the American automobile industry is in recession, partly due to competition from Japanese car makers. One of the two men is laid off, and they apparently mistake Chin as being Japanese. They will be each sentenced to three years' probation and a fine of $3,000.

Asian Americans nationwide are outraged by Chin's death and the light sentences the murderers received. The American Citizens for Justice, a community organization formed to challenge the sentences by the Wayne County circuit court, demands that the Michigan court of appeals order a new trial. The organization also requests an investigation by the federal government. The two who committed the crime will be tried in a U.S. district court again in 1984. Although one of them will be convicted for violating Chin's civil rights and be sentenced to 25 years in jail, he will win his appeal on technical grounds. A retrial will be held in Cincinnati, where the man will be acquitted. Neither man will spend time in jail for the crime.

ECON. The first Han Ah Reum, a Korean food market, opens for business in Queens, New York. In more than a decade, Han Ah Reum stores, also known as H Mart or Super H Mart, will develop into a giant ethnic supermarket chain, with stores in California, Colorado, New York, New Jersey, Pennsylvania, Maryland, Virginia, Georgia, Illinois, Washington, Oregon, Texas, Washington, D.C., and Canada. This supermarket chain is owned by the family of former South Korean President Chun Doo Hwan.

LAWS. The Amerasian Immigration Act is enacted, making it possible for children of American military personnel and Asian women to come to the United States. Many of these children are of mixed racial heritage, and they arrive from Southeast Asia, Korea, Thailand, and the Philippines without the accompaniment of their mothers and half-siblings. About 4,500 Amerasians will leave Vietnam under this law between 1982 and 1987.

1983

EDUC. Chinese American architect I. M. Pei establishes a scholarship fund for Chinese students to study architecture in the United States, using his $100,000 cash award for the Laureate of the Prizker Architecture Prize. The scholarship recipients are expected to practice architecture in China after the completion of their studies in the

United States, although some of them will later settle in the United States.

FOOD. Chinese American Andrew J. C. Cheng opens the first Panda Express fast food restaurant in Glendale, California. Born in Jiangsu, China, Cheng relocated with his family to Taiwan when he was five. He came to the United States in 1966 as a student and received a master's degree in applied mathematics from the University of Missouri. In 1973, Cheng and his father opened a restaurant in South Pasadena, but it is the Chinese fast food chain that will gain Cheng the fame and economic success. By 2008, Panda Express will become the largest Asian food corporation in America, with more than 900 restaurants in 38 states. Cheng will receive an honorary doctoral degree from California State Polytechnic University at Pomona, in recognition of his business success, his philanthropic activities, and his contribution to the university's culinary program.

LAWS. Fred Korematsu, who refused to report to the internment camp during World War II, has his case reversed by the federal district court of San Francisco.

POLI. The Commission on Wartime Relocation and Internment of Civilians investigates the harm done against Japanese Americans during the war and concludes in its report, *Personal Justice Denied,* that the exclusion of Japanese Americans from American society, the expulsion of Japanese Americans from their homes, and the internment of Japanese Americans in camps were not justified by military necessity, and that the government's decision was based on racial prejudice, war hysteria, and a failure of political leadership. The report recommends that the government recognize the grave injustice done to Japanese Americans and offer an official apology. It also recommends a one-time compensation of $20,000 to each of the approximately 60,000 surviving Japanese Americans who were interned under Executive Order 9066.

PUBL. Cathy-Lynn Song, daughter of Chinese and Korean immigrant parents, publishes a collection of poetry, *Picture Bride.* This book brings the author the Yale Series of Younger Poets Award. Song's second poetry book, *Frameless*

Windows, Squares of Light, will be published in 1991. She will receive the Shelley Memorial Award from the Poetry Society of America and the Hawaii Award for Literature.

SCIE. South Asian American astrophysicist Subrahmanyan Chandrasekhar (1910–1995) is awarded the Nobel Prize in physics along with William A. Fowler. Chandrasekhar's prizewinning theory, which lays the groundwork for the discovery of black holes, concerns the structure and evolution of white dwarf stars. Born in Lahore, India in 1910, Chandrasekhar completed college before attending the University of Cambridge in England. He received his Ph.D. in physics in 1933. He came to the United States in 1937 to join the faculty at the University of Chicago, where he became the Morton D. Hull Distinguished Service Professor of Theoretical Astrophysics in 1952. He will retire from the university in 1985 and pass away in 1995 at the age of 84.

1984

CRIM. Henry Liu, a prominent Chinese American journalist and the author of a biography of Taiwan's President Chiang Ching-kuo, is murdered outside of his home in Daly City, California. The case receives international attention, especially when it becomes evident that the crime is committed by three gang leaders from Taiwan following the order of the military intelligence bureau of the ministry of defense. It is alleged that Chiang

Professor Subrahmanyan Chandrasekhar of the University of Chicago, 1939. [AP Photo]

Hsiao-wu, the son of President Chiang, is involved.

CRIM. Vietnamese American Thong Hy Huynh is stabbed to death on the Davis High School campus in Davis, California, in a fight with two white students. This tragic incident is believed to be racially motivated. The campus community will plant a tree in honor of Thong Hy Huynh. It will also initiate a Friendship Day designed to break down racial, ethnic, and class barriers among the students.

ECON. Roger H. Chen, a Chinese immigrant from Taiwan, opens the first 99 Ranch Market store in Westminster, California. In two decades, this giant supermarket chain's stores will have become the centerpiece in suburban Chinese malls in California, Arizona, Nevada, and Washington. These stores stand in sharp contrast to the crowded grocery stores in old Chinatowns. Equipped with huge parking lots, long rows of tall shelves, specialized lighting systems, and large refrigeration and freezer units, the spacious, high-ceilinged 99 Ranch Markets set the standard for contemporary Chinese supermarkets.

FOOD. C. C. Yin becomes the first Chinese American to own a McDonald's franchise. A civil engineer from Taiwan, Yin confronts many difficulties when he tries to become a member of the giant American fast food family. The reviewing board has doubts about Yin's ability, and he has to start in a less desirable location in Oakland, California. But Yin and his wife will win the confidence of local customers. They will add 23 franchise stores in the next 24 years in 9 cities of northern California. Yin will become well known for his service to the community and his charity work.

POLI. S. B. Woo, a Chinese American physicist, is elected as the lieutenant governor of Delaware. Born in Shanghai in 1937, Woo came to the United States from Hong Kong at age 18. A graduate of Georgetown College in Kentucky, Woo received a Ph.D. in physics from Washington University in St. Louis. He became a part of the faculty in physics and astronomy at the University of Delaware in 1966. After serving as the lieutenant governor of his state from 1985 to 1989, Woo will become involved in Asian American community activism, serving as the first president of the 80-20 Initiative.

SOCI. The Vietnamese-American Civic Association, Inc. is founded in Boston. This mutual assistance association provides a wide range of services, including English to Speakers of Other Languages classes, citizenship classes, health education, counseling, youth programs, elderly services, and employment services to refugees. Similar organizations will also be founded in other regions.

SPOR. Tommy Kono, a Japanese American weight lifter, is voted the greatest weight lifter of all time by the International Weightlifting

A Chinese American shopping center in Los Angeles. [Photo by H. Lin]

Federation. Born in Sacramento, California, Kono and his family were interned in Tule Lake, California during World War II. He started weight lifting while interned to improve his own strength. After the war he entered a few local competitions. In the Junior Nationals in 1952, he set three U.S. records and one world record. At the 1952 Olympics in Helsinki, Finland, Kono brought home a gold medal and set a new world record. He set nine U.S. and four world records in the next two years. In the 1956 Olympics, he won another gold medal and set a new world record. Kono also won eight world championship titles and was crowned as Mr. Universe.

SPOR. Samoan American diver Greg Louganis, a student of former Olympic gold medalist Sammy Lee (see entry in 1948), wins a gold medal in platform diving in the Summer Olympics in Los Angeles, receiving a historically high score of above 700 (710.91). He will win the event again in the 1988 Olympics in Seoul, Korea and take a second gold medal in springboard diving. Louganis's gold medal performance in Seoul in the springboard event will capture the attention of the world as he hits his head on the diving board during the competition in front of television cameras. After receiving medical treatment for a three-inch gash, he will return to the platform to finish the competition, receiving an Olympic Spirit Award. This Olympic performance will become a subject of controversy years later, when it is revealed that before the games he tested positive for HIV, the virus that causes AIDS.

1985

EDUC. Chinese language schools begin to develop at a fast pace, responding to the demand of the fast-growing Chinese American population. After 1965, most Chinese language schools were operated by immigrants from Taiwan, but change has taken place gradually as the Chinese population has become more diverse. The pinyin system, which is used in mainland China to romanize Chinese characters, will replace the traditional system that is commonly used in Taiwan. In addition to language training, some Chinese schools also teach art, dancing, and martial art classes, as well as create programs to

Platform-diving gold medal winner Greg Louganis stands on the victory podium during the medal awards ceremony at the Summer Olympic Games in Seoul, South Korea, 1988. He is flanked by silver medal winner Xiong Ni of China, left, and bronze medal winner Jesus Mena of Mexico. [AP Photo/Ed Reinke]

enhance students' academic performances in regular schools. These language schools also provide opportunities for parents to socialize and share information and expertise on parenting. After 2000, an increasing number of non-Chinese students will enroll in some of the Chinese language schools in the United States.

LAWS. A federal district court in Oregon overturns Minoru Yasui's conviction for violating a curfew order during World War II.

MED. Asian-language television begins to play an important role in the immigrant community. There are three Chinese-language television networks: Asian American Television, Chinese Television Network, and North American Television. All three television stations have created both Mandarin and Cantonese language programs. Through satellite, their news reports, special classes and services, and various cultural and entertainment programs can reach Chinese living in different parts of the United States. Other Asian American communities will also create their own television networks. These television networks keep new immigrants well informed of events on both sides of the Pacific. They also help younger generations of Asian Americans to learn Asian languages and become familiar with their traditional cultures.

MED. Haing S. Ngor wins an Oscar for best supporting actor at the 57th annual Academy Awards for his role in *The Killing Fields*. Ngor, the son of a Khmer mother and an ethnic Chinese father, is the first Asian American actor to receive an Oscar award.

POLI. Filipina American Irene Natividad becomes the first Asian American elected to head the National Women's Political Caucus. Founded in 1971, the caucus is a political feminist organization advocating for women in electorate politics and other appointed political posts.

SCIE. Ellison Onizuka, the first Asian American astronaut, is selected to orbit in space aboard the *Discovery* shuttle. Born in Hawaii, Onizuka dreamed of becoming an astronaut at a young age. A member of the U.S. Air Force, he worked as an aerospace flight test engineer and later became a colonel and worked as a flight instructor. He began astronaut training in 1978. After the *Discovery* mission, Onizuka will join the crew of the *Challenger* in 1986 for his second opportunity to travel in space. He will perish when the space shuttle explodes during the takeoff of its 10th mission to space.

SCIE. Chinese American physicist Taylor Gun-Jin Wang becomes the second Asian American and first Chinese American to travel in space. Born in Shanghai, China, Wang lived in Taiwan and Hong Kong before coming to the United States. At the University of California, Los Angeles, he received a doctoral degree in 1971. He is selected as a payload specialist on the *Challenger* space shuttle crew while working at the California Institute of Technology as a senior scientist; in this role he travels 2.9 million miles in 110 earth orbits in one of the space shuttle's early missions. Wang will later become a physics professor at Vanderbilt University.

1986

ECON. In New York, the largest center of the garment industry, 27,000 workers are employed by 600 Chinese-owned garment factories. An additional 2,000 Chinese-operated garment factories are found outside New York, in the Los Angeles and San Francisco Bay areas, as well as in Chicago, Seattle, and Honolulu.

LAWS. A federal district court in Seattle overturns Gordon Hirabayashi's 1942 conviction for violating wartime internment orders.

LAWS. The Immigration Reform and Control Act is endorsed by President Ronald Reagan. This legislation allows aliens who were in the United States before January 1, 1982 to apply for permanent status and eventually become U.S. citizens.

MED. South Asian American Ismail Merchant, in collaboration with his long-term life partner, director James Ivory, as well as screenwriter Ruth Prawer Jhabvala, produces an adaptation of E. M. Forster's novel *A Room with a View* that wins an Academy Award. Born Ismail Noormohamed Abdul Rehman in Mumbai, India in 1936, Merchant became interested in filmmaking while in college. He left India for graduate school in the United States at age 22, earning an M.B.A. from New York University. His 1961 short film, *The Creation of Woman*, which premiered at the Cannes Film Festival, was nominated for an Academy Award. Merchant Ivory Productions will produce about 40 films and win 6 Academy Awards in a period of more than 40 years. In addition to producing and directing films, Merchant will go on to write several cookbooks, filmmaking books, and an autobiography, *My Passage From India: A Filmmaker's Journey from Bombay to Hollywood and Beyond*. Merchant will pass away in 2005 at age 68.

MED. Chinese American Joan Chen lands a leading role in a Hollywood feature film, *Tai-Pan*. An immigrant from Shanghai, China, Chen established a successful career in acting at age 14. She won the Hundred Flowers Award for best actress in 1979 for her role in the highly acclaimed *Little Flower* and starred in several other Chinese films. In the United States in the early 1980s, Chen searched for opportunities in Hollywood while studying at California State University in Northridge, but she would not get good movie offers until many years later. Her performance in the Oscar award-winning film *The Last Emperor* (1987) will be a turning point.

After that, Chen will maintain an acting career in both the United States and China, appearing in the television series *Twin Peaks* (1990–1991) and in the films *Temptation of a Monk* (1993), *Heaven and Earth* (1993), *Red Rose, White Rose* (1994), *On Deadly Ground* (1994), *Judge Dredd* (1995), *Saving Face* (2004), *Lust, Caution* (2007), and several others. Chen will also direct films, including *Xiu Xiu: The Sent Down Girl* (1998) and *Autumn in New York* (2000).

MED. Tamlyn Tomita, an actress of Japanese and Filipino heritage who was born in Okinawa, Japan in 1966, debuts in *The Karate Kid, Part II*. Before her acting debut, Tomita won the beauty queen title at the Nisei Week Pageant in Los Angeles in 1984. She will star and play roles in 19 films by 2008, including the *Joy Luck Club* and *Picture Bride*. She will also appear in more than 10 television shows.

MUSI. Fourteen-year-old Japanese American violinist Midori receives a long standing ovation for her performance of Leonard Bernstein's "Serenade" at the Tanglewood Music Festival in Massachusetts. During this performance her E-string breaks twice, but she continues the program with the concertmaster's violin at first and then the instrument of the assistant concertmaster. Born in Japan, Midori debuted with the New York Philharmonic at age 10. Starting as a child prodigy, she will be recognized as a world class artist and perform with the world's most distinguished symphonic ensembles.

OBIT. The space shuttle *Challenger* explodes at the launching of its last mission. All seven crew members on board perish, including Ellison Onizuka, the first Asian American astronaut to travel in space.

PUBL. Chinese American Sucheng Chan publishes the award-winning *This Bittersweet Soil: The Chinese in California Agriculture, 1860–1910*. Born in Shanghai, China, Chan spent her childhood and early teen years in China and Malaysia and came to the United States to attend high school. A graduate of Swarthmore College, she received her master's and Ph.D. degrees from the University of California (UC) at Berkeley in political science. She was a professor in Berkeley's Ethnic Studies Department and the provost at UC Santa Cruz's Oaks College before joining the faculty at UC Santa Barbara, where she will build the Asian American Studies Program and later the Asian American Studies Department. A pioneer in the field of Asian American studies, she is the author or editor of more than a dozen books and recipient of numerous awards for her scholarly endeavors. Her award-winning books include *This Bittersweet Soil: The Chinese in California Agriculture, 1860–1910; Asian Americans: An Interpretive History; Quiet Odyssey: A Pioneer Korean Woman in America; Claiming America: Constructing Chinese American Identities During the Exclusion Era;* and *Survivors: Cambodian Refugees in the United States*. Chan will receive a Lifetime Achievement Award from the Association of Asian American Studies in 1997.

SCIE. Chinese American Yuan T. Lee of the University of California at Berkeley wins a Nobel Prize in chemistry, along with Dudley R. Herschbach and Canadian scientist John C. Polanyi, for their joint work in crossed beam molecular research. The research makes it possible to analyze large and complex chemical molecules. Born in Hsin-chu, Taiwan in 1936, Lee became a student in chemistry at the National Taiwan University in 1959. He later earned a master's degree there and worked as a research assistant at Tsinghua University. In 1962, Lee came to the United States to study at the University of California at Berkeley, earning a Ph.D. in three years. He is a professor at Berkeley when the Nobel Prize is awarded. Lee will later renounce his U.S. citizenship and return to Taiwan to head the Academia Sinica. There, Lee will become involved in politics and issues of educational reform.

SOCI. The National Congress of Vietnamese in America (NCVA) is founded. Initiated by four major Vietnamese associations, the NCVA will grow to become a federation of about 200 Vietnamese American associations. An advocate for refugee rights, the NCVA is strongly against forced repatriation. It encourages participation of its members in U.S. political processes and creates forums for Vietnamese Americans to discuss issues of education, discrimination, business development, and the situation in Vietnam.

In 2002, the organization will be renamed the National Congress of Vietnamese Americans.

1987

ASIA. The United States recognizes Mongolia. It will establish the first U.S. embassy there a year later.

ASIA. U.S. military bases in the Philippines are the second-largest employer after the Philippine government, providing jobs to more than 68,000 Filipinos. This special relationship between the United States and the Philippines will continue to pave the way for Filipino immigration. Many enlisted Filipinos are sent to bases in the United States and eventually decide to stay. Jobs in shipyards in Long Beach, California; Norfolk, Virginia; Bangor, Maine; Bremerton, Washington; and Honolulu, Hawaii are attractive to the discharged military personnel, making settlement in the United States relatively easy.

COMM. A special exhibit of Japanese American history opens at the Smithsonian Institution's National Museum of American History in Washington, D.C.

CRIM. An incident of racially-motivated crime takes place in Jersey City, New Jersey. A group of young men attacks and kills South Asian American Navroze Mody. The youths are believed to be associated with an anti-South Asian gang.

EDUC. Hoang Nhu Tran, a Vietnamese refugee, graduates first in a class of 960 students from the U.S. Air Force Academy. Tran is selected as a Rhodes Scholar and receives the College Achievement Award from *Time* magazine.

LAWS. The Amerasian Homecoming Act is enacted in December. The new legislation allows Amerasians born in Asia between January 1, 1962 and January 1, 1976, as well as their family members, including mothers, stepfathers, and siblings or half-siblings, to enter the United States.

OBIT. Japanese American Judge John F. Aiso (1909–1987) passes away in Los Angeles. A graduate of Harvard Law School in 1934, Aiso was the highest-ranked Japanese American in World War II (as a lieutenant colonel judge). In 1952, he was appointed by California Governor Earl Warren as a judge of the Los Angeles municipal court. From there he advanced to the Los Angeles superior court and become an associate justice of the California court of appeal for the second appellate district. In Little Tokyo in Los Angeles, a block of San Pedro Street between Temple Boulevard and 1st Street is named after John F. Aiso to honor his military and legal services.

POLI. Patricia Saiki is elected to Congress representing Hawaii. A former school teacher from Hilo in Hawaii, Saiki will serve until 1991, when President George H. W. Bush will appoint her administrator of the Small Business Administration.

POLI. Asian Indian American Joy Cherian is appointed by President Ronald Reagan to the U.S. Equal Employment Opportunity Commission.

PUBL. Korean American Kim Ronyoung (1926–1987) publishes *Clay Walls: A Novel*. Born in Los Angeles, California as Gloria Hahn to immigrant parents, Ronyoung is a graduate of California State University at San Francisco. Her novel, completed shortly before her death, tells the story of Korean immigrant families in the United States in the 1920s and 1930s.

1988

ASIA. The government of Burma uses military and police force to address student demonstrations, killing more than 1,000 demonstrators. A new government is organized through a military coup, which restores order by martial law, killing an additional 3,000 individuals and putting opposition leader Aung San Suu Kyi under house arrest. U.S.-Burmese relations will deteriorate in the decades to follow. The United States will impose sanctions against Burma. In 2003, Congress will pass a law to ban all imports from and export of American financial services to Burma. Representation of the United States in Burma will be downgraded from ambassador to chargé d'affaires.

LAWS. The Civil Liberties Act is signed into law by President Ronald Reagan. The act requests that the government issue an official apology to Japanese Americans interned in World War II and compensate each living internee $20,000. The redress movement started in the mid-1970s, initiated by the Japanese American Citizens League. Asian American elected officials and political activists worked closely to make the movement a great success. Responding to the request, Congress formed the Commission on Wartime Relocation and Internment of Civilians, which reviewed documents and held hearings. The commission's report is the basis for this new law. Not until November 1989 will President George H. W. Bush sign into law an entitlement program to pay the surviving internees. Eventually each one of some 80,000 survivors will receive a $20,000 redress payment accompanied by a letter of apology signed by the president.

MUSI. Indonesian Chinese American Jahja Ling receives the Seaver/National Endowment for the Arts Conductor Award. The son of Chinese parents, Ling was born in Jakarta, Indonesia. After his graduation from the Jakarta Music School, Ling studied at the Juilliard School of Music in New York City on a Rockefeller grant. He will later become the resident conductor of the Cleveland Orchestra, as well as music director of the Florida Orchestra.

SPOR. South Korea hosts the 26th Summer Olympic Games in its capital, Seoul.

1989

ARTS. Guamanian American Manny Crisostomo wins a Pulitzer Prize in feature photography for his year-long documentary of an inner-city high school in the *Detroit Free Press.* Trained in photojournalism at the University of Missouri, Crisostomo will later work at the *Sacramento Bee,* where he will launch several long-term special projects. His photo documentary on Hmong refugees will win the 2005 Robert F. Kennedy Journalism Award for international photography. In 2006, his documentary on rising childhood obesity, "The Weight," will receive the McClatchy President's Award. Crisostomo will

publish several books: *Legacy of Guam: I Kustumbren Chamoru,* a story of his native Guam; *Mainstreet: Small Town Michigan; Moving Pictures: A Look at Detroit From High Atop the People Mover;* and *Guam From the Heavens.*

CRIM. A 24-year-old Chinese American, Ming Hai Loo (Jim Loo), is killed in late July outside a swimming pool in Raleigh, North Carolina by two white brothers, in a situation similar to the murder of Vincent Chin. The brothers lost a third brother during the Vietnam War, and they have apparently mistaken Loo for being Vietnamese. Chinese Americans are quick to form the Jim Loo American Justice Coalition to represent Loo's family. The older brother will be found guilty in March 1990 and receive 37 years in prison. The younger brother will be sentenced to six months in prison.

CRIM. A 26-year-old drifter, Patrick Purdy, who is mentally retarded, guns down a yard full of children at the Cleveland Elementary School in Stockton, California before killing himself. Five children, age six to nine, are dead; all of them are refugee children from Southeast Asia.

MED. Chinese American filmmaker John Woo gains international recognition with the release of *The Killer,* the most successful Hong Kong film in the United States. Born in China in 1946, Woo grew up in the slums of Hong Kong after his family moved to the then-British colony. He entered the film industry in Hong Kong in 1969 as a script supervisor and eventually became a director and producer of action and comedy films. Teamed with his leading actor, Chow Yun-Fat, Woo and his violent gangster thrillers enjoyed great box office success. *The Killer* brings Woo attention from Hollywood. He will immigrate to the United States in 1993 and become the first Asian American director to enter the mainstream film industry. He will win the Saturn Award for best director for *Face/Off* in 1998. Woo's other Hollywood films will include *Mission: Impossible II, Windtalkers,* and *Paycheck.*

MED. Christine Choy and Renee Tajima-Peña's *Who Killed Vincent Chin* is nominated for an Academy Award for best documentary film.

Born in Shanghai, China to a Korean father and a Chinese mother, Choy spent her childhood in China and Korea before winning a scholarship to study in the United States at age 14. A graduate of Princeton University, she discovered film while studying at Washington University in St. Louis. Choy will later found the Third World Newsreel in New York. In 1994, she will be appointed chair of the graduate film program at New York University. Choy is the producer of many films, including *Mississippi Triangle* (1984), *Homes Apart: The Two Koreas* (1991), *Out in Silence* (1994), and *In the Name of the Emperor* (1994).

Renee Tajima-Peña was born in Chicago. In addition to *Who Killed Vincent Chin,* she will produce and direct a number of highly acclaimed documentaries, including *My America . . . or Honk If You Love Buddha, Jennifer's In Jail,* and *The Best Hotel on Skid Row.* In 2000 she will begin teaching at the University of California, Santa Cruz.

MIGR. About 90,000 Amerasians and their family members from Vietnam have been admitted since 1982.

MIGR. An agreement between the United States and the Vietnamese government known as Humanitarian Operation allows individuals who have spent three or more years in re-education camps to come to the United States. More than 166,000 individuals and their family members will enter the United States in the 1990s under the agreement.

MUSI. Eight-year-old Korean American violinist Sarah Chang solos with the New York Philharmonic, conducted by Zubin Mehta. Born in Philadelphia, Pennsylvania, the daughter of Korean immigrant musicians, Chang was admitted to the Juilliard School of Music in New York at age six. Her first record will be released by EMI Classics in 1992, when she is nine years old, and become a classical best-seller. Chang will collaborate with many prestigious orchestras in the United States and Europe, including the New York Philharmonic, the Philadelphia Orchestra, the Chicago Symphony, the Boston Symphony, the Cleveland Orchestra, the Berlin Philharmonic, the Vienna Philharmonic, the principal London orchestras, and the Royal Concertgebouw Orchestra of Amsterdam. She will

work with some of the world's most prominent conductors and perform on many prestigious stages throughout the world.

MUSI. Lea Salonga, a native of the Philippines, stars in London in the musical *Miss Saigon* as Kim after a competitive audition that spanned several continents. Born in 1971, Salonga was a child star in her homeland, beginning her professional performance on stage at age seven. She also acted in movies, hosted musical television shows, and recorded albums. She was nominated for the Filipino Academy of Movie Arts and Sciences (FAMAS, the Philippine equivalent of the Oscars) award for best child actress, winning three Aliw (literally, "entertainment") Awards for best child performer. The role in *Miss Saigon* allows the singer to emerge as an international superstar, winning the Laurence Olivier Award for the best performance by an actress in a musical as well as Tony, Drama Desk, Outer Critics Circle, and Theatre World awards. Salonga will

Sarah Chang poses at the Verbier Festival and Academy in the Alpine village of Verbier, Switzerland, 2004. [AP Photo/Keystone, Olivier Maire]

later perform as Éponine to wide acclaim in the musical *Les Misérables,* both in London and on Broadway. She will also sing as Princess Jasmine in the Disney movie *Aladdin* and as Fa Mulan in *Mulan.* The song "A Whole New World" she sings as Jasmine will win an Oscar. Salonga will be invited to sing "Triumph of the One" at the closing ceremony of the 2006 Asian Games in Doha, Qatar.

POLI. The Coalition of Asian Pacific Americans, a political action committee, is founded.

POLI. Cambodian American Sichan Siv is appointed deputy assistant to President George H. W. Bush. He will hold the post until 1992. Having arrived in the United States from Cambodia as a refugee in 1976, Siv is the highest-ranking Asian American on the White House staff.

POLI. Chinese American Elaine L. Chao is appointed deputy secretary of the Department of Transportation in President George H. W. Bush's administration. Born in Taiwan, Chao arrived in the United States at age eight. A graduate of Mount Holyoke College, she received her M.B.A. from the Harvard Business School. Prior to this post as deputy secretary, Chao established a strong public and government service record, including serving as director of the Peace Corps, as president and chief executive officer of United Way of America, as a White House Fellow, as chairman of the Federal Maritime Commission, and as the deputy maritime administrator in the U.S. Department of Transportation. In 2001, she will be appointed by President George W. Bush as the secretary of labor of the United States, making her the first Asian American woman appointed to a president's cabinet in U.S. history.

POLI. Julia Chang Bloch is appointed U.S. ambassador to Nepal by President George H. W. Bush. She is the first Asian American ambassador in U.S. history.

PUBL. Asian Indian American writer Bharati Mukherjee publishes her novel *Jasmine.* Born in Calcutta, India, Mukherjee spent part of her childhood in Europe. She attended college in India before coming to the United States,

Labor Secretary Elaine Chao, left, poses with her father, Dr. James Chao, as they arrive at the White House for a reception honoring the recipients of the Kennedy Center Honors awards for 2007. [AP Photo/ Manuel Balce Ceneta]

receiving her M.F.A. degree from the Writers' Workshop in 1963 and a Ph.D. in comparative literature in 1969 from the University of Iowa. In addition to co-authoring two works of fiction with her husband, Clark Blaise, Mukherjee will write several other books, including *The Holder of the World* (1993), *Leave It to Me* (1997), *Desirable Daughters* (2002), and *The Tree Bride* (2004).

PUBL. Vietnamese American Phung Le Ly Hayslip publishes her first book, *When Heaven and Earth Changed Places: A Vietnamese Woman's Journey from War to Peace,* an autobiographical account of the author's early life in war-torn Vietnam and her first return to her homeland in 1986. Born in Vietnam as Phung Thi Le Ly, Hayslip came to the United States in 1970 to join her American husband. She will later publish a second memoir, *Child of War, Woman of Peace,* in 1993. Hayslip is also known as the founder of the East Meets West Foundation, which she established to improve the health and welfare of Vietnamese refugees in the United States.

Oliver Stone's 1993 film *Heaven & Earth,* starring Joan Chen, will be based on Hayslip's life story.

PUBL. Historian Ronald Takaki's *Strangers from a Different Shore: A History of Asian Americans* receives a number of awards and recognitions, including the Gold Medal for Nonfiction from the Commonwealth Club of California and the Notable Book of 1989 honors from the *New York Times Book Review.* After receiving his Ph.D. from the University of California at Berkeley in 1967, Takaki became a professor in the university's Ethnic Studies Department. He is the author or editor of several books and volumes, including *A Different Mirror: A History of Multicultural America; Race at the End of History; A Pro-Slavery Crusade; Violence in the Black Imagination; Iron Cages: Race and Culture in 19th-Century America; Hiroshima: Why America*

Seventeen-year-old Michael Chang reacts after scoring a decisive point during the final match of the French Open tennis championship in 1989, where he becomes the youngest man to win a Grand Slam tournament. [AP Photo/Lionel Cironneau]

Dropped the Atomic Bomb; Debating Diversity: Clashing Perspectives on Race and Ethnicity in America; A Larger Memory: A History of Our Diversity with Voices. Takaki will be granted a Lifetime Achievement Award by the Asian Pacific Council in 2005.

PUBL. Amy Tan, a second-generation Chinese American writer, publishes *The Joy Luck Club.* The book is a blockbuster on the *New York Times* best-selling list for seven months. It is a finalist for the National Book Award and the National Book Critics Circle Award, and it will be adapted into a critically acclaimed film. Born in Oakland, California of immigrant parents, Tan became a business writer after earning a Ph.D. in linguistics from the University of California at Berkeley. She started to write full time in the late 1980s. Tan will publish several other novels, including *The Kitchen God's Wife* (1991), *The Moon Lady* and *The Chinese Siamese Cat* (1995), *The Hundred Secret Senses* (1995), and *The Bonesetter's Daughter* (2001).

SPOR. Chinese American Michael Chang wins the French Open tennis tournament, becoming the youngest male and the first American winner of the event since 1955. Chang will enter the International Tennis Hall of Fame in 2008, becoming the first Chinese American to receive such an honor.

1990

AGRI. Farming is important in the Hmong culture. The Hmong farmers have their own tradition in farming, and they integrate farming into family life. The main challenge for the Hmong is to continue their farming tradition in a new manner that can meet the standards and regulations of the United States. With assistance from the federal government and several nonprofit organizations, many Hmong are using western methods in commercial farming.

ARTS. Chinese American Vera Wang opens her Vera Wang Bridal House in New York City, featuring her trademark bridal gowns. A graduate from Sarah Lawrence College, Wang's childhood dream was to become a figure skater. Failing to make the U.S. Olympic figure skating team in 1968, Wang entered the fashion industry instead. She worked as a senior fashion editor for *Vogue* for 16 years before starting her own designing salon. Most well known for her wedding gown collection, Wang will also create her brand name fragrance, jewelry, shoe, and other collections. She will author *Vera Wang on Wedding,* which will be published in 2001. Wang will design dresses for celebrities and film/television characters, and she will guest-star in a few television shows.

CRIM. Xan Than Ly, a Laotian American restaurant employee in Yuba City, California, is attacked by two white men. The attackers vandalize Ly's car after seeing him giving rides to two white female co-workers.

ECON. The median family income of Asian Americans is higher than that of white Americans. However, a higher proportion of Southeast Asian, Korean, and Chinese families are at the poverty level than white Americans.

ECON. A large proportion of Indian and Filipino Americans are professionals. By contrast, a significant proportion of Southeast Asian immigrants are laborers, service workers, and farmers. Social mobility is achieved by most second- or third-generation Chinese Americans, but a high proportion of recent Chinese immigrants are service workers.

ECON. Asian Americans are well-represented in professional occupations and small businesses. The self-employment rate is especially high among Korean and Chinese immigrants. Korean immigrants are concentrated in the grocery business, dry cleaning, convenience stores, and food service. The Chinese are most dominant in the garment industry, and a significant number of entrepreneurs are in the Chinese restaurant business.

EDUC. Chinese American Chang-Lin Tien is appointed as the eighth chancellor of the University of California at Berkeley. Tien is the first Asian American to head a major university in the United States, and he will serve in the position until 1997. Born in China, Tien moved with his family to Taiwan in 1949 after the Communist takeover. He came to the United States for postgraduate study in 1956, earning a master's degree in 1957 from the University of Louisville

and a Ph.D. in mechanical engineering from Princeton University in 1959. He then joined the faculty of the Mechanical Engineering Department at the University of California at Berkeley. An expert in thermal science, Tien will author more than 300 research articles and write 1 book, and he will edit 16 volumes. He will receive the prestigious title of University Professor from Berkeley in 1999.

EDUC. An increasing number of Asian American children attend prestigious universities in the United States. Asian Americans constitute over 30 percent of the students at several University of California campuses and over 15 percent at many prestigious state and private universities. Some universities take measures to slow down the increase of Asian American students.

EDUC. Asian immigrants have higher levels of education than the general American population. Southeast Asian immigrants are less educated than other Asian immigrants. A high proportion of Filipino and Asian Indian immigrants that have come after 1970 are college graduates.

FOOD. Thai cuisine gains increasing popularity in America. In urban areas, especially cities of California, Thai restaurants are not difficult to find. The owners and service workers of these restaurants include Thai, Laotians, and Thai Chinese. Similar to South Asian cuisine, Thai dishes are heavily spiced. Curry, basil, and chili pepper are commonly used in cooking. Other ingredients of Thai American cuisine include coconut, peanut butter, and pineapples.

FOOD. The 1990s witness a few new features in Chinese cuisine in the United States. Regional variety increases significantly, as entrepreneurs from Taiwan, Hong Kong, and different regions of mainland China bring with them many new regional specialties. Eateries featuring noodles, dumplings, and steamed buns of northern China; Taiwanese treats; Cantonese dim sum; Chaozhou specialties; Shanghai and Yangzi River Delta cooking; and Hong Kong-style western dishes can be found in cities and towns throughout the country, catering to both Chinese and non-Chinese customers. Small take-out restaurants are popular in inner cities, catering to residents in mainly African American and Latino neighborhoods. The new immigrants from the Fujian Province in south China, many of whom arrive in the 1990s, are also well known in their buffet-style restaurants, which offer a combination of Chinese and western dishes. Soft drinks and western desserts are commonly served in these restaurants. Pearl tea, a nontraditional cold drink that adds tapioca into milk tea or other flavored beverages, gains popularity among children and teenagers.

FOOD. Rice, pork, beef, chicken, and seafood are main ingredients in Vietnamese cuisine; these can be grilled, sautéed, steamed, or stewed. In the United States, noodle soups and spring rolls are the most well-known Vietnamese dishes. Vietnamese noodle soup is made of rice noodles served in a rich and tasty broth. Beef, seafood, or vegetables are often used to make the broth. The most popular noodle soup is *pho,* which is a noodle soup with a rich and clear beef or chicken broth. Shredded meat, seafood, fresh vegetables, and herbs are common ingredients for spring rolls, which are wrapped in thin layers of rice paper. Fish sauce, soy sauce, and many herbs and spices are used to add flavor to the dishes. Unlike other Asian cooking, vegetables and herbs are often served fresh as side dishes in Vietnamese restaurants. A popular Vietnamese beverage is *cafe sua da,* an iced coffee mixed with sweetened condensed milk.

HEAL. Available data indicate that Asian Americans are underrepresented among mental health patients. Moderately disturbed Asian Americans are often reluctant to seek help from mental health professionals. The immigrant-heavy Asian American population is expected to have a high level of stress and other mental health issues. Elderly Asian immigrants, middle-aged immigrant women, and Southeast Asian refugees and immigrants are identified as high-risk groups, but they are underrepresented among mental health service users.

HEAL. A significant proportion of professional immigrants from the Philippines and South Asia are medical professionals.

LAWS. The U.S. Congress passes the Hate Crime Statistics Act to allow the gathering and publication of data concerning crimes against persons based on discriminatory characteristics. An increasing number of hate crimes against Asian Americans are reported.

POLI. Daniel K. Akaka, a native of Hawaii and a member of the U.S. House of Representatives, is appointed to fill the senate seat of "Spark" Masayaki Matsunaga after the senior senator's sudden death.

POLI. Cheryl Lau, a native of Hawaii, is elected Nevada secretary of state.

POLI. Filipino American David M. Valederrama is elected as a delegate of the Maryland General Assembly. He will serve at this post until 2003. Born in Manila in the Philippines, Valederrama came to the United States to study law at George Washington University. Before the election he was a judge in Prince George's County in Maryland.

POLI. President George H. W. Bush signs a proclamation designating May as Asian/Pacific American Heritage Month. The ceremony of designation takes place in the Rose Garden at the White House; participating are several Asian American dignitaries such as Taylor Wang (astronaut), Virginia Cha (1989 Miss Maryland and first runner-up in the Miss America pageant), I. M. Pei (architect), Sammy Lee (Olympic diver and physician), Nancy Kwan (actress), and Tsung-dao Lee (Nobel laureate in physics).

POPU. The U.S. Census Bureau reports that the Asian Pacific American population in the United States has increased from 3,500,439 in 1980 to 7,273,662 in 1990. Asian Americans count for 3 percent of the U.S. population.

POPU. The Chinese are the largest Asian ethnic group, with a population of 1,645,472 in the United States. The next largest group is the Filipinos, with a population of 1,460,770. There are 847,562 Japanese Americans, 815,447 Asian Indian Americans, 798,849 Korean Americans, 614,547 Vietnamese Americans, 149,014 Laotians, 149,047 Cambodians, 94,439 Hmong, and 365,000 Native Hawaiians and Pacific Islanders in the United States.

PUBL. Chinese American Ha Jin publishes his first book of poems, *Between Silences*. Born in China of a military family, Ha joined the People's Liberation Army during the Cultural Revolution before attending college. In the United States, he studied at Brandeis University and will receive a Ph.D. in 1992. Ha will become a prolific writer. His novel *Waiting* wins the National Book Award and PEN/Faulkner Award. His collection of short stories, *Under the Red Flag*, wins the Flannery O'Connor Award for short fiction, and his *Ocean of Words* wins the PEN/Hemingway Award. In 2004 Ha will publish *War Trash*, which will win him another PEN/Faulkner Award and make him a finalist for the Pulitzer Prize. In 2007, he will publish another novel, *A Free Life*. Ha will hold a teaching position at Emory University in Atlanta, Georgia before joining the faculty at Boston University.

PUBL. Japanese American author and illustrator Allen Say publishes the critically acclaimed *El Chino*. Say will base his second book, *Grandfather's Journey*, on his own and his grandfather's lives in Japan and America. It will win the 1994 Caldecott Medal for most distinguished American children's picture book.

SCIE. Doctor and AIDS researcher David D. Ho is appointed to head the Aaron Diamond AIDS Research Center—the world's largest AIDS research facility—in New York City. Born in Taiwan, Ho immigrated to the United States at age 12. A graduate of the California Institute of Technology, he received his M.D. from the Harvard-MIT Division of Health Sciences and Technology in 1978. After years of clinical training at the University of California, Los Angeles School of Medicine and the Massachusetts General Hospital, Ho became a resident doctor at Cedars-Sinai Medical Center in Los Angeles in 1981, where he first came in contact with some of the earliest reported cases of AIDS patients.

Ho began AIDS research in 1984. He is one of the first scientists to discover that AIDS is caused by a virus. In 1996, Ho will be named *Time* magazine's Man of the Year for his contribution to the basic understanding of AIDS and his pursuit of therapeutic treatment of the disease. He will be the first scientist since 1960 to receive such an honor. Ho's research team will later focus on vaccine development to prevent the spread of the AIDS epidemic as well as the treatment of early-stage patients.

SETT. California continues to be the most desirable settlement area for Asian Americans. Los Angeles, San Francisco, San Jose, and San Diego are common destinations for new Asian immigrants. An increasing proportion of Chinese, Indian, and Korean immigrants also settle in the New York-New Jersey area.

SETT. Many post-1965 immigrants live in ethnic enclaves. Chinese from Hong Kong and mainland China, for example, are highly concentrated in Chinatowns in New York and California. Koreans in Los Angeles build a Korean Town about three miles west of downtown Los Angeles. There are several ethnic enclaves

Twelve-year-old David Ho poses with his younger brother Phillip at Disneyland, shortly after his family immigrated to the United States in 1965. [Courtesy of Phillip Ho]

established by Southeast Asian immigrants in Orange County, California. The area along Bolsa Avenue from Magnolia to Bushard in Westminster, for example, is officially designated as "Little Saigon." Filipino and Asian Indian immigrants are more scattered in urban and suburban areas. Overall, Asian Americans are more represented in suburban residential areas than the general American population.

SOCI. The Committee of 100, a group of prominent Chinese Americans, is founded to build cultural exchange between the United States and China and to provide a forum for issues concerning Chinese Americans. Permanent members of the committee are well known in the United States and overseas and include architect I. M. Pei, Yahoo! CEO Jerry Yang, cellist Yo-Yo Ma, and others. The goal of the committee is to use the strengths and influences of the members to address concerns of Chinese American community and to foster the exchange of ideas among community members and with the government.

SPOR. Japanese American golfer David S. Ishii wins the Hawaiian Open PGA tournament. Growing up in Hawaii, Ishii turned professional in 1979. He will have the most success on the Japan Golf Tour, winning 14 victories.

1991

ARTS. The Vietnamese American Arts and Letters Association, a community-based nonprofit organization, is established. Located in Westminster, California, the association organizes exhibits, book fairs, book readings and signings, lecture series, cinema symposia, and the Vietnamese International Film Festival.

ARTS. Japanese American photojournalist Paul Kuroda is named Newspaper Photographer of the Year by the National Press Photographers Association and the University of Missouri School of Journalism.

EDUC. Japanese American Bob H. Suzuki is selected as the fourth president of California State Polytechnic University, Pomona. Born in Portland, Oregon to Japanese immigrant parents, Suzuki was interned with his family in Minidoka, Idaho during World War II when he first started school. A graduate of the University of California at Berkeley, where he earned bachelor's and master's degrees, Suzuki received a Ph.D. from the California Institute of Technology in 1967. Beginning his career as a professor with the Department of Aerospace Engineering at the University of Southern California, Suzuki was deeply involved in civil rights and public and community affairs and eventually decided to devote himself to public service full time. Returning to academic administration, Suzuki was named dean of graduate studies and research at California State University, Los Angeles and then vice president for academic affairs at California State University, Northridge. He is an advocate for the inclusion of Asian Americans in federally-mandated affirmative action programs and has served on many science and educational committees at state and national levels. Suzuki will serve as the president of California State Polytechnic University, Pomona until his retirement in 2003.

MED. Japanese American Steven Okazaki's *Days of Waiting* wins the Academy Award for best documentary (short subject). The film documents American artist Estelle Ishigo's experience during World War II as she followed her Japanese American husband to the internment camp.

POLI. Major General John Liu Fugh is appointed as the judge advocate general of the U.S. Army, a post he will hold until his retirement in 1993. Born in Beijing, China, Fugh immigrated to the United States in 1950 when he was 15. A graduate of Georgetown University and the U.S. Army War College, he obtained a law degree from George Washington University. Serving the army in San Francisco, Vietnam, Europe, and Taiwan, he was eventually promoted to the rank of major general. After his retirement, Fugh will return to private practice and work with several companies to cultivate relationships with China. He will head the Committee of 100 in 2004 and receive the Chinese American Pioneer Award from the Organization of Chinese Americans.

POLI. Patricia Saiki, former representative to Congress from Hawaii, is appointed to head the

U.S. Small Business Administration by President George H. W. Bush.

PUBL. Chinese American Gus Lee publishes the semi-autobiographical novel *China Boy.* The book wins him a Literary Guild selection and a place on the *New York Times* "Best 100 of 1991" list. Lee, a lawyer, writes the book at his daughter's request. He will publish *Honor and Duty* in 1994.

PUBL. Asian Indian American Dinesh D'Souza publishes *Illiberal Education: The Politics of Race and Sex on Campus,* his first best-selling book. Born in Mumbai, India, D'Souza arrived in America in 1978 to attend high school and then college, graduating from Dartmouth College in 1983. He was the editor of Dartmouth's conservative monthly, *The Prospect.* D'Souza's conservative views were further spread when he served as the editor of *Policy Review,* an influential conservative journal, in the mid-1980s. He was a policy advisor in President Ronald Reagan's administration between 1987 and 1988. As a popular author and public speaker, D'Souza is known for his bold arguments against affirmative action, social welfare, multiculturalism, and feminism. In addition to *The Catholic Classics* (1986), he will publish many books, including *The End of Racism* (1995), *The Virtue of Prosperity* (2000), *Letters to a Young Conservative* (2003), and *The Enemy at Home: The Cultural Left and Its Responsibility of 9/11* (2007).

1992

ARTS. Chinese American designer and artist Doug Chiang wins an Academy Award for the creation and design of special effects in the 1992 film *Death Becomes Her.* Born in Taiwan in 1962, Chiang grew up in the United States and studied film and industrial design at the University of California, Los Angeles. At Industrial Light and Magic as a creative director, he will work on a number of high-profile films, including *Terminator 2* and *Forrest Gump.* Chiang will be a co-founder of Ice Blink Studio in 2004.

CIVI. The Asian Pacific American Labor Alliance (APALA), part of the American Federation of Labor and Congress of Industrial Organizations (AFL-CIO), is established. The first and only national organization of Asian Pacific union members, the APALA recruits and trains union organizers and labor activists, and it advocates for Asian Pacific American participation in the political process. It also works to forge ties with internal unions. With 11 chapters and offices, the APALA will have 600,000 Asian Pacific American union members a decade later.

FAMI. Lillian Kimura becomes the first woman to be elected as president of the Japanese American Citizens League.

HEAL. Native Hawaiian oncologist Reginald C. S. Ho becomes the first Asian American to head the American Cancer Society.

LAWS. The Voting Rights Language Assistance Act is enacted, requiring bilingual voting materials to be made available to citizens speaking a language other than English. This law encourages Asian immigrants with limited English proficiency to participate in local and national elections.

MILI. The United States withdraws its military facilities at Clark Base, Subic Bay Naval Complex, and several small subsidiary installations in the Philippines, ending a 45-year long U.S. base-era in the islands.

POLI. Asian Americans are underrepresented in politics. There are only 4 U.S. Congress members of Asian ancestry, compared to 38 blacks and 20 Hispanics. Outside Hawaii, only five Asian Americans are elected to state legislatures. Asian Americans are also underrepresented in local politics. Although Los Angles has the largest Asian American population, only one city council member is Asian American. New York, which has an Asian American population of more than half a million, does not have a single Asian American city council member.

POLI. Korean American businessman Jay Kim is elected to Congress from California, becoming the first Korean American member of the U.S. House of Representatives. Born in Seoul, South Korea, Kim was educated in both Korea and the United States, receiving his bachelor's and master's degrees from the University of Southern California in Los Angeles and his Ph.D. from

Han Yang University in Seoul. Before serving in Congress he was the mayor of Diamond Bar, California. Corruption, however, prevents Kim from succeeding in politics. In 1997, Kim will plead guilty to accepting $230,000 in illegal campaign contributions. He will be convicted and sentenced to a one-year probation and a $5,000 fine.

POLI. Chinese American Clayton Fong is appointed deputy assistant to President George H. W. Bush.

RACE. The Los Angeles riots start on the evening of April 29, triggered by the Rodney King incident. African American Rodney King is severely beaten by four police officers after a long chase on the highway. Although the beating is videotaped and televised nationwide, the attackers are acquitted and set free. After the verdict is announced, thousands of angry people gather on the streets; they loot the stores, beat bystanders, destroy property, and set the city on fire. The riots last for several days. Stores owned by Korean immigrants suffer the most damage.

SCIE. Filipino American physician Lillian Gonzalez-Pardo is elected president of the American Medical Women's Association. She is the first Asian American to hold the position.

SCIE. Vietnamese American physicist Eugene Huu-Chau Trinh travels in space for 14 days as a payload specialist on the STS-50/United States Microgravity Lab-1 Space Shuttle. A graduate from Columbia University, Trinh received his Ph.D. in applied physics from Yale University. A senior science researcher, he will later become the director of the Physical Sciences Research Division in the Biological and Physical Research Enterprise at NASA Headquarters.

SPOR. Kristi Yamaguchi, one of Americans' favorite ice skaters, wins a gold medal for women's figure skating at the 1992 Winter Olympics in Albertville, France. A third-generation Japanese American, Yamaguchi is the first Asian American woman to bring home an Olympic gold medal in this event. In addition, Yamaguchi is the winner for both the 1991 and 1992 World Figure Skating Championships and the 1992 U.S. Nationals. She will also win the World

Gold medalist Kristi Yamaguchi, center, waves during the medals ceremony of the figure skating competition at the Winter Olympic Games in Albertville, France, 1992. Silver medalist Midori Ito of Japan stands to her left, and bronze medalist Nancy Kerrigan is on her right. [AP Photo/Lionel Cironneau]

Professional Figure Skating Championships four times between 1992 and 1997. In 1998, Yamaguchi will be inducted into World Figure Skating Hall of Fame.

SPOR. Korean American Eugene Chung joins the New England Patriots professional football team.

1993

ARTS. Chinese American fashion designer Anna Sui wins the Perry Ellis Award for new fashion talent. The Michigan-born Sui studied fashion at Parson's School of Design in New York. She launched her first runway show in 1991 and her first boutique shop in New York a year later. Her boutiques will expand to Japan, China, Taiwan, South Korea, Hong Kong, Singapore, Thailand, and the Philippines. She will be named by

Time magazine as one of the top five fashion icons of the decade.

ARTS. Japanese American Eiko Ishioka wins the Academy Award for best costume design for her work in *Bram Stoker's Dracula.*

ARTS. Korean American comedian Margaret Cho becomes the first Asian American to star in her own television series, *All-American Girl.* Born Moran Cho in San Francisco in 1968, Cho graduated from the San Francisco School of the Arts, where she performed with the school's comedy group. Starting her career as a comedian in clubs in San Francisco, she appeared in a few television shows; she will win the American Comedy Award for best female comedian in 1994. But *All-American Girl* is hardly a success. In 1999, Cho will develop her first one-woman show, *I'm the One That I Want,* which will be filmed and released in 2000. Another show of hers, *Revolution,* will be released in 2004. In addition to acting, Cho will publish two books: *I'm the One That I Want* (2000) and *I Have Chosen to Stay and Fight* (2005). She will be the recipient of many awards for her performances and community activities.

ASIA. The United States officially establishes diplomatic relations with the Kingdom of Cambodia. The embargo against Cambodia was lifted a year earlier.

FOOD. P. F. Chang's China Bistro, Inc., a restaurant chain, opens for business, offering Chinese cuisine in upscale American suburbs. Based in Scottsdale, Arizona, China Bistro restaurants target middle-class American diners with attractive architectural design and elaborate, village-style décor; life-size terracotta soldiers and horses are some of the main features. The company is able to expand at a fast pace. It will have over 100 restaurants in more than 30 states a decade later. The company will also develop the Pei Wei Asian Diner, a fusion restaurant chain offering cuisines of China, Hong Kong, Japan, Vietnam, and Thailand. Over 130 Pei Wei Asian Diners are eventually in business in 18 states.

LAWS. In Joint Resolution 19 of Public Law 103, which passes on November 23, the government offers a formal apology to Native Hawaiians for the overthrow of the Kingdom of Hawaii a hundred years ago.

MIGR. With 286 passengers on board, the *Golden Venture,* a human smuggling ship, runs aground in New York Harbor. Eight of the Chinese die in their attempt to swim ashore. The incident captures Americans' fascination with human smuggling from China. Since the late 1980s, many Chinese have been smuggled into the United States by multinational operations. For a fee of about $20,000 (which will increase to as much as $80,000 after 2000), prospective emigrants, most of them from Fujian Province in China, are led by professionals through Hong Kong or Thailand before a long journey to come to the United States through Central America. Others arrive by sea like those on the *Golden Venture.* According to a study that will be conducted by the United Nations, smuggling Chinese to the United States will have generated $3.5 billion by the mid-1990s. The exact number of Chinese to make the crossing successfully is unknown.

MILI. Japanese American Master Sergeant Roy H. Matsumoto is inducted into the U.S. Army Ranger Hall of Fame for his extraordinary service during World War II.

MILI. Frederick F. Y. Pang, a native of Hawaii, becomes an assistant secretary of the navy for manpower and reserve affairs, the highest-ranking Asian American in the U.S. military.

SCIE. Asian Indian scientist Arati Prabhakar is appointed by President Bill Clinton to head the National Institute of Standards and Technology.

SPOR. Samoan American Tiaina "Junior" Seau, a San Diego Chargers linebacker, is voted as the National Football League Players Association Player of the Year. Born in 1969 in San Diego, Seau played for the University of Southern California for three years before being drafted by the San Diego Chargers. Considered one of the best linebackers in professional football in the 1990s, he will be named to all-pro teams by the Associated Press, *Football Digest,* the Pro Football Writers Association, *Sporting News, College & Pro Football Newsweekly,* and *Sports Illustrated.* In 2000, Seau will be named to the Pro Football Hall of Fame's All-Decade Team for the 1990s and as the NFL Alumni Association's Linebacker of the Year. Seau is a role model for young Samoan Americans.

SPOR. Hawaii-born Chad Rowan, better known as Akebono, becomes the first American to win the title of *yokozuna,* the highest rank in professional sumo, in Japan. He will win a total of 11 tournaments before his retirement in 2001.

1994

ARTS. The Asian American comedy troupe 18 Mighty Mountain Warriors is founded in San Francisco. It grows out of an ensemble called the New Godzilla Theater, an affiliate of the Asian American Theater Company. The group produces stage shows and workshop productions around the San Francisco Bay area and tours nationally and internationally. It also performs at bars and clubs in San Francisco's Japantown and Tenderloin districts.

EDUC. Chinese American Henry Yang is appointed as the chancellor of the University of California at Santa Barbara. He is the second Asian American to head a university in the University of California system.

HEAL. One nationwide survey reveals that about 41 percent of Asian Pacific Americans 18 years and older are having difficulty paying for medical care. This rate is higher than that of the total U.S. population (29 percent). It is higher than both white and black populations (26 and 35 percent, respectively) and slightly lower than that of the Hispanic population (45 percent).

POLI. Asian Indian American Prema Mathai-Davis is appointed to head the Young Women's Christian Association (YWCA). Born in India, Mathai-Davis received a master's degree in India before attending Harvard University, where she earned a Ph.D. in human development. She is well known as an advocate for social service programs for the elderly.

POLI. Benjamin J. Cayetano is elected governor of Hawaii, becoming the first Filipino American to serve as a state governor in the United States. Born in 1939 in Honolulu, Cayetano grew up in the city's Filipino neighborhood. After high school, he worked in several menial jobs such as metal-packer in a junkyard, truck driver, apprentice electrician, and draftsman. Moving to California with his family in 1963, he graduated from the University of California, Los Angeles in 1968 and obtained a law degree from Loyola Law School. Before his governorship, he was Hawaii's lieutenant governor for 12 years.

POLI. A relatively low percentage of Asian Americans participate in electoral politics. Only 39.4 percent of eligible Asian Americans vote. The rate will be even lower four years later in 1998, when only 32.4 percent of Asian Americans cast their votes. The voting rate for eligible white Americans in 1998 will be 46.3 percent.

SOCI. The National Association of Korean Americans, a civil and human rights organization of concerned Korean Americans, is founded in New York City. This national association is formed out of concerns after the 1992 riot in Los Angeles. It works to protect civil rights for Korean Americans, promote communication with other racial and ethnic groups, and develop traditional cultural programs. It also advocates for a peaceful and independent reunification of Korea.

SPOR. South Korean baseball pitcher Chan Ho Park signs with the Los Angeles Dodgers as an amateur free agent and starts his career in professional baseball in the United States. Beginning in 2002 he will pitch for the Texas Rangers, the San Diego Padres, the New York Mets, and finally the Houston Astros before returning to the Dodgers in 2007.

1994–1997

MIGR. The United States increases the annual immigration quota for Hong Kong to the same amount as given to any other nation, to facilitate immigration of Hong Kong residents before the British colony is taken over by the People's Republic of China in 1997.

1995

ASIA. The United States officially normalizes diplomatic relations with Vietnam on July 11.

ECON. Chinese American Eleanor Yu is chosen as the 1995 recipient of the Entrepreneur of the Year award by the U.S. Small Business Administration. She is the first Asian American, first woman, and youngest person to receive this award. Yu is the head of Adland Worldwide, a multimillion-dollar advertising agency.

ECON. Chinese American Jerry Yang, together with David Filo, founds Yahoo! Inc. in April. Born in Taiwan in 1968, Yang immigrated to the United States with his family at age 10. At Stanford University, he received his college and master's degrees in electrical engineering. While pursuing a doctoral degree, he and Filo created an Internet Web site consisting of a directory of other Web sites—Jerry's Guide to the World Wide Web—which laid the foundation for Yahoo! (Yet Another Hierarchically Officious Oracle!). The popularity of the search engine encourages Yang and Filo to postpone their studies indefinitely. They will move Yahoo! out of Stanford University's servers and incorporate it as an independent company. Yang will serve as CEO of the company from 2007 to 2008.

EDUC. The University of California, Santa Barbara, establishes the first Asian American Studies Department in a major American research university.

FOOD. *Yan Can Cook,* the long-running Chinese cooking television show hosted by Martin Yan, receives the James Beard Award for best television food journalism. Yan later will also win a Daytime Emmy Award. The television show is immensely popular and will run a total of 1,500 episodes. Yan's charisma and his convincing knowledge of Chinese food preparation introduce traditional Chinese cooking methods to American households. Born in Guangzhou, China, Yan moved to Hong Kong at age 13,

where he worked in his uncle's restaurant and received some cooking instruction. After coming to the United States, Yan studied culinary arts at the University of California at Davis and received a master of science degree in food science. He is the author of more than a dozen cookbooks.

HEAL. Asian Indian American medical doctor Deepak Chopra founds the Chopra Center for Wellbeing with Doctor David Simon in Carlsbad, California. One of the world's greatest leaders in the field of alternative medicine and one of the most sought-after speakers, Chopra combines western medicine with traditional natural healing techniques developed in Asia, emphasizing a connection between body, mind, spirit, and healing. He was the chief of staff at Boston Regional Medical Center in the 1980s, establishing a successful career in endocrinology practice. Chopra is the author of more than four dozen books and more than 100 audio, video, and CD-ROM titles. His work is translated into 35 languages. A recipient of many awards, Chopra is also the founding director and president of the Alliance for a New Humanity.

LAWS. Japanese American Los Angeles Superior Court Judge Lance Ito receives national publicity during the 133-day televised courtroom testimony of the O. J. Simpson murder trial. The Hall of Fame football player Simpson is charged of murdering his ex-wife, Nicole Brown Simpson, and her friend, Ronald Goldman.

MED. Chinese American Wayne Wang's independent feature film *Smoke* wins the Silver Bear at the Berlin International Film Festival. Born in Hong Kong, Wang received training in film and television at the California College of Arts and Crafts in Oakland. His earlier films include *Chan Is Missing* (1982), *Dim Sum: A Little Bit of Heart* (1985), *Eat a Bowl of Tea* (1989), and

---

Bill Clinton's Remarks at the State Dinner in New Delhi, India, March 21, 2000

"My country has been enriched by the contributions of more than a million Indian Americans, from Vinod Dahm, the father of the Pentium chip; to Deepak Chopra, the pioneer of alternative medicine; to Sabeer Bhatia, creator of the free mail system, Hotmail—the e-mail system."

The Joy Luck Club (1993). Wang will later direct many other films, including *Anywhere But Here* (1999), *Maid In Manhattan* (2002), and *A Thousand Years of Good Prayers* (2008).

MED. Actor Pat Morita (1932–2005) leaves his mark on the Hollywood Walk of Fame. Born in California to Japanese immigrant parents, Morita developed acting skills as a teenager, entertaining customers in his parents' restaurant in Sacramento, California. After high school he worked at an aerospace company for many years but eventually decided to quit and start a career as a standup comedian. He was a member of a Los Angeles improvisational comedy troupe—The Groundlings—and appeared in some television shows. During his career Morita had roles in more than 70 movies and television shows. He is most well known for the role of Arnold on the television production *Happy Days* and later as Mr. Miyagi in the *Karate Kid* movie trilogy, for which he was nominated for an Academy Award for best supporting actor. Morita will die in 2005 at age 73.

MED. Two Asian American scientists gain national publicity through the televised O. J. Simpson trial. Chinese American Henry Chang-Yu Lee is the world's most prominent expert in forensic science. His testimony creates high drama for the courtroom marathon and provides critical support for the defense team. Born in China and raised in Taiwan, Lee was a police officer in Taiwan before coming to the United States to study forensic science and biochemistry. Lee was Connecticut's chief criminologist. He also helped to establish the Henry C. Lee Forensic Institute at the University of New Haven. Lee will provide expert testimony in many high-profile cases and investigations, including the JonBenét Ramsey and Laci Peterson murder cases, the post-9/11 forensic investigation, and the Washington, D.C., sniper shootings. He will also be invited to Taiwan to investigate the shooting of former President Chen Shui-bian. Lee will also have a television show, *Trace Evidence: The Case Files of Dr. Henry Lee.*

Senior criminologist of the Los Angeles Police Department Dennis Fung, a Chinese American, also testifies during the Simpson trial in relation to crime scene evidence. He spends a total of nine days on the stand as the prosecution's witness, although some of his testimonies are apparently more helpful to the defense team.

MED. After early success in two Taiwanese American films, Chinese American Ang Lee gains recognition in Hollywood. *Sense and Sensibility* brings Lee a Golden Bear at the Berlin International Film Festival, seven Academy nominations, and the Golden Globe Award for best motion picture-drama. Born in Taiwan, Lee failed the national university entrance exam twice and had to attend the National Arts School instead. He came to the United States in 1979. At the University of Illinois at Urbana-Champaign, Lee completed his college degree in theater in 1980. He then went to graduate school at New York University. Although his thesis work won an award for best director in the university's student film festival and was selected for the Public Broadcasting Service, Lee could not find work after graduation. As a full-time "house husband" for six years, he wrote screenplays. In 1990, Lee's two screenplays *Pushing Hands* and the *Wedding Banquet* took first and second places in a competition sponsored by Taiwan's Government Information Office. As a result Lee was invited to direct these films. *Wedding Banquet* brought Lee his first Golden Bear in the Berlin film festival and was nominated as the best foreign language film in the Golden Globe Awards and the Academy Awards. In 2000, Lee will successfully assemble a team of talents from Taiwan, Hong Kong, and China for a martial art and chivalry movie, *Crouching Tiger, Hidden Dragon*. This worldwide blockbuster will win Academy Awards for best foreign language film and three other technical categories. In 2005, Lee will become the first Asian American to win the best director Academy Award for *Brokeback Mountain*. As an established director, Lee will test the boundaries of filmmaking constantly. His 2007 film *Lust, Caution* will be highly controversial.

MIGR. The normalization of U.S.-Vietnam relations allows Vietnamese to come to the United States through normal immigration processes. Former refugees with U.S. citizenship status can now sponsor their family members and relatives. Increased trade between the United

States and Vietnam will also facilitate Vietnamese immigration to the United States.

POLI. Chinese American law enforcement officer Fred Lau is named police chief by the mayor of San Francisco, Willie Brown. He is the first Asian American to hold the post.

POLI. Gary Locke is elected governor of the state of Washington and becomes the first Chinese American governor in U.S. history. A third-generation Chinese American, Locke was born in Seattle, Washington. He graduated from Yale University in 1972 and received a law degree from the Boston University School of Law in 1975. Before his governorship, Locke served as a house representative of the state of Washington between 1982 and 1993 and as county executive of King County in 1993. Locke will hold the state governor position until 2004. In 2009, Locke will be appointed by President Barack Obama as secretary of commerce of the United States.

POPU. An estimated 120,000 Thai immigrants and their descendents are living in the United States, including Thai Chinese.

PUBL. Chinese American historian Judy Yung publishes her award-winning monograph *Unbound Feet: A Social History of Chinese Women in San Francisco*. A professor of American studies at the University of California, Santa Cruz, Yung is the author of a number of books on Chinese American history and Chinese American women, including *Chinese Women of America: A Pictorial History; Island: Poetry and History of Chinese Immigrants on Angel Island, 1910–1940* (with Him Mark Lai); *Chinese American Voices: From the Gold Rush to the Present* (with Him Mark Lai and Gordon Chang); *San Francisco's Chinatown; Unbound Voices: A Documentary History of Chinese Women in San Francisco; The Adventures of Eddie Fung: Chinatown Kid, Texas Cowboy, Prisoner of War.*

SETT. The vast majority of Thai Americans settle in Los Angeles, where they build a Thai Town, the only one in the United States. Smaller numbers of Thai can also be found in Chicago, Houston, and Philadelphia.

SOCI. The National Alliance of Vietnamese American Service Agencies is established. The alliance is built upon 34 community-based and religioous organizations nationwide. It provides leadership training and other services through affiliated organizations and student organizations.

SPOR. Japanese baseball player Hideo Nomo turns into a permanent Major League Baseball player in the United States after freeing himself from his contract in Japan. Born in 1968, Nomo enjoyed early success in baseball in Nippon Professional Baseball, playing with the Kintetsu Buffaloes from 1990 to 1994. In the United States, he plays with the Los Angeles Dodgers. His move from Japan to the United States paves the way for other Japanese players after him to enter Major League Baseball and draws Japanese and Japanese American fans to Major League Baseball games.

Washington State Governor Gary Locke's Remarks on His Family

"Many of you know my story. My family's journey began when my grandfather came to the U.S. from China as a teenager more than 100 years ago. He worked as a servant for a family in exchange for English lessons. Today I live in the governor's mansion—just one mile from the house where my grandfather swept floors, cooked, and washed dishes. We joke that it took our family 100 years to travel one mile.

Our family's journey, like the journey of all Asian Pacific American families, has been one of hard work and hope. We have been sustained by a belief in the promise of America: freedom, equality, and opportunity."

Governor Gary Locke, public speech at Asian Pacific American Institute for Congressional Studies, May 6, 2004.

1996

AGRI. The Hmong American Community (HAC) is founded to address economic issues affecting the Hmong people, with an emphasis on farming issues. To help the Hmong farmers adjust to the U.S. agriculture system, the HAC founds a farming cooperative and runs a training center to teach about farming technology, pesticide regulations, and marketing. Graduates from the HAC training center receive loans and start-up expenses with the assistance of the U.S. Department of Agriculture.

POLI. John Huang, a Democratic National Committee fund-raiser and former Commerce Department official, is alleged to have made illegal campaign contributions to President Bill Clinton. Numerous reports by the media cast suspicion about Asian contributors and Asian American intermediaries, and some of the stories try to link China with some of the donations.

SCIE. Asian Indian American Sabeer Bhatia starts Hotmail, a Web-based e-mail system. Born in India in 1968, Bhatia started college in India and completed it at the California Institute of Technology in the United States in 1989. He later received a master's degree in electrical engineering from Stanford University. Together with Jack Smith, Bhatia officially launches the Hotmail project on July 4. It will attract over one million subscribers within six months and will be sold to Microsoft for $400 million in 1997. Bhatia will be named as Entrepreneur of the Year by the venture capital firm Draper Fisher Jurveston in 1997, and he will receive many other awards.

SPOR. Golfer Tiger Woods, born to a Thai mother and an African American father, turns pro and is named Sportsman of the Year by *Sports Illustrated* magazine. Born Eldrick T. Woods in 1975 in California, Woods was taught by his father to play golf when he was one year old. At age two, he made an appearance on *The Mike Douglas Show*. Before age 15, he won 6 junior championships. And at age 18, he became the youngest U.S. junior amateur champion in history. He turns pro while a student at Stanford University. He will win the U.S. Masters with a record score of 270 a year later and tie the Troon

Tiger Woods tees off during the fourth round of the U.S. Open championship at Torrey Pines Golf Course in San Diego, 2008. [AP Photo/Charlie Riedel, File]

course record of 64 at the British Open. He will win 14 major titles by 2008, capturing U.S. PGA titles in 1999, 2000, 2006, and 2007; U.S. Open titles in 2000, 2002, and 2008; Open Championship titles in 2000, 2005, and 2006; and the U.S. Masters in 1997, 2001, 2002, and 2005. He will have more PGA titles than any other active golfer. Woods will be the subject of his father Earl Woods's book, *Training a Tiger: A Father's Guide to Raising a Winner in Both Golf and Life* (1997).

SPOR. Chinese American figure skater Michelle Kwan captures a gold medal in the World Figure Skating Championship. Born in Torrance, California in 1980, Kwan began skating at age five, winning a skating competition two years later. At age 13, she earned a spot as an alternate for the 1994 Winter Olympic Games. And within two years, she became a dominant athlete in the event. Kwan will be favored to win gold at the Nagano Olympics in 1998, but she will have to settle for silver when fellow U.S. skater Tara Lipinski takes first place. She will let another gold medal slip away at the Salt Lake City Olympics in 2002, when she finishes third after American skater Sarah Hughes (gold medalist) and Irina Slutskaya of Russia (silver medalist). But Kwan will continue to compete, withdrawing from the 2006 Olympic Games in Torino, Italy only because of an injury. Although Kwan will end her career without an Olympic gold medal, as a five-time world champion (1996, 1998, 2000–2001, 2003) and nine-time U.S. national champion (1996, 1998–2005), she is no doubt the most accomplished figure skater in the United States and one of the very best in the world. Her autobiography, *Michelle Kwan: Heart of a Champion,* will be published in 1997. She will also author a children's book and appear in several television series. After her retirement from figure skating, Kwan will transfer from the University of California, Los Angeles to the University of Denver to study political science and international studies. In 2006, Secretary of State Condoleezza Rice will name Kwan as a public diplomacy ambassador. Kwan will join a U.S. government delegation to the Beijing Summer Olympics in 2008.

SPOR. Chinese American gymnast Amy Chow and her teammates bring home the first American team Olympic gymnastics gold medal. The first Asian American woman to take an Olympic gold medal in gymnastics, she also wins an individual silver medal on the uneven bars. Born in 1978, Chow began gymnastics training in 1981 at age five. She entered national and international competitions when she was 12. In addition to being a gymnast, Chow plays the piano, and she is also an athlete in diving and pole vaulting.

1997

ASIA. Hong Kong returns to China, as a 99-year lease between China and Britain expires. Under the Visa Waiver Program, the United States offers visa-free entry status to Chinese nationals who are permanent residents of Hong Kong.

HEAL. Available data reveal that Asian Americans are more likely to be uninsured compared with white Americans. A large proportion of new immigrants do not have health insurance;

many self-employed individuals also do not opt to buy health insurance. Koreans and Southeast Asians have the lowest rates of health insurance coverage.

MED. Chinese American Jackie Chan leaves the imprint of his hands, feet, and nose in the cement outside Mann's Chinese Theatre in Hollywood. Born in 1954 in Hong Kong, Chan studied at the Chinese Drama Academy as a young child and trained rigorously in martial arts and acrobatics. His first film appearance was in *Big and Little Wong Tin Bar* (1962), at age eight. He was a stuntman in two Bruce Lee films, *Fist of Fury* (1972) and *Enter the Dragon* (1973). Chan's career in Hollywood began in 1980, although he continued to be most popular in East Asia. Not until the late 1980s and early 1990s was Chan able to establish himself in Hollywood. Over Chan's career he will have roles in more than 100 movies produced in Hong Kong, the United States, and China and be the recipient of many awards.

MIGR. As part of the Resettlement Opportunities for Returned Vietnamese (RORV) program, under an agreement that the United States and the Vietnamese government reaches in January, repatriated Vietnamese are given opportunities to be interviewed by American immigration officials in Vietnam to determine whether they are qualified to be admitted to the United States. More than 20,000 applicants are interviewed and almost all of them eventually will come to the United States.

POLI. Japanese American Rose M. Ochi is appointed to the Department of Justice as assistant attorney general by President Bill Clinton. Attorney General Janet Reno assigns Ochi to coordinate race relations matters for the Department of Justice. Prior to Ochi's appointment, she was the associate director at the White House Office of National Drug Control Policy for two years. An advocate for interracial understanding, Ochi receives much recognition, including the U.S. Department of Justice Award for distinguished public service, the YWCA Silver Achievement Award for women leaders, and the Women of Courage Award from the City of Los Angeles.

PUBL. Vietnamese American Lan Cao, a law professor at the College of William and Mary, publishes *Monkey Bridge,* a novel based on Cao's own experience of leaving Vietnam on a journey to the United States with her mother. This is the first novel by a Vietnamese American about the impact of the Vietnam War on ordinary Vietnamese women and their journey to the United States.

SCIE. Chinese American scientist Steven Chu shares the Nobel Prize in physics for the development of methods to cool and trap atoms with laser light. Born in 1948 in St. Louis, Missouri, where his father taught at Washington University, Chu followed his family tradition to study science. He graduated from the University of Rochester and received a Ph.D. from the University of California at Berkeley. His award-winning work was conducted at Bell Laboratories, before Chu became a faculty member at Stanford University. Chu will be appointed as the director of the Lawrence Berkeley National Laboratory in 2004. In 2009, President Barack Obama will appoint Chu as the 12th United States secretary of energy.

SPOR. Nineteen-year-old Chinese American Dennis Fong wins a Ferrari sports car at a video game tournament. He will receive sponsorship from Microsoft and eventually win world championship titles and hundreds of thousands of dollars in prize money. Fong will later start his own

President-elect Barack Obama listens as energy secretary nominee Steven Chu addresses the media at a news conference in Chicago, December 2008. [AP Photo]

Internet company, GX Media, which will operate two video game Web sites.

1998

ARTS. Cambodian photojournalist Dith Pran (1942–2008), who covered the fall of the capital Phnom Penh to the Khmer Rouge in 1975, receives the Ellis Island Medal of Honor and the International Center in New York's Award of Excellence. Born in Siem Reap, Cambodia, Dith began his career as a photojournalist in 1975 when he met *New York Times* reporter Sydney Schanberg, from whom he learned to take pictures. Under the Khmer Rouge regime, Dith endured much hardship and witnessed the death of countless people. As a refugee and Cambodian genocide survivor, he is the subject of the Academy Award-winning film *The Killing Fields.* Dith started to work as a photojournalist with the *New York Times* in 1980. He will die of cancer in 2008, at age 33. (Also see entry in 2008)

COMM. Chang Le (Changle) American Association is founded in New York by new Chinese immigrants from Changle in Fujian Province. Beginning in the 1980s, some Changle natives began to leave their home villages through arrangements made with smugglers. In less than two decades, immigrants from Changle have become the fastest-growing Chinese American regional group. The organization is formed to create a positive public image of and provide mutual aid to its members. Built upon family and village ties back in China and an extensive network of entrepreneurship in the United States, this new regional community organization will emerge as a powerful force in New York's Chinatown, posing a direct challenge to the existing traditional Cantonese-dominated community organizations.

CRIM. Rishi Maharaj, a man of Asian Indian-Caribbean descent, is attacked by three white men who use baseball bats to beat the 20-year-old Maharaj while shouting anti-Indian epithets.

HEAL. According to information from the Centers for Disease Control, Asian Americans experienced the highest increase in cancer deaths compared to other racial and ethnic groups

Chang Le American Association in New York. [Photo by H. Lin]

between 1980 and 1993. While overall cancer death rates declined in America in the 1990s, cancer is the leading cause of death for Asian American and Pacific Islander women. Apparently Asian American women have the lowest screening rates for pap smears and mammogram examinations. Asian American men have a high rate of liver cancer. The fact that Asian Americans have high rates of chronic hepatitis B cases is probably associated with liver cancer occurrences.

MED. Chinese American Lucy Liu's impressive performance in one episode of Fox's *Ally McBeal* allows her to secure a position as a permanent cast member of the series. It also earns her an Emmy Award nomination for Outstanding Supporting Actress in a Comedy Series. Born in New York of Chinese immigrant parents, Liu started acting in 1989. She will enjoy great success in many roles in Hollywood films, especially *Charlie's Angels* (2000) and *Charlie's Angels: Full Throttle* (2003). She will win an MTV Movie Award for best movie villain for her role in *Kill Bill* (2003) and play key roles in several other movies and television sitcoms. Liu will also be an executive producer for the 2006 documentary *Freedom's Fury.*

MILI. Richard Sakakida, a Japanese American counterintelligence agent during World War II, is posthumously awarded the Distinguished Service Cross from the U.S. Air Force.

POLI. The U.S. Department of Justice announces that it will apologize and offer monetary compensation to more than 2,200 individuals of Japanese ancestry who were forcibly removed from Latin American countries and interned in the United States during World War II. About $1.6 billion in reparations will be disbursed by the government to the surviving internees and their heirs.

POLI. Fred Korematsu is awarded the Presidential Medal of Freedom by President Bill Clinton, for his lifelong commitment to civil rights and his fight against the wrongful imprisonment of Japanese Americans during World War II.

POLI. The Asian American Legal Defense and Education Fund leads a march in the Queens borough of New York City to protest the September attack on Rishi Maharaj.

PUBL. Chinese American Jeff Yang pens the autobiography of action star Jackie Chan, *I Am Jackie Chan: My Life in Action.*

PUBL. *A. Magazine* editors Jeff Yang, Diana Gan, and Terry Hong publish *Eastern Standard Time,* a book about Asian American influences on popular culture.

1999

ECON. Chinese American Jenny Ming becomes the president of Old Navy, a chain of clothing stores owned by Gap, Inc. Born in Canton, China in 1955, Ming spent her childhood in Macao, on the coast of China's Guangdong Province, then a Portuguese colony, before immigrating to the United States. After graduating from the State University of California at San Jose, where she majored in arts and clothing merchandising, she found work at Mervyn's. She was recruited by Gap, starting as a buyer for its activewear division. Within three years she became the vice president of Gap. When Gap's spin-off, Old Navy, opened its first store in 1994, Ming was the senior vice president of merchandising.

FAMI. The Hmong Women's Circle Program is organized by Kashia Moua. The program provides assistance to Hmong women and girls through 30 middle and elementary schools in California, Wisconsin, and Minnesota.

LAWS. President Bill Clinton signs Executive Order 13125, increasing participation of federal programs to improve the quality of life of Asian Americans and Pacific Islanders in areas where they may be underserved, such as health, human services, education, housing, labor, transportation, and economic and community development.

PUBL. Asian Indian American writer Jhumpa Lahiri's collection of short stories, *Interpreter of Maladies,* is published. The book wins an O. Henry Award, a PEN/Hemingway Award, and a Pulitzer Prize for fiction. Born in London, Lahiri grew up in Rhode Island and eventually received a Ph.D. in Renaissance studies from Boston University. She is the author of a many short stories and will write several novels. Her first novel, *The Namesake,* will be published in 2003 and adapted into a movie in 2007.

RACE. Chinese American Wen Ho Lee, a scientist at the Los Alamos National Laboratory of the University of California, is accused of stealing U.S. nuclear arms secrets for China. He is arrested and loses his job. Although accusations of espionage are dropped, the government will later conduct a new investigation and charge Lee with improper handling of restricted data. Lee will plead guilty to this charge. Supporters of Lee will believe he is singled out because of his ethnic background, although he immigrated to the United States from Taiwan, not China. No other national lab employees who handled restricted data improperly will be charged or fired.

RELI. A large number of Pakistanis are Muslims. Pakistanis and other South Asians account for about one quarter of the six million Muslims in the United States.

SETT. A Thai Town is officially created in October in Los Angeles, in an area between Normandie and Western avenues. This ethnic business district provides Thai Americans and tourists a good selection of restaurants, shops, and some forms of entertainment, and it works to help young Thai Americans maintain a sense of cultural identity. The Thai community also makes an effort to attract more entrepreneurs to the ethnic enclave; it provides assistance to immigrants with little capital to get started.

SPOR. Thai Culture Day is celebrated in Thai Town in Los Angeles on the last Sunday in September each year. A parade featuring Thai costumes, exhibitions of traditional arts, and performances of martial arts—*muay Thai*—are organized for the celebration.

SPOR. Vietnamese American Dat Nguyen signs with the Dallas Cowboys and becomes a professional football player. He is the very first Vietnamese professional football player in the United States.

TWENTY-FIRST CENTURY

2000

ARTS. The National Japanese American Memorial to Patriotism in Washington, D.C., is dedicated during the Veteran's Day memorial weekend. This memorial pays tribute to Japanese American World War II veterans as well as all the Japanese Americans who were interned from 1942 to 1945. The centerpiece of the memorial is a sculpture of a bronze crane created by Japanese American artist Nina A. Akamu.

ARTS. Pin Chong, a theater director, playwright, choreographer, and video artist, wins an Obie Award (Off-Broadway Theater Award) for sustained achievement.

ARTS. Korean martial artist Jhoon Rhee is named one of the 200 most famous immigrants of all time by the National Immigration Forum.

ASIA. A president's executive order legalizes most transactions between Americans and North Koreans. It allows many products to be exported to North Korea and eases restrictions on U.S. investments there. It also allows American citizens to travel to North Korea. This executive order ends a total economic embargo on North Korea. Without formal diplomatic relations, U.S. interaction with North Korea is still limited.

ECON. About 71 percent of Asian men aged 16 and over and 57 percent of Asian women of the same age are in the labor force. This is about the same rate as the general American population.

ECON. About 45 percent of Asians are employed in management, professional, and related occupations, in comparison to 34 percent of the total U.S. population. This suggests that Asians are more likely to be in management, professional, and related occupations. The distribution, however, is uneven among the Asian groups. About 60 percent of Asian Indians are employed in these jobs, compared with less than 20 percent of Cambodians, Hmong, and Laotians.

ECON. Median earnings for full-time employed Asian Americans age 16 or older are $36,051, with males earning $40,650 and females $31,049. Median earnings for male Asian American groups are $51,900 for Asian Indians; $50,900 for Japanese; $44,831 for Chinese; $40,277 for Pakistanis; $38,776 for Koreans; $35,560 for Filipinos; $32,879 for Thais; $31,258 for Vietnamese; $28,706 for Cambodians; $26,664 for Laotians; $25,187 for Hmong; and $36,247 for others. Median earnings for female Asian American groups are $35,998 for Japanese; $35,173 for Asian Indians; $34,869 for Chinese; $31,450 for Filipinos; $28,403 for Koreans; $28,315 for Pakistanis; $25,403 for Thais; $24,028 for Vietnamese; $21,911 for Cambodians; $21,857 for Laotians; $20,237 for Hmong; and $29,966 for others. Median earnings for Native Hawaiians and Pacific Islanders are $28,457, with $31,030 for men and $25,694 for women.

ECON. The median earnings of Asian men are 9 percent higher than those of the U.S. population, and the median earnings of Asian women are 14 percent higher than those of all U.S. women. Median earnings for Native Hawaiians and Pacific Islanders lag behind. Their median earnings for both men and women are lower than the general U.S. population.

ECON. Hmong Americans, who are concentrated in agriculture, enter local farmers' markets in large numbers. In California, Minnesota, and other states, Hmong vendors provide a variety of fresh produce that is most welcomed by Asian American customers.

ECON. Hmong Americans have the highest individual poverty rates (37.8 percent), followed by Cambodian Americans (29.3 percent). The poverty rate for the total American population is 12.4 percent.

ECON. Pacific Islanders have a relatively high rate of unemployment. The unemployment rate for Native Hawaiians and Pacific Islanders is 10.4 percent for males and 10.9 percent for females. In comparison, the unemployment rate for the general U.S. population is 5.7 percent.

EDUC. About 80 percent of Asian Americans 25 and older have at least a high school diploma, which is similar to the rate of the total U.S. population. Forty-four percent of Asian Americans, however, have at least a bachelor's degree, which is a much higher percentage than that of the total population (24 percent). About 64 percent of Asian Indians have a bachelor's degree. About 60 percent of Hmong and about half of Cambodians and Laotians have less than a high school education. Native Hawaiians have lower levels of educational attainment: only 16 percent of them have attended college. Even at the University of Hawaii, Native Hawaiians are underrepresented. Lower educational attainment has a negative impact on their living standard. Native Hawaiians tend to earn less and are less able to save money and become homeowners.

FAMI. The median income of Asian families is $59,300, which is about $9,000 higher than the $50,000 median family income for American families. Asian Indian and Japanese American families' median incomes are higher than those of other Asian groups.

FAMI. About 60 percent of all Asians are married, compared with 54 percent of the total population.

FAMI. The labor force participation rate for Filipino women is 65 percent, higher than that of Asian women and of American women in general.

FOOD. There are 69,903 Asian-owned restaurants in the United States; 54 percent are owned by Chinese. Chinese food can be found in virtually every corner. Due to the wide acceptance of Chinese food, some typical Americanized Chinese dishes are often listed in the menus of Korean, Japanese, Thai, or Vietnamese restaurants. Pan-Asian soup-noodle joints like Zao Noodle Bar or Long Life Noodle House offer Asian fusions of noodle, won ton, and dumpling options. Chinese dim sum and Japanese sushi, considered rather trendy in the 1980s and 1990s, become almost as common as pizza, available not only in food courts in shopping plazas and airports, but also in college dining halls and supermarkets, especially in California.

HEAL. The Asian American Network for Cancer Awareness, Research and Training is established to address cancer concerns specific to the Asian community. Cancer is the number two cause of death, next to cardiovascular disease, among female Asian Americans.

LANG. According to the census, almost four-fifths of Asians speak a language other than English at home, but about three-fifths of them are fluent in English. After Spanish, Chinese is the most widely spoken non-English language in the country. Tagalog and Vietnamese have more than one million speakers each.

MED. Chinese American martial artist Jet Li (Li Lianjie) plays his first Hollywood lead role in *Romeo Must Die.* Born in China, Li became a national martial art champion as a teenager. He won national and international fame as an actor in kung fu films in China and Hong Kong before coming to the United States. Li will star in many Hollywood action films.

MED. The Ammy Awards are established to honor Asian American films and actors in Hollywood.

The winners are determined through online and mail-in votes.

MILI. In a White House ceremony, President Bill Clinton presents the Medal of Honor to 21 Asian American veterans of World War II. The Medal of Honor recipients are inducted into the Pentagon's Hall of Heroes.

POLI. Asian Americans vote at relatively low rates. Because a large number of Asian Pacific Americans are immigrants or have not yet reached voting age, only 59 percent of Asian Pacific Americans are eligible to vote, and only 43 percent of them vote in this year's presidential election. This is the lowest among all ethnic groups and far below the 65 percent rate among eligible whites.

POLI. The number of Asian American elected officials continues to grow, with 328 Asian Americans serving in local, state, and federal offices, from members of school boards to mayors, governors, and members of Congress. In addition to Chinese and Japanese Americans, elected officials also include Asian Indian, Filipino, Vietnamese, Cambodian, and Hmong Americans, as well as Native Pacific Islanders.

POPU. The U.S. Census finds that 11.9 million people, or 4.2 percent of the entire population, are Asian. This number includes 10.2 million Asians and 1.7 million people of mixed ancestry. Sixty-nine percent of all Asians are foreign born. Among the Asian groups, Asian Indians, Pakistanis, and Thais are the three groups with the highest proportions of noncitizens. The majority of the foreign-born Asians have arrived in the United States in the past 20 years.

POPU. The census counts 1,855,590 Asian Indians in the United States; 75 percent of them are foreign born.

POPU. The census counts 212,633 Cambodians in the United States; 34 percent of them were born in the United States.

POPU. The census counts 2,858,291 Chinese living in the United States, making the Chinese the largest Asian ethnic population group in the United States. Ethnic Chinese arrive from mainland China, Hong Kong, Taiwan, Southeast Asia, and other parts of the world. Only 29 percent of the population was born in the United States.

POPU. The census counts 2,385,216 Filipinos in the United States; 32 percent of the population is native born. The Philippines send more immigrants to the United States each year than any other Asian nation.

POPU. The census reports 184,842 Hmong Americans in the United States. Forty-four percent of the Hmong population was born in the United States. The majority of Hmong Americans are clustered in five states: California, Minnesota, Wisconsin, North Carolina, and Michigan.

POPU. There are 1,152,324 Japanese in the United States. The majority of the population (61 percent) is native born.

POPU. The census counts 1,226,825 Koreans in the United States. Only about 22 percent of the Korean Americans were born in the United States.

POPU. The Laotian population is 196,893, 31 percent of which was born in the United States.

POPU. The Pakistani population is 209,273. More than 75 percent of the Pakistanis are immigrants.

POPU. About 150,093 Thai people are in the United States; only 22 percent of them were born in the United States. A third of the Thai in America live in southern California, and Los Angeles has the largest Thai American community. The Thai population in the United States is relatively dispersed, and a growing number of new immigrants now reside on the east coast, especially in New Jersey. Thai and Lao culture and language are very similar. It is common for Laotians to work in Thai-operated businesses.

POPU. There are 1,212,465 Vietnamese in the United States; 24 percent of them are U.S.-born.

POPU. For the first time the census identifies Native Hawaiians and Pacific Islanders separately from Asian Americans. About 399,000 Pacific Islanders are counted; 45 percent of them are Native Hawaiian. This number includes multiethnic and multiracial people; half of the Pacific Islanders are of mixed ethnic/racial heritage.

PUBL. Vietnamese American writer Monique Truong wins a Bard Fiction Prize, the Stonewall Book Award-Barbara Gittings Literature Award, and the Young Lions Fiction Award for her first novel, *The Book of Salt.* The book is a national best-seller. Born in Saigon, Vietnam in 1968, Truong came to the United States at age six. She is a graduate of Yale University and Columbia University School of Law.

RELI. An estimated three million Buddhists are in the United States; the vast majority of them, if not all, are people of Asian descent.

RELI. Sixty-five percent of Asian Indian Americans are Hindu; the rest include Sikh believers, Christians, and others.

RELI. An increasing number of Asian Americans are Christians. As many as 75 percent of Koreans in the United States are Christians; most of them are Protestants. Most Filipino and almost a third of Vietnamese Americans are Catholics. A significant proportion of Chinese Americans are Catholics or Protestants.

SETT. More than half of the Native Hawaiians and Pacific Islanders reside in Hawaii and California. Washington, Texas, New York, Nevada, Florida, and Utah also have large Hawaiian and Pacific Islander populations.

SETT. Fifty-three percent of Asian-occupied housing units are owned by their occupants, which is lower than the 66 percent homeownership rate of the total U.S. population. The majority of Chinese, Filipino, Japanese, Laotian, and Vietnamese American families own their homes, while the majority of other Asian American families rent. Hmong, Korean, Pakistani, and Cambodian Americans have the highest proportions of renter-occupied housing units.

SETT. Forty-eight percent of Asians still live on the west coast of the United States. Thirteen percent of California's population is Asian.

SOCI. South Asian American Leaders of Tomorrow is founded in New York City. This nonprofit organization organizes lectures and workshops,

publishes its own newsletters, and campaigns to raise public awareness about hate crimes against South Asians.

SPOR. Samoan American Tiaina "Junior" Seau, linebacker for the San Diego Chargers, is named the NFL Alumni Association's Linebacker of the Year. (Also see entry in 1993)

SPOR. Ichiro Suzuki, a Japanese baseball player, signs a contract with the Seattle Mariners and becomes the first Japanese position player in Major League Baseball. He will set several MLB records in 2004, including a new all-time, single-season major league record of 262 hits. He is a seven-time Gold Glove winner and will make the all-star selection six times.

SPOR. Along with his partner Sanjay Kumar, Charles Wang, a Shanghai-born Chinese American raised in Queens, New York, purchases the New York Islanders hockey team for $190 million.

2001

ARTS. Thai writer and composer Somtow Sucharitkul debuts his first opera, *Madana,* a work inspired by a fairy tale written by King Rama VI of Siam and dedicated to his wife, Queen Indrasaksachi. Born in Thailand and raised in Europe, Sucharitkul eventually settled in the United States. He is a world famous musician and prolific writer, authoring about 40 published books. He commutes between Los Angeles and Thailand.

CRIM. One study reveals 349 hate crimes against Asian Pacific Americans, 32 more than the year before. Cases against South Asians increase more significantly than others.

ECON. President George W. Bush appoints Cambodian American Sichan Siv to serve as the U.S. representative to the Economic and Social Council of the United Nations. (Also see entry in 1989)

LAWS. President Bush signs Executive Order 13216, extending federal programs specified in Executive Order 13125 for two more years. These programs are designed to increase opportunities and improve the quality of life for Asian Americans and Pacific Islanders.

MED. *Monsoon Wedding,* a film by Mira Nair depicting a contemporary Indian family, receives a Golden Lion Award at the Venice Film Festival and a Golden Globe nomination for best foreign language film. The India-born and New York-based film director is a graduate of Delhi University and Harvard University. Her company, Mirabai Films, has made many highly acclaimed films, including *Salaam Bombay!,* the Golden Camera winner at the Cannes International Film Festival. In 2007, she will be named the Indian Abroad Person of the Year.

POLI. Japanese American Mike Honda wins a seat in the U.S. House of Representatives. A native of California, Honda spent his early childhood in a Colorado internment camp during World War II. He developed a passion for teaching during his service with the Peace Corps in El Salvador in the late 1960s. Before his service in Congress, Honda worked as a schoolteacher and principal for several decades, also serving as a board member of the San Jose Unified School from 1981 to 1990 and with the Santa Clara County Board of Supervisors from 1990 to 1995. Between 1996 and 2000, he was a California state assembly member. In Congress, Honda will serve as chair of the Congressional Asian Pacific American Caucus. He will be elected as vice chair of the Democratic National Committee. He will be named house Democratic senior whip in 2007.

2002

OBIT. Japanese American historian Yuji Ichioka (1936–2002) of the University of California, Los Angeles dies of cancer on September 1, at age 66. Born in San Francisco in 1936, Ichioka was interned with his family during World War II. He grew up in a multiracial neighborhood in Berkeley and worked with Mexican farm laborers in the Central Valley of California. After graduating from the University of California, Los Angeles and then earning a master's degree from Berkeley, Ichioka attended Columbia University briefly. In 1969, he helped to found the Asian American Studies Center at the University of California, Los Angeles, and he became a senior researcher at the center and adjunct professor in the History Department. Considered the nation's foremost authority on Japanese American history, Ichioka

utilized many Japanese language sources for his research. He authored the award-winning monograph *The Issei: The World of the First Generation Japanese Immigrants, 1885–1924.*

OBIT. Chinese American Chang-Lin Tien (1935–2002), former chancellor of the University of California at Berkeley (1990–1997), dies on October 29. The Chang-Lin Tien Center for East Asian Studies will be established to honor him. (Also see entry in 1990)

OBIT. Japanese American Patsy Matsu Takemoto Mink (1927–2002), who served as a U.S. congresswoman from Hawaii for a total of 12 terms, dies at age 75. In 1964, Mink became the first nonwhite woman to be elected to Congress. (Also see entry in 1964)

OBIT. Actress Nobu McCarthy (1934–2002), the first artistic director of the theater group the East West Players, dies at age 67. Born Nobu Atsumi, McCarthy came to the United States in 1955 as the wife of an American serviceman. She appeared in a number of films.

POLI. Mee Moua is elected to the Minnesota state senate, representing the East Side neighborhood of St. Paul. She is the first Hmong American to win a seat in a state legislature and will be reelected in 2006. Born in Laos in 1969, Moua fled from her homeland with her parents when she was five. She came to the United States from a refugee camp in Thailand in 1978.

POLI. Asian Americans are still underrepresented in Congress. Only eight Asian Pacific Americans are in Congress, comprising 1.5 percent of the total membership.

POLI. Jeanne Hong is appointed as associate judge for the district court of Maryland. She is the first Korean American female judge.

POLI. Madison Nguyen becomes the first Vietnamese American woman elected to public office in California. Beginning as a trustee of the Franklin-McKinley School District Board of Education in San Jose, she will become the president of the board two years later. She will be elected to the city council of San Jose in 2005.

POLI. Korean American Hoon-Yung Hopgood, who was adopted at a young age from South Korea by an American couple, is elected to represent the 22nd house district in Detroit. Hopgood is the first Asian American to serve in Michigan's legislature.

POLI. Madeleine Z. Bordallo is the first woman in Guam's history to be elected to Congress. Prior to the election, she served as lieutenant governor of Guam for two terms and as a legislator for Guam for several terms.

PUBL. Korean American author Linda Sue Park's *A Single Shard* wins the John Newbery Medal for American children's literature. The daughter of immigrants, Park is the author of many other works of fiction and poetry. Her other published books include *Seesaw Girl* (1999), *The Kite Fighters* (2000), *When My Name was Keoko* (2002), *The Firekeeper's Son* (2004), and *Project Mulberry* (2005).

SCIE. Flossie Wong-Staal is named one of the 50 most extraordinary women scientists by *Discover* magazine. Born Yee Ching Wong in China in 1947, Wong-Staal is a graduate of the University of California, Los Angeles. She received a Ph.D. in molecular biology from the same university in 1972. She is most known for her work at the National Cancer Institute, where her team discovered the HIV virus as the cause of AIDS. Wong-Staal is the scientist who completed genetic mapping of the virus. She held the Florence Riford Chair in AIDS Research at the University of California, San Diego before becoming the chief scientific officer and vice president of genomics for Immusol.

SPOR. Yao Ming, a Chinese basketball player, is drafted by the Houston Rockets as the overall number one draft pick of the National Basketball Association. Although many observers consider the choice a gamble, the seven-foot-six Yao erases these doubts quickly and emerges as an international basketball sensation. Hundreds of thousands of Asian Americans are now fans of the Houston Rockets. Yao's likability and good sense of humor make him one of the NBA's most popular and marketable players, and he is

featured in big commercials for companies such as Apple computers and VISA.

SPOR. Japanese American Apolo Anton Ohno wins a gold medal in 1,500-meter short-track speed skating at the Salt Lake Winter Olympics. He also wins a silver medal in the 1,000-meter event.

SPOR. Chin-Feng Chen becomes the first Taiwanese athlete to play in Major League Baseball by signing with the Los Angeles Dodgers. He will be followed by several others from Taiwan, including Chin-Hui Tsao of the Dodgers and Chien-Ming Wang of the New York Yankees.

2003

ARTS. A historic art exhibition, "Dreams and Reality: Korean American Contemporary Art Exhibit to Celebrate 100 Years of Korean Immigration to the U.S." opens at the International

Houston Rockets center Yao Ming (11), of China, puts up a shot against Indiana Pacers forward Troy Murphy during the second quarter of an NBA basketball game, 2009. [AP Photo/Darron Cummings]

Gallery at the Smithsonian Institution. Works of 18 Korean American artists are featured in the exhibit.

COMM. President George W. Bush signs a proclamation commemorating the hundred-year anniversary of Korean immigration to the United States and calls on Americans to celebrate the occasion.

CRIM. Katrina Leung (Wenying Chen), regarded as a pillar of the Chinese American community, is arrested and charged with being a double agent for China during her two-decade career as a highly valued FBI agent. Born in China in 1954, Leung attended high school in New York before entering Cornell University. She has a master's degree from the University of Chicago. In 1995, she became an FBI agent. She is charged for unauthorized copying of national defense information with intent to benefit a foreign nation. The main concern is whether she is loyal to the United States. The case will later be dismissed. Leung will enter a plea bargain on one count of lying to the Federal Bureau of Investigation and one count of filing false federal taxes. She will receive three years' probation, 100 hours of community service, and a fine of $10,000.

HEAL. The media coverage of the SARS (Severe Acute Respiratory Syndrome) epidemic originating in rural China causes concerns among American consumers. Chinese American businesses in New York's and San Francisco's Chinatowns suffer great losses as patrons stay away in fear of contracting the disease.

LAWS. Twenty-eight Asian American organizations nationwide file an amicus curiae (friend of the court) brief in an affirmative action case before the U.S. Supreme Court involving admissions policies at the University of Michigan. The brief offers support to the university's affirmative action stance.

MED. Korean Canadian actress Sandra Oh begins to gain recognition in Hollywood and win audiences in the United States by her role in *Under the Tuscan Sun*. Born in Ontario, Canada in 1971 to Korean immigrant parents, Oh has developed an interest in acting since her high school years. Following her own instinct, she turned down a four-year scholarship to study journalism in order to pursue training in drama at the National Theatre School of Canada in Montreal. She starred in several stage productions, films, and television programs in Canada, but American audiences are not familiar with her until her appearances in a few popular Hollywood movies. Her performance in *Sideways* in 2004 will receive high marks. Oh will become well known to American audiences for her role in the ABC medical series *Grey's Anatomy,* for which she will win a 2006 Golden Globe Award for best supporting actress and Screen Actors Guild Award for outstanding performance by a female actor in a drama series. She will be nominated for the Emmy Award four times.

MED. Bill Moyers produces the documentary series *Becoming American: The Chinese Experience.* The three-part documentary runs four and a half hours on PBS. It also includes six interviews of notable Chinese Americans.

MED. Justin Lin's *Better Luck Tomorrow,* a film about Asian American teens involved in criminal activities, is released. The film offers a sharp contrast to media images of Asian American highschoolers as nerdy overachievers.

MILI. Filipino American Stephen Eagle Funk, a U.S. Marine reservist in San Jose, stands out publicly to resist returning to duty in the war against Iraq. He is followed by many others.

MUSI. Chinese American rapper Jin tha MC, the first Asian American to sign with a major hip-hop record label (Virgin Records), releases his debut album.

OBIT. The U.S. space shuttle *Columbia* breaks up over Texas upon its reentry into Earth's atmosphere. All seven crew members disappear, including Asian Indian American astronaut Kalpawna Chawla. Chawla is the first Asian American woman, and the first Asian Indian American, to fly in space.

SPOR. Korean American golfer Michelle Sung Wie becomes the youngest-ever winner of the U.S. Women's Amateur Public Links. Born in Honolulu of immigrant parents, Wie started golfing at age four. She won many tournaments by age 11. Wie will become the youngest person, and just the fourth woman, to play at the Sony Open, a PGA tour event. Her talent and charisma, as well as her determination to play against both female and male players, make her a sensational figure in golf.

SPOR. *Sports Illustrated* publishes a list of "101 Most Influential Minorities in Sports" for the first time. Golfer Tiger Woods is ranked number two and basketball player Yao Ming number seven. Also on the list are Charles Wang, co-owner of the New York Islanders hockey team; sports agent Don Nomura; golfer Se Ri Park of Korea, the second-highest-ranked female in LPGA; Ichiro Suzuki, Major League Baseball's Most Valuable Player of the Year; and Kim Ng, vice president and assistant general manager of the Los Angeles Dodgers.

2004

HEAL. Many former Wat Tham Krabok camp residents from Thailand suffer acute respiratory illnesses and skin diseases, because these Hmong refugees had no access to international assistance and had few resources for health needs while in Thailand. Mental health of these refugees is of special concern to social workers.

MIGR. In the last major settlement of refugees, about 15,000 Hmong from the Wat Tham Krabok camp in Thailand are resettled in the United States. They are sent to well-established Hmong communities in California, Minnesota, Wisconsin, North Carolina, and Michigan. The refugees arriving in the late 1970s could receive up to 36 months of financial support from the federal government, but these newcomers are expected to be on their own at the end of 8 months.

OBIT. Chinese American Hiram Fong (1906–2004), a member of the U.S. Senate from 1959 to 1977, passes away at age 97. (Also see entry in 1959)

OBIT. Chinese American author Iris Chang commits suicide on November 9 at age 36. Born in Princeton, New Jersey in 1968, Chang graduated from the University of Illinois at Urbana-Champaign and received a master's degree in writing from Johns Hopkins University. After working as a journalist for the *New York Times,* the Associated Press, and the *Chicago Tribune,* she established a career as a writer. Chang is the author of three books, *Thread of the Silkworm, The Rape of Nanking* (a best-seller), and *Chinese Americans.* She will be the subject of the 2007 biographical book *Finding Iris Chang.*

POLI. Asian Indian American Piyush "Bobby" Jindal is elected to succeed David Vitter in the U.S. Congress, representing Louisiana's first congressional district. Born in Baton Rouge, Louisiana of Punjab immigrant parents, Jindal attended high school there before going to college at Brown University. Although Jindal was admitted to Harvard Medical School, he chose to pursue a political career instead by getting a master's degree in political science from New College in Oxford, as a Rhodes Scholar. Jindal will be elected to Congress for the second time in 2006. And in 2007, at age 35, Jindal will be elected governor of Louisiana and become the first elected Indian American governor in U.S. history. Jindal will later emerge as a rising star of the Republican Party.

SOCI. The Union of North American Vietnamese Student Associations (uNAVSA) is founded. The union provides networks for Vietnamese American/Canadian college and university

Bobby Jindal, shown here with his wife and son during the Inaugural Prayer Service on January 13, 2008. Jindal, elected in 2008, became the nation's first elected Indian-American governor and the first nonwhite governor of Louisiana since Reconstruction.
[AP Photo/Tim Mueller]

New York Yankees pitcher Chien-Ming Wang at Yankee Stadium in New York, 2008. [AP Photo/Kathy Willens]

students. It holds annual conferences and serves as a special forum for community service and leadership skills.

2005

ARTS. Vietnamese American artist Dinh Q. Le's works are exhibited at Asia Society in New York City. Born in Cambodia in 1968, Le and his family came to the United States as refugees in 1978. The exhibition includes the artist's woven photographs, sculptures, and mixed media projects.

OBIT. Robert Takeo Matsui (1941–2005), a member of the U.S. House of Representatives for California's third and fifth districts from 1979 to 2005, dies at age 64.

POLI. Thai American Gorpat Henry Charoen is elected to the La Palma city council in California. He will become the mayor of the city a year later.

SPOR. "Jenny" Lang Ping, a former volleyball superstar who led the Chinese national volleyball team to victory in the 1984 Summer Olympics, is appointed as the head coach for the U.S. Olympic volleyball team. Lang's team will receive a warm reception in China at the 2008 Beijing Games and bring home to the United States a silver medal.

SPOR. Chien-Ming Wang, a former pitcher for the Chinese Taipei national baseball team,

becomes the starting pitcher for the New York Yankees. Wang's career in the United States started in 2000, when he signed as an amateur free agent for the Staten Island Yankees. All of his games in Major League Baseball are televised on both sides of the Pacific. Large crowds will gather in Taiwan to watch Wang on big television screens.

2006

MIGR. A growing number of South Korean parents are sending their young children to study in the United States, some seeking the adoption of their children by paying American families a large sum of money. A study by the Center for Korean Education Development in Seoul reveals that one out of three Korean parents are willing to send their children abroad for better education, and an American education is most desired.

OBIT. Chinese American Chi Mui (1952–2006), the mayor of San Gabriel City in southern California, dies on April 27 at age 54. Congress will pass a law in 2008 to dedicate the San Gabriel Post Office to Mui.

2007

CRIM. A massacre takes place on the campus of Virginia Polytechnic Institute and State University in Blacksburg, Virginia on April 16. Twenty-three-year-old Korean American student Seung-Hui Cho, an English major, guns down 32 people and wounds many others in two separate attacks on the same day before taking his own life. Cho immigrated to the United States with his family at age eight. He had received therapy treatment as well as special education support for an anxiety disorder and severe depression in junior high and high school. The crime shocks the nation and receives international media coverage. It also will lead to passage of a federal gun control measure in 2008.

OBIT. Benazir Bhutto (1953–2007), Pakistan's former prime minister (1988–1990 and 1993–1996), is assassinated on December 27. Born in Pakistan, Bhutto graduated from Harvard and Oxford universities. After her father, former President and Prime Minister Zulfikar Ali Bhutto, was executed, Bhutto headed the Pakistan Peoples Party and became the Muslim world's first female prime minister. A woman of tremendous courage and strength, the American-trained Bhutto is viewed in the west as a voice for democracy and women's rights, but she was twice forced to leave office due to accusations of corruption. After years in exile, Bhutto had returned to Pakistan to enter the election a third time when the assassination takes place.

2008

COMM. Six Korean American investors purchase a shopping mall in the Little Tokyo section of downtown Los Angeles—the largest indoor Japanese shopping mall in the country—with plans to convert the three-story structure into a Korean American shopping and entertainment center. For several decades, Little Tokyo has been the historical and cultural center of the Japanese American community in southern California and a tourist attraction to visitors from Japan. The infusion of non-Japanese establishments reflects demographic changes of Asian Americans in the Los Angeles area, while causing concerns among long-time residents and community supporters.

ECON. A group of scholars at the University of Maryland finds that Chinese Americans occupy two ends of the socioeconomic spectrum. Challenging common portraits of Chinese Americans as affluent and well-educated model minorities, this study finds that although a large proportion of Chinese Americans work in managerial and professional occupations, a substantial number of them have blue collar jobs. The top three occupations for Chinese American men, for example, are cooks, computer software developers, and managers and administrators.

MED. Chinese American Arthur Dong's *Hollywood Chinese* wins a Golden Horse Award in Taiwan for best documentary film. The film took the San Francisco-born Dong 12 years to complete. It documents the dilemma of Chinese American actors and actresses in the American movie industry for several decades. The film also records interviews with non-Chinese actors and actresses who created stereotypical images of Chinese in early Hollywood films. A prominent documentary filmmaker, Dong has made several other films, including *The Sewing Women* (1983, nominated for Academy Award for short

subject); *Forbidden City, USA* (1989); *Coming Out Under* (1994, Best documentary at the Berlin International Film Festival); *Licensed to Kill* (1997); and *Family Fundamentals* (2002).

OBIT. Cambodian photojournalist Dith Pran (1942–2008), the subject of the highly acclaimed film *The Killing Fields,* dies on March 30. (Also see entry in 1998)

POLI. Vietnamese American Anh "Joseph" Cao is elected as U.S. representative from Louisiana's second congressional district and becomes the first Vietnamese American to serve in Congress. Born in 1967 in war-torn Vietnam, Cao fled to the United States after the fall of Saigon in 1975 when he was eight years old. After graduating from Baylor University in Waco, Texas, he became a Jesuit seminarian and studied religion and philosophy at Fordham University in New York, earning a master's degree in 1995. In 2000, Cao received a law degree from Loyola School of Law in New Orleans and began legal practice on immigration issues. He became involved in politics as residents in New Orleans rebuilt their homes in the aftermath of Hurricane Katrina (2005). In 2007 Cao ran an unsuccessful race as an independent. He wins his seat in Congress on a Republican ticket in an overwhelmingly Democratic district by defeating nine-term Democratic U.S. Representative William Jefferson, who is facing federal investigation of bribery charges.

Republican Anh "Joseph" Cao became the first Vietnamese-American in Congress when he defeated William Jefferson for the fourth congressional district in New Orleans in 2008. He is shown here with his wife and daughter at his victory party. [AP Photo/Alex Brandon]

SCIE. Japanese American scientist Yoshiro Nambu of the University of Chicago is awarded the Nobel Prize in physics. Born in Tokyo in 1921, Nambu developed his interest in science while in high school. Nambu graduated from the University of Tokyo in 1942 and received his doctoral degree from the same university in 1952. In the United States, Nambu worked at Princeton University for two years before joining a team of scientists in Chicago in 1954. A theoretic physicist who is one of the founders of string theory, Nambu completed work that forms an essential cornerstone of what physicists call the Standard Model, which explains three of the four fundamental forces of nature: strong, weak, and electromagnetic. He is the Harry Pratt Judson Distinguished Service Professor Emeritus in physics at the Enrico Fermi Institute and is seen as one of the leading scholars in the deployment of modern particle physics. Nambu shares the Nobel Prize in physics with two Japanese scholars, Makoto Kobayashi and Toshihide Maskawa.

SCIE. Japanese American scientist Osamu Shimomura wins the Nobel Prize in chemistry for his discovery of a green fluorescent protein. Born in Kyoto, Japan in 1928, Shimomura graduated from Nagasaki College of Pharmacy in 1951 and earned a Ph.D. in organic chemistry from Nagoya University in 1960. From 1960 to 1982, he worked as a research biochemist at Princeton University before joining the Marine Biological Laboratory in Woods Hole, Massachusetts, from where he retired in 2001. Shimomura was the first to discover a green molecule in the jellyfish, and he purified and isolated it as a protein in 1961. This protein fluoresces green under ultraviolet light. The discovery of the green fluorescent protein (GFP) was a major scientific breakthrough in that it allows scientists to examine inside living cells or animals and observe molecules interacting in real-time. Shimomura shares the Nobel Prize with two other scientists, Martin Chalfie and Roger Tsien, who later developed the GFP into a useful tool for scientific research.

SCIE. Chinese American scientist Roger Tsien wins the Nobel Prize in chemistry for his research

that helps develop and expand the use of fluorescent proteins. After Japanese American chemist Osamu Shimomura discovered the green fluorescent protein (GFP) from a jellyfish in 1961, biologist Martin Chalfie demonstrated in the mid-1990s that the GFP could be used as a tool for researchers. Tsien's background in both chemistry and biology allows him to take it a step further by finding ways to make the GFP glow more brightly and consistently and by creating many more colors and making the color change. His contribution makes the tool far more powerful and accessible to thousands of cell biologists. Born in 1952 in Livingston, New Jersey, Tsien developed an interest in scientific research beginning in his childhood years. He graduated from Harvard College in chemistry and physics at age 20 and received his Ph.D. in physiology from Cambridge University in England. A professor of pharmacology at the University of California, San Diego, Tsien has also produced other promising research results which will allow the application of fluorescent proteins in the treatment of human diseases such as cancer. Tsien shares the Nobel Prize in chemistry with Osamu Shimomura and Martin Chalfie.

SPOR. China hosts the 29th Summer Olympics in Beijing, generating great excitement among Chinese in the United States. On the U.S. team are four Chinese American coaches, including "Jenny" Lang Ping of the women's volleyball team, Liang Chaw of the women's gymnastics team, Wenbo Chen of the men's diving team, and Li Li of the men's track team.

SPOR. Bryan Clay brings the United States a gold medal at the Beijing Olympics in the decathlon and is seen by some sports commentators as the world's greatest all-around athlete. Born in Texas of African American and Japanese American parents in 1980, Clay grew up in Hawaii and attended Azusa Pacific University in southern California. He was a silver medalist at the 2004 Olympics and the winner of the 2005 world championships.

2009

POLI. Chinese American Christopher P. Lu is appointed by President Barack Obama as the

Bryan Clay of the United States bites his gold medal after winning the decathlon in the National Stadium at the 2008 Olympics in Beijing. [AP Photo/Luca Bruno/ FILE]

cabinet secretary for his new administration. Born in New Jersey in 1966 of immigrant parents from Taiwan, Lu graduated from Princeton University and Harvard Law School. Before this appointment he was legislative director and acting chief of staff in Obama's senate office, and he worked as a policy advisor during the presidential campaign. Lu is also known for his love of running marathons.

POLI. Asian American educators and political activists criticize a new University of California (UC) admissions policy. Although the UC system claims that the policy is adopted to increase campus diversity, critics say it can actually increase the number of white students on campuses while driving down the Asian population. Asian American educators and community leaders argue that the policy is ill-conceived and discriminatory. Some note that the new policy will lead to a slight increase in African American and Latino students at the UC campuses, while reducing 7 percent of the Asian American student population and increasing up to 10 percent of the white student population.

GLOSSARY

Cafe sua da. A popular Vietnamese beverage made of iced coffee and sweetened condensed milk.

Chop suey. A Chinese American dish; a stir-fry of a mixture of sliced meat and vegetables.

Cohong. A government-licensed Chinese trading company. Before the Opium War in 1839, foreign merchants were only allowed to trade with western merchants through the cohong system.

Dim sum. Means "snacks" in Cantonese. A variety of dim sum dishes are served in some Cantonese restaurants, usually for brunch.

Ghadar (also Gadar or Ghadr). Means "revolution" in Hindi. The Ghadar Party was an advocate for the independence of India in the early twentieth century.

Gurdwara. A Sikh temple. The gurdwara in Hong Kong was a stopover place for Indian immigrants to North America in the early twentieth century.

Hui. Rotating credit associations in early Chinese immigrant communities. This system allowed individuals with modest means to start small businesses.

Huiguan. A district association organized by Chinese immigrants.

Issei. First generation Japanese Americans. An issei is an immigrant born in Japan.

Jati. Part of the caste system differentiating one occupational caste from another in India. Each jati has its own regional or local origin.

Jinshan (Gum San). Means "gold mountain" in Chinese. It is the name the Chinese gave to San Francisco.

Judo. A form of Japanese martial arts officially introduced to the Olympic Games in 1964.

Kae. Rotating credit associations in early Korean immigrant communities, similar to the Chinese hui.

Kenjinkai. A prefectural association organized by Japanese immigrants.

Kibei. Second-generation Japanese Americans who were born in the United States but received some education in Japan.

Kung fu. A form of Chinese martial arts; a genre in Hong Kong and Hollywood films.

Luna. Overseers hired by Hawaii's sugar plantation owners to watch the contract laborers. Most plantation workers were Asians, but the luna were usually white.

Nihonmachi. A Japanese ethnic enclave, also known as Little Tokyo.

Nisei. Second-generation Japanese Americans. A nisei is an American-born Japanese of immigrant parents.

Paper son/daughter. A young Chinese who gained entry by making a false claim as the offspring of a merchant or U.S. citizen. This practice was common during the Chinese exclusion.

Pensionados. Filipinos attending colleges and universities overseas. Most pensionados of the early twentieth century came to the United States with scholarships from their government, and many returned to the Philippines after the completion of their programs.

Pho. A popular Vietnamese noodle soup made of a rich and clear beef or chicken broth.

Picture bride. A Japanese or Korean woman who gained entry to the United States in the early twentieth century as the wife of an immigrant already residing in Hawaii or the U.S. mainland after Japanese and Korean laborers were excluded. Although they came as wives of immigrants, many picture brides had not met their husbands before they gained entry. The brides and grooms usually got to know each other by exchanging pictures and letters.

Schoolboys. Young male Japanese or Filipinos who came to the United States in the early twentieth century with the intention of obtaining an American education. These young men came without government assistance. To support themselves they often worked as domestics or farm laborers. Some later became labor contractors.

Sushi. A Japanese dish popular in the United States. Rice, raw fish, and seaweed are some of the main ingredients of sushi.

Tanomoshi. Rotating credit associations in early Japanese immigrant communities similar to hui (Chinese) or kae (Korean).

Tet. Vietnamese Lunar New Year.

Tong. A Chinese immigrant fraternal organization. The tongs in old Chinatowns often controlled the Chinese American underground.

War bride. A wife of an American war veteran or a woman married to a U.S. military serviceman.

Yamato Colony. A farming community established by Japanese immigrants.

Yangban. Korea's ruling class during the Yi dynasty.

SELECTED BIBLIOGRAPHY

U.S. GOVERNMENT PUBLICATIONS

Commission on Wartime Relocation and Internment of Civilians. *Personal Justice Denied: Report of the Commission on Wartime Relocation and Internment of Civilians.* Washington, DC, 1982.

U.S. Bureau of the Census. *United States: Census of 2000.*

U.S. Immigration and Naturalization Service. *Statistical Yearbook of the Immigration and Naturalization Service.*

BOOKS

Abelmann, Nancy, and John Lie. *Blue Dreams: Korean Americans and the Los Angeles Riots.* Cambridge, MA: Harvard University Press, 1995.

Anderson, Robert N., Richard Collier, and Rebecca F. Pestano. *Filipinos in Rural Hawaii.* Honolulu: University of Hawaii Press, 1984.

Azuma, Eiichiro. *Between Two Empires: Race, History, and Transnationalism in Japanese America.* New York: Oxford University Press, 2005.

Bao, Xiaolan. *Holding Up More Than Half the Sky: Chinese Women Garment Workers in New York City, 1948–1992.* Urbana: University of Illinois Press, 2006.

Bonus, Rick. *Locating Filipino Americans: Ethnicity and the Cultural Politics of Space.* Philadelphia: Temple University Press, 2000.

Bulosan, Carlos. *America Is in the Heart.* Seattle: University of Washington Press, 1973.

Cariaga, Roman R. *The Filipinos in Hawaii: Economic and Social Conditions, 1906–1936.* Honolulu: Filipino Public Relations Bureau, 1937.

Chan, Sucheng. *Asian Americans: An Interpretive History.* New York: Twayne Publishers, 1991.

———. *Not Just Victims: Conversations with Cambodian Community Leaders in the United States.* Urbana: University of Illinois Press, 2003.

———. *Survivors: Cambodian Refugees in the United States.* Urbana: University of Illinois Press, 2004.

———. *This Bittersweet Soil: The Chinese in California Agriculture, 1860–1910.* Berkeley: University of California Press, 1986.

———. *The Vietnamese American 1.5 Generation: Stories of War, Revolution, Flight, and New Beginnings.* Philadelphia: Temple University Press, 2006.

Chen, Yong. *Chinese San Francisco: A Trans-Pacific Community, 1850–1943.* Stanford, CA: Stanford University Press, 2000.

Choy, Catherine Ceniza. *Empire of Care: Nursing and Migration in Filipino American History.* Durham, NC: Duke University Press, 2003.

Conroy, Hilary F. *The Japanese Frontier in Hawaii, 1868–1898.* Berkeley: University of California Press, 1953.

Daniels, Roger. *Asian America: Chinese and Japanese in the United States since 1850.* Seattle: University of Washington Press, 1988.

———. *Concentration Camps, North America: Japanese in the United States and Canada during World War II.* Malabar, FL: Krieger, 1981.

———. *The Politics of Prejudice: The Anti-Japanese Movement in California and the Struggle for Japanese Exclusion.* Berkeley: University of California Press, 1978.

Donnelly, Nancy D. *Changing Lives of Refugee Hmong Women.* Seattle: University of Washington Press, 1994.

Dorita, Mary. *Filipino Immigration to Hawaii.* San Francisco: R&E Research Associates, 1975.

Espana-Maram, Linda. *Creating Masculinity in Los Angeles's Little Manila: Working Class Filipinos and Popular Culture, 1920s–1950s.* New York: Columbia University Press, 2006.

Espiritu, Yen Le. *Filipino American Lives.* Philadelphia: Temple University Press, 1995.

———. *Home Bound: Filipino American Lives across Cultures, Communities, and Countries.* Berkeley: University of California Press, 2003.

Fong, Timothy P. *The First Suburban Chinatown: The Remaking of Monterey Park, California.* Philadelphia: Temple University Press, 1994.

Freeman, James A. *Hearts of Sorrow: Vietnamese-American Lives.* Stanford, CA: Stanford University Press, 1989.

Fujino, Diane C. *Heartbeat of Struggle: The Revolutionary Life of Yuri Kochiyama.* Minneapolis: University of Minnesota Press, 2005.

Glenn, Evelyn Nakano. *Issei, Nisei, War Bride: Three Generations of Japanese American Women in Domestic Service.* Philadelphia: Temple University Press, 1986.

Glick, Clarence E. *Sojourners and Settlers: Chinese Migrants in Hawaii.* Honolulu: University of Hawaii Press, 1980.

Hayslip, Le Ly, and Jay Wurts. *When Heaven and Earth Changed Places: A Vietnamese Woman's Journey from War to Peace.* New York: Doubleday, 1989.

Horton, John. *The Politics of Diversity: Immigration, Resistance, and Change in Monterey Park, California.* Philadelphia: Temple University Press, 1995.

Hsu, Madeline Y. *Dreaming of Gold, Dreaming of Home: Transnationalism and Migration between the United States and Southern China, 1882–1943.* Stanford, CA: Stanford University Press, 2000.

Ichioka, Yuji. *The Issei: The World of the First Generation Japanese Immigrants, 1885–1924.* New York: The Free Press, 1988.

Jensen, Joan. *Passage from India: Asian Indian Immigrants in North America.* New Haven, CT: Yale University Press, 1988.

June, Moon-Ho. *Coolies and Cane: Race, Labor, and Sugar in the Age of Emancipation.* Baltimore: Johns Hopkins University Press, 2006.

Kessler, Lauren. *Stubborn Twig: Three Generations in the Life of a Japanese American Family.* New York: Penguin Books, 1994.

Kibria, Nazli. *Family Tightrope: The Changing Lives of Vietnamese Americans.* Princeton, NJ: Princeton University Press, 1993.

Kim, Claire Jean. *Bitter Fruit: The Politics of Black-Korean Conflict in New York City.* New Haven, CT: Yale University Press, 2000.

Kim, Elaine H. *Asian American Literature: An Introduction to the Writings and Their Social Context.* Philadelphia: Temple University Press, 1982.

Kingston, Maxine Hong. *China Men.* New York: Alfred A. Knopf, 1980.

———. *The Woman Warrior: Memoirs of a Girlhood among Ghosts.* New York: Alfred A. Knopf, 1976.

Kwong, Peter. *Forbidden Workers: Illegal Chinese Immigrants and American Labor.* New York: New Press, 1997.

———. *The New Chinatown.* New York: Hill and Wang, 1987.

Kwong, Peter, and Dušanka Miščević. *Chinese America: The Untold Story of America's Oldest New Community.* New York: The New Press, 2005.

La Brack, Bruce. *The Sikhs of Northern California, 1904–1975.* New York: AMS Press, 1988.

Lai, Eric, and Dennis Arguelles, eds. *The New Face of Asian Pacific America: Numbers, Diversity & Change in the 21st Century.* San Francisco: AsianWeek, 2003.

Lai, Him Mark, Genny Lim, and Judy Yung. *Island: Poetry and History of Chinese Immigrants on Angel Island, 1910–1940.* San Francisco: HOC DOI, 1980.

Lee, Erika. *At America's Gate: Chinese Immigration during the Exclusion Era, 1882–1943.* Chapel Hill: University of North Carolina Press, 2003.

Leonard, Karen. *Ethnic Choices: California's Punjabi-Mexican Americans, 1910–1980.* Philadelphia: Temple University Press, 1991.

Lien, Pei-ti. *The Making of Asian America through Political Participation (Mapping Racism).* Philadelphia: Temple University Press, 2001.

Light, Ivan, and Steven J. Gold. *Ethnic Economics.* San Diego: Academic Press, 2000.

Ling, Huping. *Emerging Voices: Experiences of Underrepresented Asian Americans.* New Brunswick, NJ: Rutgers University Press, 2008.

Lowe, Lisa. *Immigrant Acts: On Asian American Cultural Politics.* Durham, NC: Duke University Press, 1996.

Lui, Mary Ting Yi. *The Chinatown Trunk Mystery: Murder, Miscegenation, and Other Encounters in Turn-of-the-Century NYC.* Princeton, NJ: Princeton University Press, 2005.

Lukes, Timothy J., and Gary Y. Okihiro. *Japanese Legacy: Farming and Community Life in California's Santa Clara Valley.* Cupertino: California History Center, 1985.

Lydon, Sandy. *Chinese Gold: The Chinese in the Monterey Bay Area.* Capitola, CA: Capitola Book Co., 1985.

Matsumoto, Valerie. *Farming the Home Place: A Japanese American Community in California, 1919–1982.* Ithaca, NY: Cornell University Press, 1993.

McClain, Charles J. *In Search of Equality: The Chinese Struggle against Discrimination in Nineteenth-Century America.* Berkeley: University of California Press, 1994.

Mukherjee, Bharati. *Jasmine.* New York: Grove Press, 1989.

Nee, Victor G., and Brett De Bary Nee. *Longtime Californ': A Documentary Study of an American Chinatown.* New York: Pantheon Books, 1972.

Ngai, Mae M. *Impossible Subjects: Illegal Aliens and the Making of Modern America.* Princeton, NJ: Princeton University Press, 2004.

Noda, Kesa. *Yamato Colony, 1906–1960: Livingston, California.* Livingston, CA: Japanese American Citizens League, 1981.

Omi, Michael, and Howard Winant. *Racial Formation in the United States: From the 1960s to the 1990s.* New York: Routledge, 1994.

Ong, Paul. *Beyond Asian American Poverty: Community Economic Development Policies and Strategies.* Los Angeles: Leadership Education for Asian Pacifics, 1993.

Osorio, Jonathan Kay Kamakawiwoʻole. *Dismembering Lahui: A History of the Hawaiian Nation to 1887.* Honolulu: University of Hawaii Press, 2002.

Parreñas, Rhacel Salazar. *Servants of Globalization: Women, Migration, and Domestic Work.* Stanford, CA: Stanford University Press, 2001.

Peffer, George Anthony. *If They Don't Bring Their Women Here: Chinese Female Immigration before Exclusion.* Urbana: University of Illinois Press, 1996.

Ronyoung, Kim. *Clay Walls.* Sag Harbor, NY: The Permanent Press, 1987.

Saito, Leland T. *Race and Politics: Asian Americans, Latinos, and Whites in a Los Angeles Suburb.* Urbana: University of Illinois Press, 2001.

Salyer, Lucy E. *Laws Harsh as Tigers: Chinese Immigrants and the Shaping of Modern Immigration Law.* Chapel Hill: University of North Carolina Press, 1995.

See, Lisa. *On Gold Mountain: The One-Hundred-Year Odyssey of My Chinese-American Family.* New York: Vintage Books, 1995.

Shah, Nayan. *Contagious Divides: Epidemics and Race in San Francisco's Chinatown.* Berkeley: University of California Press, 2001.

Shukla, Sandhya. *India Abroad: Diasporic Cultures of Postwar America and England.* Princeton, NJ: Princeton University Press, 2003.

Sone, Monica. *Nisei Daughter.* 1953. Reprint, Seattle: University of Washington Press, 1979.

Takaki, Ronald. *Strangers from a Different Shore.* New York: Little, Brown and Company, 1989.

Tan, Amy. *The Joy Luck Club.* New York: Ballantine Books, 1989.

Wong, Jade Snow. *Fifth Chinese Daughter.* Reprint, Seattle: University of Washington Press, 1989.

Wong, Sau-ling. *Reading Asian American Literature: From Necessity to Extravagance.* Princeton, NJ: Princeton University Press, 1993.

Yang, Fenggang. *Chinese Christians in America: Conversion, Assimilation, and Adhesive Identities.* University Park: Pennsylvania State University Press, 1999.

Yee, Alfred. *Shopping at Giant Foods: Chinese American Supermarkets in Northern California.* Seattle: University of Washington Press, 2003.

Yoo, David. *Growing Up Nisei: Race, Generation, and Culture among Japanese Americans of California, 1924–49.* Urbana: University of Illinois Press, 2000.

Yu, Renqiu. *To Save China, to Save Ourselves: The Chinese Hand Laundry Alliance of New York.* Philadelphia: Temple University Press, 1992.

Yung, Judy. *Unbound Feet: A Social History of Chinese Women in San Francisco.* Berkeley: University of California Press, 1995.

Zhao, Xiaojian. *Remaking Chinese America: Immigration, Family, and Community, 1940–1965.* New Brunswick, NJ: Rutgers University Press, 2002.

Zhou, Min. *Chinatown: The Socioeconomic Potential of an Urban Enclave.* Philadelphia: Temple University Press, 1992.

Zia, Helen. *Asian American Dreams: The Emergence of an American People.* New York: Farrar, Straus and Giroux, 2000.

ONLINE RESOURCES

General

Asian American History Timeline (Loni Ding)
  http://www.cetel.org/timeline.html
Asian Americans in Washington State (Washington State University)
  http://www.aapifsa.wsu.edu/default.asp?PageID=1568
Asian Media Watch
  http://www.goldsea.com/Mediawatch/mediawatch.html
AsianWeek (national English-language newspaper)
  http://www.asianweek.com/
Association for Asian American Studies
  http://www.aaastudies.org/aaas/index.html
National Asian American Telecommunications Association
  http://www.museum.tv/archives/etv/N/htmlN/nationalasia/nationalasia.htm
Smithsonian Asian Pacific American Program
  http://www.apa.si.edu/
Wing Luke Asian Museum, Seattle
  http://www.wingluke.org/

Census 2000 Briefs

The Asian Population: 2000
    http://www.census.gov/prod/2002pubs/c2kbr01-16.pdf
The Native Hawaiian and Other Pacific Islander Population: 2000
    http://www.census.gov/prod/2001pubs/c2kbr01-14.pdf

Immigration and Refugees

Asian Immigration to Hawaii (Pacific University)
    http://mcel.pacificu.edu/as/students/hawaii/index.html
Immigration Records at the Library of Congress
    http://lcweb2.loc.gov/ammem/ndlpedu/features/immig/immigration_set2.html
U.S. Citizenship and Immigration Services (formerly the Immigration and Naturalization Service)
    http://www.uscis.gov/portal/site/uscis

Chinese Americans

Angel Island Immigration Station Foundation
    http://aiisf.org/
Chinese American Museum (Los Angeles)
    http://www.camla.org/
Chinese Americans in Tuscon, Arizona (University of Arizona)
    http://parentseyes.arizona.edu/promise/
Chinese Historical Society of America
    http://www.chsa.org/
Chinese Historical Society of Southern California
    http://www.chssc.org/index.shtml
Documents on the Chinese in California (San Francisco Museum)
    http://www.sfmuseum.org/hist1/index0.html
Gateway to Gold Mountain Exhibit (Smithsonian)
    http://www.wright.edu/admin/ahna/gateway%20pictures.htm
    http://www.maiwah.org/gateway.htm
On Gold Mountain Online Exhibit
    http://www.apa.si.edu/ongoldmountain/
Portrait of Chinese Americans (University of Maryland)
    www.aast.umd.edu/ocaportrait.html
Readings in Chinese Canadian History (Prof. Henry Yu)
    http://www.sscnet.ucla.edu/05W/asian130a-1/readings.html
San Diego Chinese Historical Museum
    http://www.sdchm.org/

Filipino Americans

Carlos Bulosan Memorial Exhibit (Seattle)
    http://www.bulosan.org/
Filipino American National Historical Society
    http://www.fanhs-national.org/
Filipino American Photographs of Ricardo Ocreto Alvarado (Smithsonian)
    http://www.tfaoi.com/aa/6aa/6aa220.htm
Filipino Links (Filipino American National Historical Society, Stockton)
    http://www.geocities.com/tokyo/pagoda/4534/filipino.html
Spanish-American War in Motion Pictures (Library of Congress)
    http://lcweb2.loc.gov/ammem/sawhtml/sawhome.html

Hawaiians and Immigration to Hawaii

Annexation of Hawaii Documents (University of Hawaii)
    http://libweb.hawaii.edu/digicoll/annexation/annexation.html
Asian Immigration to Hawaii (Pacific University)
    http://mcel.pacificu.edu/as/students/hawaii/index.html
Hawaiian Sovereignty Movement
    http://www.hawaii-nation.org/
Hawaii Kingdom History
    http://www.hawaiiankingdom.org/political-history.shtml
Hawaii's Story, by Hawaii's Queen Liliuokalani (1898)
    http://digital.library.upenn.edu/women/liliuokalani/hawaii/hawaii.html
Perspectives on Hawaiian Sovereignty (Institute for the Advancement of Hawaiian Affairs)
    http://www.opihi.com/sovereignty/
Women and Work in Hawaii (Hawai'i Women's Heritage Project)
    http://www.soc.hawaii.edu/hwhp/hawork/itm.open.html

Japanese Americans

Ansel Adams's Photographs of Internment at Manzanar (Library of Congress)
    http://memory.loc.gov/ammem/collections/anseladams/
Chronology of Japanese American History
    http://web.mit.edu/21h.153j/www/chrono.html
Documents, Reports, and Letters Related to Relocation on Bainbridge Island, Washington (University of Washington)
    http://www.lib.washington.edu/exhibits/harmony/documents/
Hirabayashi v. United States (1943)
    http://supreme.justia.com/us/320/81/case.html
Japanese American Exhibit and Access Project (University of Washington)
    http://www.lib.washington.edu/exhibits/harmony/default.html
Japanese American National Museum
    http://www.janm.org/
Japanese American Network
    http://www.janet.org/
Japanese Americans in San Francisco (San Francisco Museum)
    http://www.sfmuseum.org/hist1/index0.1.html#japanese
Japanese American Internment Camps in Utah (University of Utah)
    http://www.lib.utah.edu/portal/site/marriottlibrary/menuitem.350f2794f84fb3b29cf
    87354d1e916b9/?vgnextoid=2f2b1c769fcfb110VgnVCM1000001c9e619bRCRD
Kiyoshi Hirabayashi v. United States (1943)
    http://caselaw.lp.findlaw.com/cgi-bin/getcase.pl?court=us&vol=320&invol=81
Korematsu v. United States (1944)
    http://caselaw.lp.findlaw.com/scripts/getcase.pl?court=US&vol=323&invol=214
Minoru Yasui v. United States (1943)
    http://caselaw.lp.findlaw.com/scripts/getcase.pl?navby=search&court=US&case=/data/
    us/320/115.html
A More Perfect Union—Japanese Americans and the Constitution (Smithsonian)
    http://americanhistory.si.edu/perfectunion/non-flash/index.html
100th Battalion/442nd Regimental Combat Team Nisei Veterans
    http://www.katonk.com/442nd/442/page1.html
Photographs by Dorothea Lange (Library of Congress)
    http://www.loc.gov/exhibits/wcf/wcf0013.html

War Relocation Authority Camps in Arizona, 1942–46 (University of Arizona)
    http://parentseyes.arizona.edu/wracamps/camplife.html
War Relocation Authority Publication, "The Relocation of Japanese Americans," 1943 (University
    of Washington)
    http://www.lib.washington.edu/exhibits/harmony/documents/wrapam.html

Korean Americans

Korean Adoptee Adoptive Family Network
    http://www.kaanet.com/
"Korean Adoptees Remember," in Finding Home: Fifty Years of International Adoption (American
    Public Radioworks)
    http://americanradioworks.publicradio.org/features/adoption/a1.html
Korean American Historical Society
    http://www.kahs.org/
Korean American History Timeline (AsianWeek)
    http://www.asianweek.com/2003_01_10/feature_timeline.html
Korean American Museum
    http://www.kamuseum.org/
Korean Americans: A Century of Experience (Smithsonian)
    http://www.apa.si.edu/Curriculum%20Guide-Final/index.htm
Korean Quarterly
    http://www.koreanquarterly.org/Home.html

South Asian Americans

Little India
    http://www.littleindia.com/
Masala.com
    http://www.masala.com/
Sikh American Legal Defense and Education Fund
    http://www.saldef.org/default.aspx
Sikh Community: Over 100 Years in the Pacific Northwest (Wing Luke Asian Museum)
    http://www.wingluke.org/pages/sikhcommunitywebsite/introduction.html
South Asian American Link (University of Texas)
    http://asnic.utexas.edu/asnic/countries/india/linta.html
South Asian Women's Network
    http://www.sawnet.org/

Southeast Asian Americans

Cambodian Genocide Program (Yale University)
    http://www.yale.edu/cgp/
Hmong Studies Internet Resource Center
    http://www.hmongstudies.org/
Hmong Studies Journal
    http://www.hmongstudies.org/HmongStudiesJournal
Lao Census Data
    http://www.hmongstudies.org/LaoCensusData.html
Lao Family Community of Minnesota
    http://www.laofamily.org/
Lao Language and Culture Learning Resources (Northern Illinois University)
    http://www.seasite.niu.edu/lao/lao3.htm
LaoNet Community Home Page
    http://home.vicnet.net.au/~lao/

Lao Studies Review
    http://home.vicnet.net.au/~lao/laostudy/laostudy.htm
Laos WWW Virtual Library
    http://home.vicnet.net.au/~lao/laoVL.html
Southeast Asian Archive (University of California–Irvine)
    http://www.lib.uci.edu/libraries/collections/sea/sasian.html
WWW Hmong Homepage
    http://www.hmongnet.org/

FILMS AND VIDEOS

Anatomy of a Springroll. Produced by Paul Kwan and Arnold Iger, 1980 (Vietnamese American).

Ancestors in the Americas: Coolies, Sailors, and Settlers. Produced by Loni Ding, 1998 (Chinese American).

Another America. Produced by Michael Cho, 1995 (Korean American).

Asians in America. Produced by Jade Productions, 1986 (Vietnamese American).

As Seen by Both Sides: American and Vietnamese Artists Look at the War. Produced by Larry Rottmann and Mark Biggs, 1995 (Vietnamese American).

Back to Bataan Beach. Directed by Ernesto M. Foronda, 1995 (Filipino).

Becoming American. Produced by Ken Levine and Ivory Waterworth Levine, 1996 (Hmong American).

Becoming American: The Chinese Experience. Produced by Bill Moyers, 2003 (Chinese American).

Between Two Worlds. Produced by Siegel Productions, 1986 (Laotian/Cambodian).

Bittersweet Survival: Southeast Asians in America. Produced by J. T. Takagi and Christine Choy, 1983 (Southeast Asian American).

Blue Collar & Buddha. Produced/directed by Taggart Siegel and Kati Johnston, 1987 (Laotian).

Carved in Silence. Produced/directed by Felicia Lowe, 1988 (Chinese American).

The Color of Honor. Produced by Loni Ding, 1989 (Japanese American).

Daughter from Danang. Produced by Gail Dolgin and Vicente Franco, 2002 (Vietnamese and mixed race American).

Dollar a Day, Ten Cents a Dance. Produced by Cinima Guild, 1985 (Filipino American).

Do 2 Halves Really Make a Whole? Produced by Martha Chono-Helsley, 1993 (Multiracial/ethnic).

Dreaming Filipinos. Produced by Manny Reyes and Herky Del Mundo, 1990 (Filipino American).

Eat a Bowl of Tea. Directed by Wayne Wang, 1989 (Chinese American).

A Family Gathering. Produced by Lisa Yasui and Ann Tegnell, 1988 (Japanese American).

Forbidden City USA. Produced/directed by Arthur Dong, 1989 (Chinese American).

From Hollywood to Hanoi. Produced by Tiana (Thi Thang Nga), 1993 (Vietnamese American).

The Girl Who Spelled Freedom. Directed by Simon Wincer, 1985 (Cambodian American).

A Hand Up: The Vietnamese Nail Salon Success Story. Produced by Rob Amato and Jody Hammond, 2003 (Vietnamese American).

Hollywood Chinese: The Chinese in American Feature Films. Produced/directed by Arthur Dong, 2008 (Chinese American).

In No One's Shadow: Filipinos in America. Produced by Naomi and Antonio De Castro, 1988 (Filipino American).

The Joy Luck Club. Directed by Wayne Wang, 1993 (Chinese American).

Khush Refugees. Produced by Nidhi Singh, 1991 (South Asian American).

Letter Back Home. Produced by Nith Lacroix, 1994 (Laotian/Cambodian).

Letters to Thien. Produced by Trac Minh Vu, 1997 (Vietnamese American).

Mai's America. Produced by Marlo Poras, 2002 (Vietnamese American).

Miss India Georgia. Produced by Daniel Friedman and Sharon Grimberg, 1997 (Asian Indian).

Mississippi Triangle. Produced by Christine Choy, 1984 (Chinese American).

Monterey's Boat People. Produced/directed by Spencer Nakasako and Vincent DiGirolamo, 1982 (Vietnamese American).

My America . . . or Honk If You Love Buddha. Directed by Renee Tajima-Peña, 1997 (Asian American).

New Puritans: The Sikhs of Yuba City. Produced by Ritu Sarin and Tenzing Sonam, 1985 (South Asian American).

Omai Fa'atasi: Somoa Mo Samoa. Directed by Takashi Fujii, 1974 (Samoan American).

A Personal Matter: Gordon Hirabayashi v. the U.S. Produced by John DeGraff, 1992 (Japanese American).

Picture Bride. Directed by Kay Hatta, 1995 (Japanese American).

Precious Cargo. Produced by Janet Gardner, 2001 (Vietnamese American).

The Price You Pay. Christine Keyser (NAATA, distribution@naatanet.org), 1998.

Quiet Passages: The Japanese American War Bride Experience. Directed by Tim Depaepe and produced by Chico Herbison and Jerry Schultz, 1991 (Japanese American).

The Rabbit in the Moon. Directed by Emiko Omori and produced by Emiko Omori and Chizuko Emiko, 1999 (Japanese American).

Rebuilding the Temple: Cambodians in America. Produced by Direct Cinema, 1992 (Cambodian American).

Reflections: Returning to Vietnam. Produced by KCSM, 1992 (Vietnamese American).

Saigon, U.S.A. Produced by Lindsey Jang and Robert G. Winn, 2000 (Vietnamese American).

Sewing Woman. Produced/directed by Arthur Dong, 1982 (Chinese American).

Sin City Diary. Produced by Rachel Rivera, 1992 (Filipino American).

Thousand Pieces of Gold. Directed by Nancy Kelly, 1991 (Chinese American).

Unfinished Business. Directed by Steven Okazaki and produced by Mouchette Films, 1985 (Japanese American).

Visible Target. Produced by Cris Anderson and John DeGraaf, 1985 (Japanese American).

The Wedding Banquet. Directed by Ang Lee, 1993 (Chinese American).

We Served With Pride: The Chinese American Experience in WWII. Directed by Montgomery Hom, 1999 (Chinese American).

Who Killed Vincent Chin. Produced by Christine Choy and Renee Tajima-Peña, 1988 (Chinese American).

Women Outside. Produced by Mary Beth Yarrow and Julie Thompson, 1995 (Korean American).

INDEX

About the Author

XIAOJIAN ZHAO is associate professor and has served as chair (2005–2008) of the Department of Asian American Studies at the University of California, Santa Barbara, and she has taught and conducted research in Asian American history for over a decade. She is the author of *The New Chinese America: Class, Economy and Social Hierarchy* (2009) and *Remaking Chinese America: Immigration, Family, and Community, 1940–1965* (2002), which won the 2003 History Book Award from the Association for Asian American Studies. Her research interests include twentieth-century U.S. social history, Asian American history, Chinese American history, immigration patterns, gender and race relations, transnational communities, globalization, and U.S.-China relations.